DID THEY REALLY DO IT?

DID THEY REALLY DO IT?

FROM LIZZIE BORDEN TO THE
TWENTIETH HIJACKER

Fred Rosen

THUNDER'S MOUTH PRESS

NEW YORK

DID THEY REALLY DO IT?
From Lizzie Borden to the Twentieth Hijacker

Published by
Thunder's Mouth Press
An Imprint of Avalon Publishing Group, Inc.
245 West 17th Street, 11th floor
New York, NY 10011

AVALON
publishing group incorporated

first printing, May 2006

Library of Congress Cataloging-in-Publication Data is available.

ISBN-10: 1-56025-774-1
ISBN-13: 978-1-56025-774-5

9 8 7 6 5 4 3 2 1

Book design by Maria Torres

Printed in the United States of America
Distributed by Publishers Group West

For Lori Perkins,
who helped changed my life

"I BELIEVE STRONGLY IN THE LONG ARM OF
COINCIDENCE. BECAUSE I KNOW COPS WELL,
I KNOW HOW MUCH IT CONTRIBUTES TO THE
SOLVING OF REAL POLICE CASES."

—ED MCBAIN

Contents

Acknowledgments   XI

Prologue   XIII

1   Hero or Villain? Part 1   1
1865–1869—Dr. Samuel Mudd

2   Forty Whacks of Trouble   29
1892—Lizzie Borden

3   Who Killed Mary Phagan?   57
1914–1916—Leo Frank

4   Was Bruno Framed?   77
1934—Bruno Richard Hauptmann

5   A Bullet for Pretty Boy   101
1934—Charles Arthur Floyd,
aka "Pretty Boy"

6   The Atomic Spies   119
1954—Ethel and Julius Rosenberg

7   The Murdered Civil Rights
Workers, Part I   133
1964—Victor Ray Killen

8 THE BOSTON STRANGLER   149
1962–1966—ALBERT DESALVO

9 THE TWENTIETH HIJACKER   161
9/11/01—ZACHARIAS MOUSSAOUI,
AKA "THE TWENTIETH HIJACKER"

10 HERO OR VILLAIN? PART 2   177
1868–2002—DR. SAMUEL MUDD
1865–2005

**11 THE MURDERED CIVIL RIGHTS
WORKERS, PART 2**   191
2005—EDGAR RAY KILLEN

EPILOGUE   203

**APPENDIX I—THOMAS EWING, JR.,
ARGUMENT ON THE LAW AND EVIDENCE
IN THE CASE OF DR. SAMUEL A. MUDD**   205

**APPENDIX II—JAMES SPEED, OPINION
ON THE CONSTITUTIONAL POWER OF THE
MILITARY TO TRY AND EXECUTE THE
ASSASSINS OF THE PRESIDENT**   253

BIBLIOGRAPHY   275

INDEX   279

ACKNOWLEDGMENTS

Some writers claim to hate the Internet as a research tool. Apparently, they are among the few who can travel to any library, from Alexandria, Egypt, to Washington, D.C., with unlimited time and money to do the job. Alas, Alexandria is not on my itinerary at the moment. Washington, however, always is.

Without the digitized collection of presidential papers in the National Archives, available much more quickly online than putting on my wings and flying over the Ohio Valley to Washington, I would not have had such ready access to President Jimmy Carter's presidential papers, which proved invaluable in solving the mystery of Dr. Mudd.

A special thank you to President Carter for taking time out to answer my questions. The Nobel Laureate responded, personally, within a week of being queried. I don't know how it is with other writers, but when I saw the president's handwritten response to my questions, I was thrilled. He signed it "Jimmy C."

The only other president to be awarded the Nobel Peace Prize was T. R. Roosevelt. That places "Jimmy C." in good company indeed. Class shows. Likewise publisher John Oakes. In an industry that more and more thinks of "product" and not books, Mr. Oakes provided unqualified support, ideas, editing, and historical knowledge.

That's why his name is in the same paragraph as the president's.

PROLOGUE

By the end of June 2005, two of the biggest criminal cases in United States history had finally been adjudicated by lower courts: Zacharias Moussaoui aka "the Twentieth Hijacker," and Edgar Ray Killen, the former KKK Kleagle who was convicted of murdering the three civil rights workers, James Chaney, Andrew Goodman and Michael Schwerner in 1964. Yet, questions lingered about the guilt of both.

Did Moussaoui really plan to be the twentieth hijacker on 9/11?

Did Killen really finger the civil rights workers, marking them for death?

Did they really do it?

Because most criminal convictions are based on circumstantial evidence, such questions will always linger. When cases have reached the last level of appeal, the courts sign off; the cases are relegated to the history bin. Truth is lost. People who did it are found innocent. Worse, people who didn't do it are found guilty and are executed or forced to serve prison terms for crimes they did not commit.

In 1946, Erle Stanley Gardner formed the Court of Last Resort, a group of criminal justice experts who looked into closed cases, where a defendant alleged he was convicted for a crime he didn't commit. Unfortunately, it has long ceased to exist. But the work needs to be done.

It's time, then, to take a second look at eleven of those cases. They have been chosen both for their historical relevance and contemporary significance. It is no coincidence, for example, that the case of Dr. Mudd began in 1865 and didn't end until the latter part of the twenty-first century. Forever having their family bname besmirched, the Mudd family had taken their case all the way to the president to prove their forebear's innocence. Nor can any investigator taking a look at the canon of these cases ignore the more popular ones that continue to generate controversy, including Lizzie Borden, Bruno Richard Hauptmann, and the Rosenbergs.

Did they really do it? Let's find out.

HERO OR VILLAIN? PART I

1865–1868 DR. SAMUEL MUDD

A heavily armed patrol of Union soldiers filled the front yard of the rural Maryland farm. Inside the farmhouse, Colonel H. H. Wells, an investigator for the Judge Advocate General's Office, interrogated one of the suspects in the conspiracy to kill President Abraham Lincoln.

"Have two strangers been here recently?" Colonel Wells asked Dr. Samuel Mudd. Before answering, Mudd became "very much excited, and got pale as a sheet of paper and blue about his lips, like a man frightened at something he had done," Wells later recalled.

"It was about 4 o'clock on Saturday morning, the 15th of April, when I was aroused by a loud knock at my door," Dr. Mudd began.

Going to the window, he pulled back the curtain. There at the door was a young man holding the reins of two horses. On one of them, a second man sat, slumped over in pain. Mudd opened the door. The man who held the horses was talkative and wore a dusty, cutoff jacket and a huge ribbon of a bow tie.

"My companion has broken his leg, and desires medical assistance," the young man said.

Mudd helped bring the injured man into his house and laid him on a sofa in the front parlor.

"I fell from a horse," volunteered the injured man, apparently in response to Mudd's unarticulated question. "Did either man identify himself?" Wells asked.

Mudd shook his head. The injured man lay there awhile on Mudd's couch, catching his breath, until his companion and Dr. Mudd carried him upstairs into the front bedroom and set him on the bed. Carefully, Mudd removed the dusty black boot and gave it to his wife for safekeeping. Examining the injured leg, he saw that the front bone of the foot was broken at right angles about two inches above the instep.

"It was a light break that could have been worse," Mudd told his interrogator. That made no sense to Wells. It seemed odd that a broken bone in the foot would stick out at right angles if it was just a light break. Dr. Mudd proceeded to dress the limb, "as best as I was able to do with the limited facilities I had available."

That also seemed odd to Wells. Mudd had a thriving and well-stocked medical practice. He was used to calls for help at all hours of the day and night.

"I called in a white servant to make a pair of crutches," Mudd continued.

He would not trust the job to one of his newly freed black slaves who still worked his farm. While Lincoln's Emacipation Proclamation had been issued in 1863, it did not apply to Maryland. It wasn't until the following year that Maryland passed a new constitution outlawing slavery.

With the white servant beginning to make the crutches, all retired for the night. The next morning at breakfast, the young man, who had still not given his name, ate with a hearty appetite. Not so the patient. The sleep had apparently done him no good. He wore a muffler constantly over his face. Mudd didn't get a look at his features, or so he claimed.

As breakfast ended, the young man made some remark

about procuring a carriage for his friend. A short time later, he came down and asked for a razor. He said his friend wished to shave himself. When Mudd went up later to check on his patient, he saw that the wounded man had indeed shaved off his moustache. He still kept a shawl about his neck, for the purpose of concealing the lower part of his face.

There's something odd about these men, Mudd thought.

Later that morning, they tried to get a carriage at Mudd's father's home nearby. On the way there, they ran into Mudd's brother, who told them that the carriage wasn't available. The young man decided to go back to Mudd's house and see how his friend was doing. Mudd took the opportunity to go into Bryantown to see some friends and patients.

Mudd was certain that it was only when he went to town that he heard of the murder of President Lincoln in Washington city the day before. Mudd claimed that all he heard was that along with an accomplice, the unidentified assassin had fled across the Potomac into Maryland and vanished into the night. It had taken many hours for the news to come down the line from Washington. Bryantown, like the rest of the country, was in a state of shock.

"No one mentioned the name of the assassin?" Wells asked,

"No," Mudd answered firmly.

Returning home in late afternoon, the young man confronted Mudd and asked for directions to Dr. John Wilmer's who lived nearby. He claimed to be acquainted with the doctor. Mudd told him to take the main road.

"Is there not a nearer way?"

Mudd replied that there was a road across the swamp. That's when the young man helped his limping companion onto their horses. They spurred their mounts into the swamp, off toward Dr. Wilmer's house.

"That is all I know about them," Dr. Mudd finished.

"Did you recognize the wounded man?" Wells asked, his voice rising slightly.

"I did not," Mudd answered not too convincingly.

Knowing Mudd to be a former "slaver," who openly supported the Confederacy during the late war, Wells figured him for a liar. From a folder, Wells took out a daguerreotype. He carefully placed the photograph on the table in front of Mudd.

"Was this the man who came to your door, John Wilkes Booth?"

Mudd began to fidget. Wells noticed he was having trouble maintaining eye contact.

"I do not recognize him from that photograph. I *had* been introduced to Booth at church, some time in November last, as wanting to buy farming lands," he added. "We had some little conversation on the subject. Booth then asked, 'Are there any desirable horses that could be bought in the neighborhood cheaply?' I mentioned a neighbor of mine who had some horses that were good drivers."

"What happened then?" Wells asked.

"Booth remained with me that night, and next morning purchased one of those horses."

"Do you now recognize the person you treated that night as the same person you had been introduced to—Booth?"

"Yes," Mudd admitted, his memory suddenly coming back to him, "But I never saw Booth from the time he was introduced to me in church until that Saturday morning he came to my door. The young man I never saw before."

Wells told him that the "young man's" real name was David Herold. Mudd didn't flinch.

"He was Booth's accomplice."

Mudd claimed to have never heard the name.

"Dr. Mudd, you know by now that Booth shot the president. I believe you are concealing the facts of the case, which would be considered the strongest evidence of your guilt, and might endanger your safety."

If ever an investigator had told a suspect to come clean before it was too late, it was Wells. If Mudd was charged, he would be tried before a military tribunal. President Johnson had made certain of that. Days after Lincoln's assassination, Johnson signed an executive order establishing a special military tribunal to prosecute the men charged in the conspiracy to assassinate President Lincoln. The country was angry. Whoever killed Lincoln deserved swift retribution.

Mudd's wife came into the room. "The penalty for conviction will be death," Wells explained calmly, his demeanor lending the words their power.

Responding to Wells's very real threat, the wife raced upstairs and promptly returned with a boot. It was the same one Mudd had taken off the injured man that night. Wells looked inside.

A tag bearing the initials "JWB" had been sewn in just below the lip.

Up until the night of April 14, 1865, no president had ever been assassinated, although in 1832 an assassin had tried to shoot President Andrew Jackson on the steps of the Capital— twice. Both times, his pistols misfired. All he got for his efforts was a caning from Jackson and confinement to an insane asylum. Booth, however, was a new breed of American: the presidential assassin who knew how to put together a conspiracy.

John Wilkes Booth was an intelligent, educated criminal. Born into a prominent theatrical family, his father Junius had been the most popular and respected actor in America. John Wilkes, handsome, dashing, debonair, had inherited the mantle. By the time he snuck into the back of President Lincoln's box at Ford's Theatre with a .40 caliber derringer in his pocket, Booth was the most famous actor in America—his face known far and wide. He was paid the ungodly sum of $20,000 a year to act, well over a million dollars by today's standards.

John Wilkes Booth had grown up in Maryland, a border state; his family supported slavery. By the time he was an adult, he hated "niggers" so much, he made sure to be in attendance when John Brown was hanged in 1859 for fomenting insurrection among Virginia's slaves. During the Civil War, he became a member of the Confederate underground of border-state sympathizers who conducted Confederate dispatches up and down the east coast, and to Europe when necessary.

To Booth, as to most Southerners, the Union was something abhorrent, to be destroyed. Lincoln was its symbol. In March 1865, when Lincoln was inaugurated at the White House for the second time, Booth was seated behind him, as the guest of an abolitionist senator's daughter, who had procured him a ticket to the event.

"What an excellent chance I had to kill the President, if I had wished, on inauguration day!" Booth would later complain to a friend.

Booth then used his talent and charisma to attract a group of what today would be termed terrorists, men whose goal it was to disrupt and, if possible, take down the federal government. The core of the conspiracy were Michael O'Laughlen, Samuel Arnold, Lewis Powell, aka "Lewis Paine," John Surratt, David Herold, and George Atzerodt.

A secret dispatch rider for the Confederates, Surratt had introduced Booth to the others. Later identified by the military commission that would try them as "the Lincoln Conspirators," these men discussed their plans at an inn in Surrattsville, Maryland, owned by Mary Surratt, John's mother. On March 15, 1865, Booth decided to meet instead at Gautier's Restaurant on Pennsylvania Avenue, about three blocks from Ford's Theatre.

The Lincoln Conspirators gathered around a table in the restaurant's dark interiror. The discussion centered on kidnapping Lincoln and holding him for a ransom of Confederate prisoners of war. Booth needed the right moment to put the plot into play. But after a kidnapping attempt failed because of a presidential schedule switch, John Surratt lost his nerve and fled to Canada. Samuel Arnold would eventually do the same.

Quoted in the *Baltimore American* in 1902, Arnold said that Booth "became a monomaniac on the success of the Confederate arms, a condition that generally follows when a man's thoughts are constantly centered upon one subject alone."

As would be expected of the commander-in-chief of a nation at war, Lincoln's schedule was constantly shifting. Booth finally abandoned the kidnapping plot. When Robert E. Lee surrendered to Ulysses S. Grant at Appomattox Court House, Virginia, on April 9, 1865, most people thought the war was over. Not Booth, not by a short shot.

Two days later, on April 11, the president delivered a speech at the White House. The crowd included a large group of former slaves. Also in the crowd were John Wilkes Booth and an acquaintance, Louis Weichmann. The president suggested giving voting rights to "the very intelligent [blacks], and on those who serve our cause as soldiers."

Booth couldn't believe it: *niggers voting?!* Booth was a Southerner through and through. He grew up in Maryland with slaves doing the family's drudgery. And now Lincoln was making them *equal?* He turned to Weichmann and said it would be "the last speech" the president ever gave.

That speech pushed Booth over the edge. Forget kidnapping; the plot he now conceived was much, much worse. It was so brilliant that in one night, he intended to destroy the United States of America.

Booth had read the Constitution. In the presidential line of succession, the vice president came after the president, then the president pro tempore of the Senate, and finally, secretary of state. By eliminating Vice President Andrew Johnson and Secretary of State William H. Seward, the only one left to assume power was the president pro tempore of the Senate, Lafayette LaSabine.

Seward and Johnson were men of real courage. Booth knew they could be relied on to follow Lincoln's policies. LaSabine was a hack Whig politician. If any greatness lurked in his character, it was pretty far back. Restoring a crippled nation to health required vision and courage. With LaSabine as president, the Union would fall.

Lincoln eschewed most of the trappings of his office. During his presidency, he could regularly be seen about Washington without bodyguards. His vow that it was Lincoln's last speech could be made true if he acted expedititously. As Booth planned it out, Louis Paine would kill Secretary of State Seward. Herold would function as his backup, holding the horse for the getaway. Atzerodt would assassinate Johnson and Booth, and, of course, the president. Booth had already worked out his escape route through northern Maryland. He knew he could stop at places along the way that were operated by members of the Confederate underground.

Booth, however, proved a better actor than criminal mastermind. He was the only one to succeed at his task that night. In Paine's case, it was not for lack of trying. Seward was wearing a leather brace around his neck from a recent riding accident. Otherwise, Paine's Bowie knife would have cut into his throat, instead of glancing off the tough leather. Paine had to settle for mutilating Seward's face instead.

• • •

Like John Wilkes Booth, Samuel Mudd was a Maryland native. Born December 20, 1833, on a large, slave-driven plantation in Charles County, the son of Henry Lowe Mudd and his wife, Sarah Ann Reeves. Sam had an idyllic childhood, replete with fishing and hunting trips with Dad. Educated by private tutors, in 1847 he began St. John's College in Frederick, Maryland at the age of 14. Two years later, he transferred to Georgetown College in Washington, D.C.

In 1854, the 21-year-old Mudd went to the University of Maryland in Baltimore to study medicine and surgery Graduating in two years, in 1856 Mudd went home to start a practice. "Home" was the plantation he grew up on, home to the Mudd family and their 89 slaves. In contemporary American money, those slaves would be valued at well over $1,000,000. Losing them to emancipation would be a devastating blow. Multiply the Mudds by all the plantation and slave owners throughout the South, and it becomes clear why the Union needed four long and bloody years before winning. As war loomed, and with economics favoring slavery, the Mudd family held unwaveringly to their proslavery position. Dr. Mudd regularly beat his slaves and even disciplined one by shooting him in the leg.

On November 26, 1857, Dr. Mudd had married his childhood sweetheart, Sarah Frances Dyer. Andrew, their first child, was born in November 1858. By 1859, the Mudds had a farm of their own, located about five miles north of Bryantown, Maryland, and thirty miles south of Washington, D.C. In 1860, the Mudds' second child, Lillian Augusta, was born. Two more sons were born in 1862 and 1864.

By the end of the war, the children totaled four, and they were as dear to Dr. Mudd as to any father in any age. And yet, Dr. Mudd did not hesitate to open the door to two strangers, one wounded on horseback, never once suspecting in any way that they could be a threat to his family. Unless . . . He knew who they were?

The Judge Advocate General was wondering the same thing. He also had access to an extensive group of investigators. He used those now. They ferreted out the first conspiracy to kidnap Lincoln and the second to murder him. As for Dr. Mudd's role, they let the indictment speak for itself:

> And in further prosecution of said conspiracy [to assassinate the president], the said Samuel A. Mudd did, at Washington City, and within the military department and military lines aforesaid, on or before the 6th day of March, A.D. 1865, and on divers other days and times between that day and the 20th day of April, A.D. 1865, advise, encourage, receive, entertain, harbor, and conceal, aid and assist the said John Wilkes Booth, David E. Herold, Lewis Payne, John H. Surratt, Michael O'Laughlin, George A. Atzerodt, Mary E. Surratt, and Samuel Arnold, and their confederates, with knowledge of the murderous and traitorous conspiracy aforesaid, and with the intent to aid, abet, and assist them in the execution thereof, and in escaping from justice after the murder of the said Abraham Lincoln, in pursuance of said conspiracy in manner aforesaid.
>
> By order of the President of the United States.
>
> J. HOLT,
> *Judge Advocate General.*

The accused conspirators were placed on one of the Navy's ironclads. Under orders from Secretary of War Stanton, their heads were hidden under canvas hoods. Mudd, a true son of the South, found himself hooded ignominiously and held prisoner aboard the ironclad *Montauk*.

Stanton, who was really running the show until Andrew Johnson got settled, urged the president to appoint a military commission to make swift work of the conspirators. Many members of Lincoln's cabinet, including Secretary of the Navy Gideon Welles, objected to the military's trying civilians. Welles had been by Lincoln's side during the death vigil and knew how his boss felt about the military's usurping the civilian functioning of the courts.

Nevertheless, Johnson acceded to Stanton.

Exproceedings of a Military Commission, Convened at Washington, D.C., by virtue of the following Orders:

Executive Chamber, Washington City, May 1, 1865

Whereas, the Attorney-General of the United States hath given his opinion:

That the persons implicated in the murder of the late President, Abraham Lincoln, and the attempted assassination of the Honorable William H. Seward, Secretary of State, and in an alleged conspiracy to assassinate other officers of the Federal Government at Washington City, and their aiders and abettors, are subject to the jurisdiction of, and lawfully triable before, a Military Commission;

It is ordered:

1st. That the Assistant Adjutant-General detail nine competent military officers to serve as a Commission for the trial of said parties, and that the Judge Advocate General proceed to prefer charges against said parties for their alleged offenses, and bring them to trial before said Military Commission; that said trial or trials be conducted by the said Judge Advocate General, and as recorder thereof, in person, aided by each Assistant and Special Judge Advocates as he may designate; and that said trials be conducted with all diligence consistent with the ends of justice: the said Commission to sit without regard to hours.

2nd. That Brevet Major-General Hartranft be assigned to duty as Special Provost Marshal General, for the purpose of said trial, and attendance upon said Commission, and the execution of its mandates.

3rd. That the said Commission establish such order or rules of proceeding as may avoid unnecessary delay, and conduce to the ends of public justice.

[Signed] ANDREW JOHNSON.

WAR DEPARTMENT, ADJ'T GENERAL'S OFFICE,
Washington, May 6, 1865

The government meant business and so did the doctor. Dr.

Mudd's attorney, Thomas Ewing, Jr., had impeccable Yankee credentials. His father, Thomas Ewing, Sr., had been a U.S. Senator from Ohio and secretary of the treasury to President Andrew Harrison and secretary of the interior to President Zachary Taylor. These credentials added a note of credibility to Ewing's defense of the southern slaver. A good advocate, Ewing saw an opportunity to knock the charges out before even getting to court.

In a precedent-setting brief, Thomas Ewing argued that the military commission was unconstitutional since President Lincoln was murdered in time of peace. Therefore, the accused should be tried by a civilian court. Only a civilian court had jurisdiction. Ewing had the misfortune that his opposite number was James Speed.

Attorney General James Speed was President Lincoln's oldest friend in Washington. His brother Joshua had been an early friend of Lincoln's in Springfield, Illinois. When Joshua returned home to Kentucky rather than stay in Springfield, Lincoln got friendly with the brother who stayed behind. Eventually, James Speed and Abraham Lincoln became good friends. Speed wasn't about to let his old friend down now.

In his brief, Speed countered that since the Union victory was barely a week old, the president's principal job was still commander in chief. It was in that capacity that President Lincoln was murdered. Therefore, the military had jurisdiction over the men and woman, who plotted and carried out the president's murder. It was a logical, well thought out argument, propelled as much by logic as it was by Speed's need for swift justice.

Not surprisingly, the federal appellate courts held for the government. How could they not? Even for judges, it was hard to stand down from four concerted years of war in a mere matter of weeks. That was how the legal precedent was set to try United States civilians by a military court in time of peace, an argument later continued by the administration of President George W. Bush.

On May 8, 1865, Generals David Hunter (first officer), David Clendenin, James Ekin, Robert Foster, T. M. Harris, Albion Howe, August Kautz, Lewis Wallace, and Colonel C. H Tomkins got together for the first time as a military commission. The venue was a spanking new courtroom made out of sweet smelling, fresh wood on the third floor of the Old Arsenal Penitentiary in Washington.

The commission's job was to judge the innocence or guilt of the civilian Lincoln Conspirators: David Herold, Lewis Paine, George Atzerodt, Samuel Arnold, Mary Surratt, Michael O'Laughlen, Edman Spangler—the man who held Booth's getaway horse outside Ford's Theatre—and Dr. Samuel Mudd. The penalty for conviction for each of them would probably be death, but the commission had the option of imposing life imprisonment should they so desire.

For its part, the prosecution had made the decision to try the conspirators all at once, employing different strategies with each to gain conviction. In Mary Surratt's and Samuel Mudd's cases, neither conviction nor execution were expected. The public saw them as weak pawns in Booth's chess game of death.

Some, like Lewis Paine, Seward's would-be assassin—stood no chance. Realizing that, when it was his turn, William Doster, Paine's attorney, passionately argued that his client was insane, even though insanity was three decades away from being accepted as a criminal defense.

"He lives in that land of imagination where it seems to him legions of southern soldiers wait to crown him as their chief commander. We know now that slavery made him immoral, that war made him a murderer, and that necessity, revenge, and delusion made him an assassin. Let him live, if not for his sake, for our own."

The Judge Advocate General decided to approach the Mudd prosecution in three ways. The first was rather obvious and totally irrelevant to the charges at hand. Mudd was an unrepentant and cruel slaver. The prosecution would bring this out at trial to show his character, or lack thereof.

Second, the prosecution felt they could show that Mudd consistently made anti-Union statements, including a public call for Lincoln's death. They would then show Mudd to be a direct part of the Confederate underground.

Third, if the government could show that Mudd knew Booth prior to the night he came to his door, which meant not only his appearance but his *voice,* conviction would be imminent. To do that, the government had some interesting evidence up its federal sleeve. It had lined up six of Dr. Mudd's former slaves to testify against him

Regardless of the questions of the constitutionality of its very existence, the military commission trying the civilian Lincoln Conspirators readily agreed to hear their testimony. "Mary Sims—Colored" was the first former slave to testify on May 25:

"I know that prisoner yonder, Dr. Samuel Mudd. I was his slave, and lived with him four years. I left him about a month before this Christmas gone," Simms began. "I heard him talk about President Lincoln. He said that he [Lincoln] was here at night, dressed in woman's clothes; that he lay in watch for him, and if he had come in right, they would have killed him. He said nothing about shooting him; he would have 'killed him,' he said."

The prosecution then led her to Mudd's clandestine activities.

"A man named John Surratt and [Confederate agent] Walter Bowie visited Dr. Mudd's last summer," the ex-slave continued. "Mr. Surratt was a young-looking man, slim made, not very tall, nor very short, and his hair was light. He came very often."

"How did you know that his name was Surratt?" the prosecutor asked.

"Dr. Samuel Mudd and his wife both called him Mr. Surratt. They all called him that. I have seen Surratt in the house, upstairs and in the parlor with Dr. Mudd. They never talked much in the presence of the family; they always went off by themselves upstairs."

It was devastating testimony that placed Mudd, prior to Lincoln's assassination, in intimate conversation with one of the other accused co-conspirators. Simms then proceeded to identify by name the other Confederate officers and spies who visited Mudd and bivouacked behind his farm.

"When they came to the house to eat," she continued, "Dr. Mudd would put us out to watch if anybody came. When we told them somebody was coming, they would run into the woods again, and he would make me take the victuals out to them. I would set them down, and stand and watch, and then the rebs would come out to get the victuals."

"What else do you remember about these men?"

"Some men were lieutenants and officers from Virginia, and brought letters to Dr. Sam Mudd. He gave them letters and clothes and socks to take back. They were dressed in gray coats, trimmed up with yellow; gray breeches, with yellow stripes down the leg."

What Simms was really claiming was that Mudd helped relay letters from the Confederates, some of whom arrived at his doorstep in uniform. Now, the prosecution turned to their other strategy, which would be repeated throughout the trial, of showing how Mudd treated his "property."

"After Dr. Mudd shot my brother, Elzee Eglent, one of his slaves, he said he should send him to Richmond, to build batteries, I think he said."

In a civilian court, there would have been an immediate

objection from the defense that the statement was prejudicial and irrelevant. The military tribunal, however, found it particularly relevant. Mudd appeared to have enough connections to send a slave behind Confederate lines during a critical time in the war.

"Call Elzee Eglent," said the bailiff.

A young black man took the stand.

"How do you know the defendant, Samuel Mudd?" the prosecutor asked.

"I know Dr. Samuel Mudd. He was my boss. Yonder he is [pointing to the accused]. I was his slave, and lived with him. I left him on the 20th of the August before the last."

"Did he say any thing to you before you left him about sending you to Richmond?"

"Yes, sir. He told me the morning he shot me that he had a place in Richmond for me."

Thomas Ewing sprang to his feet.

"I object to that question and the answer," he shouted

"Overruled, said General Hunter, the commission's presiding officer.

"He told me he had a place in Richmond for me when I should be able to go away," Eglent continued, glancing over at his former owner. "He did not say what I was to do there. That was the June before the last. He named three more that he said he was going to send to Richmond—Dick and my two brothers, Sylvester and Frank."

It was a clear threat by Mudd to send any slaves that misbehaved to the front lines in Richmond, the Confederate capital.

"What about the men who came to Dr. Mudd's house?"

"I saw men come to Dr. Mudd's, dressed some in black clothes and some in [Confederate] gray; gray jackets, coat-like, and gray breeches. One of them, [Confederate agent], Andrew Gwynn I had seen before. The others I did not know.

"They used to sleep in the woods, about a quarter of a mile off, I reckon, and would come to the house at different times, and go back to the woods. I have seen my sister, Mary Simms, carrying them. That was in the June and July before the last."

Next to the stand was Sylvester Eglent, Elzee's brother.

"I used to live about a quarter of a mile from the house of Dr. Samuel Mudd. I lived with his father."

"State whether you heard him say any thing, at any time, about sending men to Richmond and, if so, what he said, and to whom he was talking," the Judge Advocate General asked.

"Last August, about twelve-month ago, I heard him say he was going to send me, my brother Elzee, Frank, and Dick Gardner, and Lou Gardner to Richmond to build batteries."

Ewing got to his feet.

"Objection to question and answer!"

"Overruled," said General Hunter.

Mudd had to sit in his seat as a parade of the damned, the slaves he had beaten, were brought to the stand in an American court of law that had clearly been constituted to get a conviction. It must have rankled. "Melvina Washington, Colored," was called next to the stand.

"I used to live with Dr. Samuel Mudd. I was his slave. I see him there [pointing to the accused, Samuel A. Mudd]. I left him this coming October two years. The last summer I was there, I heard him say that President Lincoln would not occupy his seat long. There was a heap of gentlemen in the house at the time, but I do not know who they were.

"Some had on gray clothes, and some little short jackets, with black buttons, and a little peak on behind. Sometimes they staid in the house, and sometimes slept in the pines not far from Dr. Mudd's spring. Dr. Mudd carried victuals to them sometimes, and once he sent them by Mary Simms. I happened to be at the house one time when they were all sitting down to dinner, and they had two of the boys watching. When they were told somebody was coming, these men rushed from the table to the side door, and went to the spring [to hide]."

As for how he treated his slaves, "I heard Dr. Mudd say one day, when he got mad with one of his men, that he would send him to Richmond, but I did not hear him say what he was to do there." But on cross-examination Ewing got the witness to admit, "I do not know of any white people that saw these men but Dr. Mudd and his wife, and two colored women, Rachel Spencer and Mary Simms."

Ewing had just gotten the witness to introduce the possibility that the "colored" witnesses were conspiratorial liars. It was a good tactic with a civilian jury that thought could be more easily swayed. Milo Simms, Mary Simms brother, testified next.

"I was a slave of Dr. Samuel Mudd, and lived with him. There he is [pointing to the prisoner, Dr. Mudd]. I left his house on the Friday before last Christmas but the last summer I was there, I saw two or three men there, that sometimes staid in the house and sometimes out by the spring, up among the bushes. They had on plaid gray clothes, and one had stripes and brass buttons on.

"I saw their bed among the bushes. It was fixed under a pine tree. Rails were laid at the head and blankets spread out. They got their victuals from Dr. Samuel Mudd's. Sometimes he carried them out himself, and sometimes my sister carried them away.

"She would lay them down at the spring, and John Surratt or Billy Simms took them away. I heard John Surratt called by that name in the house. Dr. Samuel Mudd's wife called him so in Dr. Mudd's presence. He was a spare man, slim, pale face, light hair, and no whiskers. When he was in the house, Dr. Mudd told his son and some of the children to stay out of doors and watch, and if anybody was coming to tell him."

Simms description of Surratt was dead on. This was especially damaging testimony.

"Last year, about tobacco-planting time," Simms continued, "I heard Ben Gardiner tells Dr. Samuel Mudd, in Bean town [Bryantown], that Abe Lincoln was a God damned old son of a bitch, and ought to have been dead long ago. Dr. Mudd said that was much of his mind."

On cross-examination, the witness testified, "I worked in the field, but sometimes was at the house to take the horses from the men who came there. I reckon I am about fourteen years old."

Slaves couldn't be sure of their birthdays. Being property, birth certificates weren't filed with the county.

"I do not know whether I would know Mr. Surratt now. I knew him last summer. He was not shown to me by any one," he continued. The way he knew Surratt was because "Dr. Samuel Mudd came out to me and said, 'Take Mr. Surratt's horse to the stable and feed him.' He staid all night that time. I only saw him there two or three times."

As the day wore down, "William Marshall—Colored," took the stand.

"I was a slave until the year 1863, when I got away from home," said Marshall calmly, describing how he escaped from his master. "I belonged to Mr. Willie Jameston. Of late I have lived near Dr. Samuel Mudd. I see him here now [pointing to the accused, Dr. Mudd]. I know Benjamin Gardner, one of his neighbors. He was my wife's master.

"State whether you heard any conversation between Benjamin Gardner and Dr. Samuel A. Mudd about the rebels, and their battle with the Union forces on the Rappahannock," the Judge Advocate General asked the witness.

Ewing was on his feet.

"I object! I object on the ground heretofore stated by me with reference to similar questions."

General Hunter overruled the objection.

"Yes, sir, I did [hear that conversation] on Saturday, soon after the battle at the Rappahannock, I happened to be home. I had every other Saturday off. My wife being sick, the Doctor had been to see her, and when he came out, Mr. Gardiner met him at the corner of the house, and said to him, 'We gave them hell down on the Rappahannock,' and the Doctor said, 'Yes, we did.' Then he said, 'Damned if Stonewall ain't the best part of the devil. I don't know what to compare him to.' "

"Who said that he was the best part of the devil?"

"Benjamin Gardiner. The Doctor said Stonewall was quite a smart one. Then Benjamin Gardiner said, 'Now he has gone around up in Maryland, and he is going to cross over on the Point of Rocks. He will be down here and take the capital of Washington, and soon have old Lincoln burned up in his house.' And Dr. Mudd said he would not be the least surprised. He made no objection to it."

Even as this testimony was being given in court, Dr. Mudd always claimed publicly that when he set the assassin Booth's ankle, he had no idea who the man was, let alone that he had just killed the president. He was an innocent country doctor doing what a doctor does—performing his duty under the Hippocratic Oath.

Yet in the courtroom, his former slaves had delivered devastating testimony that Mudd had met regularly with known Confederate agents. He passed documents they gave him, presumably to agents further down the line. He knowingly consorted with conspirator John Surratt, who was still at large. He either made anti-Union comments or condoned them, which in a border state like Maryland was certainly common. But since Mudd was being charged with participating in *premeditated* murder, they were being used as evidence of his complicity in the conspiracy and as evidence of his homicidal feelings toward Lincoln *prior* to his death.

Now it was time to place him closer to the central character of the conspiracy: John Wilkes Booth.

Daniel J. Thomas was the first white man the prosecution called. He was one of Mudd's neighbors.

"I am acquainted with Dr. Mudd. About two months ago, some time in the latter part of March, I had a conversation with Dr. Mudd at John S. Dawning's. He lives close to me, and about a mile and quarter from Dr. Mudd's. We were engaged in conversation about the politics of the day," Thomas testified.

"I made a remark to Dr. Mudd that the war would soon be over, that South Carolina was taken, and Richmond would soon be too, and that we would soon have peace. He then said that Abraham Lincoln was an abolitionist, and that the whole Cabinet were such. He thought the South would never be subjugated by abolition doctrine, and he went on to state that the President, Cabinet, and other Union men in the State of Maryland would be killed in six or seven weeks."

There it was, what a later generation would call "the smoking gun:" a witness testifying that Mudd had knowledge aforethought of the plot to kill the president. It was devastating testimony. Ewing's only hope was to use Thomas's own testimony to raise reasonable doubt.

"Perhaps Dr. Mudd was joking?" Ewing asked the witness.

"He did not seem to be joking, but it is impossible for me to say whether or not he was earnest in what he said," Thomas replied. "He did not look as if he was angry or speak [*sic*] in malice. I can not judge whether a man is in earnest or not from the language he uses, but I should think a man in earnest to talk of the President being assassinated."

"Did you think at the time that he was in earnest?"

"No, sir. I did not think any such thing would ever come to pass. I thought the President was well guarded, and that it was a want of sense on his part saying so. I laughed to think that the man had no more sense. When Dr. Mudd first said it, I thought he meant it, but after a day or two I thought he certainly could not have meant it. But after the President was killed, and after hearing that Booth was at his house, I thought he really meant it."

"You thought it was a mere joke at the time, from the way he said it?"

"He was laughing at the time, or something like it. I know Dr. Mudd. We went to school together, and when he was a boy he was full of fun and jokes."

Dr. Mudd, the court jester of the conspiracy? What did that make Booth—a tragedian who created his own tragedy?

"Did you mention your conversation with Dr. Mudd to anyone?"

"I spoke of what Dr. Mudd had said to almost everybody I saw, but everybody laughed at the idea of such a thing."

Of course they did. Before Lincoln's homicide no president had ever been assassinated. But they weren't laughing afterward. As for Thomas, his cross-examination literally didn't stop till the end of the trial. Ewing continually tried to impeach Thomas's testimony by calling numerous character witnesses who testified to Thomas's unreliability and Dr. Mudd's trustworthiness.

However, there wasn't much the defense counsel could do when the Judge Advocate General introduced into evidence a statement that the accused co-conspirator, George Atzerodt, had previously given. On May 1, 1865, George Atzerodt had given a recorded confession to a detective on the staff of Maryland's provost marshal.

"I am certain Dr. Mudd knew all about it [the assassination], as Booth sent (as he told me) liquors and provisions for the trip . . . about two weeks before the murder, to Dr. Mudd's," Atzerodt testified.

The prosecution honed in on the relationship between Mudd and Booth. Witness after witness took the stand to testify that there was a closer relationship between Dr. Mudd, Booth, and some of the other conspirators than Mudd would readily admit. Witnesses testified that they had seen Booth and Mudd together on November 13, 1864, in Maryland at a horse sale. This was most likely the steed Booth rode after killing the president.

Louis Weichmann testified that in late December 1864 he was walking with John Surratt near the National Hotel in Washington. Mudd, strolling with Booth, hailed them this way: "Surratt! Surratt!" Booth clearly knew the secret Confederate dispatch rider. Although indicted by the commission, Surratt was still at large in Canada,.

According to Weichmann, Booth, Surratt, and Mudd later excused themselves to have a private conversation. Mudd later claimed they were just talking over Booth purchasing real estate in Maryland. Weichmann's testimony further impeached Mudd's statement that he had only met Booth once, the past November when he sold him a horse. In fact, according to Weichmann there had been another, more clandestine meeting in December.

The government was ready to close, but had one more witness to call.

"Call Marcus Norton to the stand!" yelled the bailiff.

A distinguished looking middle aged man came forward, took the oath, and sat in the witness box. He testified that his name was Marcus Norton. He was an attorney. In early March 1865, Norton was in Washington to argue a case before the Supreme Court. He was staying at the National Hotel.

While working on his brief, a man Norton did not know at the time, but who he now realized was Dr. Mudd, burst into his room. Apologizing for his hasty entry, Dr. Mudd said that he thought the room was occupied by a man called "Booth."

Norton's testimony was bolstered by the final witnesses, detectives who checked the National Hotel registry for the day Norton stayed there. On that same day, the detectives discovered that the man renting the room directly above Norton's was John Wilkes Booth.

The prosecution rested. They had presented a compelling case that Dr. Samuel Mudd was part of the Confederate Underground. That didn't make him guilty of conspiracy to kill Lincoln, but the prosecution had also produced legitimate witnesses who testified that Mudd and Booth had met on at least two occasions. Nevertheless, Mudd still claimed that because Booth had had a muffler over his face, Mudd had not recognized him during the twelve hours Booth spent in his home.

Booth was the most famous actor in America, his face known far and wide. Mudd claimed he had not recognized Booth as the man with the broken bone in his foot, even though the man stayed with him for a total of twelve hours? Even to an objective observer, that strained the concept of reasonable doubt.

Credible witnesses had put Booth and Mudd in the same room in intimate conversation, and other evidence showed that Mudd knew Surratt, another co-conspirator. Atzero had also given a written statement against him. Coupled with Mudd's clear anti-Union sentiments, the prosecution had made a strong case for a guilty verdict.

Thomas Ewing knew all this. Like a good defense attorney, Ewing repeatedly challenged the veracity of the prosecution's witnesses. When it was his turn to present his case, he did everything he could to present character witnesses to testify to Mudd's good reputation as a doctor and to challenge any testimony that showed him to be an abusive slave owner and enemy of the Union.

Ewing's best defense was to present an alternate timeline. If Ewing could show that Mudd had not been informed of the assassin's identity until *after* Booth left his farm, then maybe he could present reasonable doubt as to Mudd's complicity in the president's murder. Ewing therefore tried to show that when Mudd visited Bryantown, he only learned that the president had been shot, *not who had done it.* The defense was adamant that when Mudd returned home, he was still ignorant of the fact that it was Booth who had shot Lincoln.

When it was its turn again, the prosecution presented credible rebuttal witnesses who were in Bryantown at the same time as Mudd. In Mudd's presence, they, like everyone else, had heard from a messenger delivering news of the assassination, that the suspected assassin was Booth.

During his closing argument, Ewing reiterated to the commission Mudd's contention that he had only one prior meeting with Booth, the one in November about the horse. All the other alleged meetings that happened after that were figments of the imagination of the prosecution's unreliable witnesses. Ewing then went further, advancing the argument that Mudd's Hippocratic Oath made it imperative for him to treat *anyone,* that even if he knew Booth had shot Lincoln, he was morally and ethically obligated to still treat him.

Ewing contended that in order to find his client guilty, the government needed to find conclusively that he helped further the conspiracy to kill Lincoln in some way. Left unsaid was that even if this argument was valid, Mudd would still be an accessory after the fact for not reporting he had treated the assassin Booth after he knew who he was.

On June 29, 1865, the Military Commission met in secret session. They reviewed the evidence of the seven-week-long trial. A majority vote of five to four of the nine man commission would lead to a guilty verdict. Death sentences needed a full two-thirds majority: six votes. The next day, June 30, the commission reached its verdict.

All of the Lincoln Conspirators were found guilty of the conspiracy charges. For what the commission felt were their more egregious parts in the assassination, Lewis Paine, Mary Surratt, George Atzerodt, and David Herold were all sentenced "to be hanged by the neck until he [or she] be dead." The rest were sentenced to a worse fate.

Samuel Arnold, Dr. Samuel Mudd, and Michael O'Laughlen were sentenced to "hard labor for life, at such place at the President shall direct." Edman Spangler received a six-year sentence. Their prison would be the American version of Devil's Island, the dreaded Fort Jefferson in the Dry Tortugas off the west coast of Florida.

The Commission then forwarded its sentences and the trial record to President Johnson for his final review. Included were notes from five of the nine Commission members, recommending to the President that because of "her sex and age," Mary Surratt's sentence be commuted to life in prison. Nevertheless, on July 5 Johnson approved *all* of the Commission's sentences, including the death sentence for Surratt and life in prison for Mudd. After some legal wrangling, the condemned were sentenced to hang immediately.

Two days later at 1:30 P.M., July 7, 1865, in the courtyard of the Old Arsenal Building in the District of Columbia, Surratt, Paine, Herold and Atzerodt were led out the gallows. After they climbed the sturdy wooden steps, their feet were placed over the trapdoors. A hood was put over their heads and the noose tightened around their throats. Three of the four declined to say anything.

"May we meet in another world" were Atzerodt's last words.

A moment later, the trapdoor flew out from under them and the four Lincoln Conspirators hung out in space. That left the last four sentenced to prison. Of them all, questions continued to dog Mudd's conviction even as he entered into hell.

Did he really do it? Was Dr. Mudd a member of the conspiracy to murder Abraham Lincoln?

In 1865, with Mudd sentenced to life in prison at hard labor, his guilt or innocence should have been left to the judgment of history. History, though, has a way of biting you right on the ass when you least expect it. Because of a combination of historical events and a family's dedication to their forebear, the president of the United States in the latter part of the twentieth century, and the United States Supreme Court in the new millennium, would be asked to render a final verdict on Dr. Samuel Mudd's guilt or innocence.

FORTY WHACKS OF TROUBLE

1892—LIZZIE BORDEN

Dr. Seabury W. Bowen strode deliberately into the sitting room. He stopped short when he saw the body of Andrew Borden on a lounge. Miss Lizzie had already telephoned him and told him of the grisly discovery. As family physician and family friend, he needed to see for himself.

Without delay, Bowen determined to make a thorough investigation. He noted that the sofa upon which the dead man reclined was of mahogany with a hair cloth covering, such as was commonly manufactured for high-class parlor furniture in the 1850s. Mr. Borden lay partly on his right side, with his coat thrown over the arm of the sofa at its head. He wore a dressing gown and his feet, sheathed in shiny black boots, rested on the carpet. Bowen knew it was the man's custom to lie in just that way. To Bowen, the position was perfectly natural; it appeared as if he had just lain down to sleep.

Impressed at the manifest absence of any sign of a struggle—no piece of furniture was overturned—Bowen noticed that Mr. Borden's hands were not clenched. Also, there was no contraction of the muscles or indications of pain or fear, such as he would expect to find under circumstances where the victim knew a fatal blow was about to delivered.

"I am satisfied that he was asleep when he received the first blow, which was necessarily fatal," Bowen later wrote. "I felt for the pulse. It had ceased to beat. Then I examined the body to note its condition and the extent of the wounds."

Despite the family relationship, Dr. Bowen was purely objective in his narration. By acting like a professional when examining the bodies, he gives historians and criminologists a scientist's observations of a the long-ago crime scene.

"Mr. Borden's clothing was not disarranged, and his pockets had apparently not been touched."

This, of course, eliminated robbery as a motive.

"The blows were delivered on the left side of the head, which was more exposed than the other, by reason of the dead man's position. I do not believe he moved a muscle after being struck. The cuts extended from the eye and nose around the ear. In a small space, there were at least eleven distinct cuts of about the same depth and general appearance. In my opinion, any one of them would have proved fatal almost instantly."

Dr. Bowen was accustomed to viewing all kinds of horrible sights, from industrial accidents where limbs had been sheared off, to babies killed horribly by their parents. Yet it sickened him to look at the right side of Andrew Borden's face; it no longer existed because the skull had been shattered. Then, the professional kicked in once again.

"I am inclined to think that an axe was the instrument used. The cuts were about four and a half inches in length and one of them had severed the eye-ball and socket. There was blood from the wounds on the floor and spatters on the wall, but nothing to indicate the slaughter that had taken place. I calculated that nearly all the blows were delivered from behind with great rapidity."

Andrew Borden literally never knew what hit him, because the killer struck from behind. That is very consistent with twentieth century research by criminologists who found that when parricide is committed, the child does so when the parent or parents are at their most vulnerable. Also, the use of the word "spatter" instead of "splatter," shows that Dr. Bowen was forensically aware of what he was observing—the blood had not *splattered* all over the place but rather *spattered* in a distinct spraying pattern.

In some venues, a coroner's inquest is called prior to any criminal proceedings. The inquest itself can also serve as the basis for a criminal indictment. During the inquest, it was common at the time for medical doctors to ask questions of witnesses themselves. However, most of the detective work was left to the authorities.

Dr. Bowen was determined to get at the truth. After he left the parlor where Mr. Borden languished on the sofa, he returned to the kitchen and inquired for Mrs. Borden.

"I do not know where mother is," Miss Lizzie replied. She was Borden's eldest daughter. "I had been out to the barn, and the servant was on the third floor."

Lizzie thought her mother had received a note that morning to visit a sick friend, and had gone out.

"Would you telegraph my sister Emma?" Miss Lizzie asked Bowen, referring to her younger sister, who had a separate residence. Of course, Bowen agreed. He left to telegraph, returning within the hour. When he got back, he met Mrs. Churchill, another family friend, who Lizzie had called by telephone.

"They have found Mrs. Borden," said Mrs. Churchill excitedly.

"Where?" demanded Bowen.

"Upstairs in the front room."

Bowen climbed the stairs, and was about to enter the front bedroom when Miss Lizzie, as everyone called her, appeared at the banister downstairs.

"Mr. John Morse occupied it the night before," Miss Lizzie shouted up.

Morse was Miss Lizzie's uncle by Mr. Borden's first wife, Alice. She died in 1863, when Lizzie was only three years old. Two years later in 1865, Mr. Borden remarried, to Abby Durfree Gray.

As Bowen passed into the front upstairs bedroom, Dr. Borden was horrified to see the body of Abby Borden on the floor, between the bed and dressing-case in the northeast corner of the room. At that moment, he was not sure she had been murdered. He even thought she might have fainted.

On closer examination, however, that did not prove to be the case. Mrs. Borden's skull had sustained almost exactly the same damage as her husband's by what appeared to be the exact same weapon.

"I think she must have been engaged in making the bed when the murderer appeared with an axe or hatchet and made a slash at her," Bowen later wrote. "After that, she turned, and the fiend chopped her head as if it had been a cake of ice. One blow killed the woman but the murderer kept on hacking at her until he was well satisfied that she was dead.

"It is a mystery to me how *he* could have done so much savage work *in so short a time and made no noise* [author's italics]. The weapon must have been a *sharp one* [author's italics] for the cuts were as clean as if made by a razor."

The murderer had planned well enough to use a sharp weapon to do the dastardly work quickly and avoid detection.

"There were, however, no signs of a struggle in the surroundings."

Of course not. Bowen's examination had already shown that both victims were struck from behind; only Mrs. Borden even managed to turn her head after the first blow was struck.

"There was a large pool of blood under the dead woman's head as she lay with her hands under her. I easily made out eleven distinct gashes of apparently the same size as those on her husband's face. Some of these blows had been delivered from the rear and two or three from the front."

Then the doctor got even more specific in his examination.

"One glancing blow cut off nearly two square inches of flesh from the side of the head. In my judgment, the dead woman did not struggle. She was rendered unconscious by the first blow. Not a chair was displaced and not a towel disturbed on the rack near by."

Each victim had continued to be assaulted by blade after death. The autopsy would later confirm Bowen's initial impressions. Andrew took ten chops and Abbie eighteen, for a total of twenty-eight "whacks." So much for the veracity of the nursery rhyme.

Descending the stairs, Bowen found Miss Lizzie "in a highly nervous state. She said that her father left the house about 9 o'clock and went to the bank and the post-office. He returned about 10:30, as near as she could remember, and took off his coat to put on his dressing gown.

"She asked him about the mail, and also if he was feeling any better, as he had been sick the day before. She said he replied to her, 'I feel no better now, no worse,' and then went into the sitting room." Solicitous of her father, Miss Lizzie helped him onto the lounge, and then went to the next-door barn to slice up some "soft lead" for fishing sinkers. Miss Lizzie was an avid angler. She told Bowen she was gone not more than fifteen or twenty minutes at her task of carving up the soft lead in the barn. This would later turn out to be a key piece of testimony.

After a short time in the barn, Miss Lizzie came back into the house when she discovered the body of her father. Miss Lizzie then reminded Bowen, the family physician, that the members of her family had been sick recently.

Bowen recalled that Mrs. Borden had come to him on Wednesday morning past. She was very much frightened for she thought she had been poisoned. She and Mr. Borden had vomited all night, and she feared the poison had been from the baker's bread or the milk. Miss Lizzie and Bridget the maid had been sick with the same symptoms. It was their belief that an "enemy" had attempted to kill the whole family.

Marshal Sam Hilliard immediately dispatched two of his best detectives to see if they could find out the identity of the person or persons who had tried to poison the Borden family. Hitting the hot, summer streets of Fall River, the "flatfoots canvassed most of the drug stores in town for any person or persons attempting to buy poison. With no success, they were running down the last names on their list when they stopped in at D. R. Smith's pharmacy, on the corner of South Main and Columbia Streets.

Eli Bence, the pharmacist behind the counter, told the detectives that on the Wednesday before the murder, a young woman had come into the store and asked to buy a small bottle of hydrocyanic acid. The young woman, who did not identify herself, said she wanted the deadly poison to kill moths that were feasting on her sealskin cloak. Mr. Bence told her that he did not sell so deadly a poison except upon a doctor's certificate, and she went away empty handed.

Hydrocyanic acid (HCN), aka prussic acid, is a solution of water mixed with hydrocyanide gas. Its vapors have that distinct bitter almond smell that identifies it as part of the cyanide family of lethal poisons. When ingested, the victim feels a hot, bitter taste on swallowing, followed by throat constriction, heaviness on the chest, suffocation, dizziness, mind confusion, diminished sight, and finally death. It is not a pleasant way to die.

Because HCN is a concentrated solution, it is not necessary to give the intended victim a large dose. A small one will do. Absorbed through the stomach into the nervous system, for a murderer it is ideal—after killing the victim, HCN leaves no chemical trace. Most importantly to the Borden case, it produces none of the symptoms common to violent poisoning: vomiting, spasming, convulsions, muscle contractions, none of that. Instead, hydrocyanic acid just takes hold of the heart muscle and strangles it to death without a whimper—quick, silent, deadly.

The detectives knew that if the Borden family had been poisoned by HCN, they would have been dead, all of them, long before Andrew and Abby were chopped to death. Could the poisoning have been a dry run for the real crime? If it was, then why leave Miss Lizzie and Bridget the maid alive? Bridget had been doing some housework that morning, and when she finished, she went up to the attic to rest, and fell asleep. She woke up to Miss Lizzie's cries and the carnage downstairs.

It was also possible that whoever did the initial poisoning thought the old man and old woman would not stand up to whatever the poison was, while younger people would. What really baffled the detectives was this: Who was the young woman who tried to purchase the poison on the Wednesday *before* the murder?

The cops took Bence to the Borden house at 10 o'clock on the night following the murder. Like some Peeping Tom, the police placed Bence outside the Borden house, right on the street in front of the narrow edifice. When Miss Lizzie finally came to the downstairs window and turned toward the street, Bence positively identified her as the woman who tried to buy the hydrocyanic acid from him the previous Wednesday.

The Borden murders were less than two days old. Through careful and professional investigation, police had their prime suspect: Miss Lizzie Borden. If Bence's identification was correct, she had tried to buy a lethal poison that polished human beings off with nary a whimper. As poisons go, it couldn't be beat.

Working from that theory of the crime, Lizzie Borden's murder of her father and stepmother was actually the *second* time she had tried to kill them; and only this time by taking matters into her own hands, had she succeeded. As to her alibi that she was in the barn making sinkers, Marshal Hilliard sent some of his deputies into the rickety structure to make a search.

Miss Lizzie had claimed that she went to the loft of the barn for the lead, and that was where she did the cutting. But an officer who examined the premises said that they were covered completely with dust. No lead shavings littered the floor as would be expected if someone had been carving sinkers. There were no tracks to prove that any person had been there for weeks. The officer took particular notice of the fact, and reported back that he had walked about on the dust-covered floor on purpose to discover whether or not his own feet left any tracks.

He said that they did and thought it singular that anybody could have visited the floor a short time before him and have made no impression on the dust. The lower floor of the stable told no such tale, for it was evident that it had been used more frequently and the dust had not accumulated there.

Then there was the matter of motive. Ostensibly, that was easy: money. By all contemporary accounts, Andrew Borden was worth a minimum of $500,000, about $150,000,000 in contemporary currency. He had parlayed an undertaking business into real estate, farming, and other interests. He was one of the most powerful men in Fall River.

But as powerful as he was, and as generous as he was in his philanthropy, he was not equally spendthrift with his family. Police began to believe that by being cheap with his family, particularly his dour and unforgiving eldest daughter Lizzie, Andrew may have set up his own homicide.

While the police continued investigating, in search of a killer and an indictment, newspapers coast to coast picked up on the story. This was a criminal first. Even the robberies and murders of the James Gang, led by brothers Frank and Jesse, were never covered with that kind of reach and detail.

"When the assassination of Andrew J. Borden and Abbie [*sic*] D. Borden, his wife, was announced, not only the people of Fall River and of Massachusetts, but the public throughout the country manifested the deepest interest in the affair," wrote Edwin H. Porter in his book, *The Fall River Tragedy: A History of the Borden Murders,* published in 1893. Porter was a reporter for the *Fall River Globe*, the only newspaper to cover the case from start to finish.

"The murders soon became the theme of universal comment, both in public and private, and every newspaper reference to the affair was read with eagerness, digested and commented upon in a manner unprecedented. The crimes stand out in bold relief as the most atrocious, and at the same time, the most mystifying which the American public had ever before been called upon to discuss. They had about them that fascination of uncertainty, horrible though they were which fixes the attention and holds it continually."

By early the next afternoon, Marshal Hilliard had dispatched a medical team headed up by Medical Examiner Max Dolan to the Borden house to conduct a partial autopsy. The bodies had been removed to the sitting room. There, Dolan and his team did their initial examination. They found a total of thirteen clean wounds, made by some very sharp instrument, on Mr. Borden's head. The largest was four and a half inches long and two inches wide. Many of them penetrated the skull, and one severed the eyeball and jaw bone.

"The sight was the most ghastly I had ever seen," Dr. Dolan later said.

Abby Borden's body was in even worse shape. Chopped into ribbons of flesh, the skull broken in several places, a deep wound penetrated between the shoulder blades and had the appearance of having been made by a hatchet, the blade penetrating three inches deep. That was the indication that Abby had managed to turn even after the initial assault, but to no avail as the killer continued her, or his, deadly work.

The stomachs were neatly taken out, sealed up, and sent to Professor Edward S. Wood, a preeminent chemist at Harvard University, for analysis. There was one special question for Professor Wood to consider. Marshal Hilliard was anxious to know if there was any indication in the victim's stomachs of HCN poisoning. He also wanted to know who had been killed first, and when? No one was sure.

It was thought that the stomach contents could help provide an answer, along with the condition of the blood at the crime scene. The police had previously noted that the blood in which Mrs. Borden's head lay was coagulated, while the blood from Mr. Borden's body was still oozing from the wounds.

Unless the stomach content analysis came back otherwise, it was evident, based upon accepted times for blood coagulation, that the woman had been dead two hours before the assassin slaughtered the old man. At trial, this needed to be established beyond a reasonable doubt. In order to do so, the prosecution hoped to rely on the expert Wood's stomach analysis.

The partial autopsy was finished and the bodies delivered to the city morgue for further analysis. A few days later, after the full autopsy was completed and the findings were under review, the bodies were released to the Borden family for burial. Except for newspaper coverage of the Garfield and Lincoln assassinations, this was the first time a murder had gotten coverage coast to coast. Every major paper sent a reporter to the funeral, from the venerable *New York Times* and *New York Herald*, to the *Chicago Sun Times* and *St. Louis Post-Dispatch*. Even the *San Francisco Chronicle* had a correspondent present.

Someplace in that crowd that stood around the twin plots of the murdered Bordens was the murderer. Marshal Hilliard was sure of it. He was there, paying his last respects to the dear departed. Good cops always know more than they let on. Hilliard was no exception.

He had gotten a description of the clothes Lizzie Borden was in the habit of wearing. His thought was that if she had done it, wouldn't she have blood on her dress? Detectives discovered that Miss Lizzie had a calico dress, which she was in the habit of wearing mornings. It was a light-blue dress with a fixed figure, a geometrical figure of some sort, and the figure was not white, but was navy blue—a darker blue.

When he talked to Miss Lizzie the morning of the murder, Dr. Bowen told police she had on a cheap, drab-colored calico dress. Police had already searched the Borden home a few times. The calico dress had not turned up. If they could find it, and it had blood on it, they would have Miss Lizzie dead to rights.

Nevertheless, Lizzie Borden was a woman of impeccable breeding, and most importantly, wealth. She deserved special treatment. After all, she had just lost her parents. If it should turn out she was innocent, no one wanted to be on her bad side. Miss Lizzie was known around Fall River as a no-nonsense spinster without a shred of humor in her body.

On Saturday evening, August 6, 1892, Fall River Mayor John Coughlin called on the telephone to inform Lizzie

Borden that she was under suspicion for the murders of her parents, Andrew and Abby Borden. By the time Lizzie hung up, the maid, Bridget Sullivan, was upstairs packing. She'd overheard the conversation. Inside of minutes, Sullivan was out the door, never to return. Remaining in the Borden house that night were Lizzie's sister Emma, her friend Alice Russell, and, of course, Miss Lizzie herself.

On Sunday morning, August 7, Miss Russell came into the kitchen. There were officers outside of the house, but none inside. Lizzie stood by the stove. The skirt of a dress was upon her arm, and its waist lay upon a shelf by the side. The dress itself was a faded, light blue calico dress, the one Miss Lizzie favored wearing in the morning, the one the police were after.

"Lizzie, what are you going to do?" Miss Emma asked.

"I am going to burn this dress. It is all covered with paint," Lizzie replied.

Miss Russell turned away wordlessly. She went out, and then came back in soon after. She found Lizzie standing with the waist of the light-blue dress, tearing it in parts.

"Lizzie, I would not do that where people can see you," said Miss Russell.

Lizzie's only response was to take a step or two further out of Miss Russell's view. Miss Russell didn't stay to see anything else. Instead, she used the wealth and good sense of her position to buy the not inconsiderable support of the Pinkerton National Detective Agency.

Pike Hansom, a Pinkerton detective Miss Russell employed, arrived the next day. They entered the room where Lizzie and Emma were sitting.

"Lizzie, I am afraid the burning of that dress was the worst thing that you could have done," said Miss Russell.

"Oh, why did you let me do it, then?" Lizzie countered.

Whatever it was that Lizzie might or might not have

burned, a thorough search of the stove by Hansom disclosed nothing but ashes. When the cops found out what had happened inside the house while they were outside, there was no evident embarrassment. That would have been a tip-off to a news hungry press that the mayor had truly messed up. Instead, the state moved forward with the necessary medical inquest.

At the end of the two-day affair, enough information had been presented by the authorities in the case, from the police to the doctors, to recommend that Elizabeth Andrew "Lizzie" Borden be indicted on murder charges. While murder by women was not an unusual crime in the nineteenth century, murder by a woman using an ax was. Guns and knives were common. Black widows, women who deliberately married to inherit their husband's money after they killed them, did their dirty business with untraceable poisons.

But an ax murderess? Now that sold newspapers!

Four months after the crime, in December 1892, the Grand Jury for the County of Bristol returned to the Superior Court the following indictment against Lizzie Andrew Borden of Fall River, charging her with the murder of her stepmother, Abby Durfree Borden, and her father, Andrew Jackson Borden:

COMMONWEALTH OF MASSACHUSETTS

At the Superior Court in the year of our Lord one thousand eight hundred and ninety-two. The Jurors for the said Commonwealth on their oath present: That Lizzie Andrew Borden of Fall River in the County of Bristol, at Fall River in the County of Bristol, on the fourth day of August in the year eighteen hundred and ninety-two, in and upon one Abby Durfee Borden, feloniously, wilfully and of her malice aforethought, an assault did make and with a certain weapon, to wit a sharp cutting instrument, the name and a more particular description of which is to the Jurors unknown.

Lizzie Andrew Borden feloniously, wilfully and of her malice aforethought did strike, cut, beat and bruise, in and upon the head of her, the said Abby Durfee Borden, giving to her, the said Abby Durfee Borden, by the said striking, cutting, beating and bruising, in and upon the head of her, the said Abby Durfee Borden, divers, to wit, twenty mortal wounds, of which said mortal wounds the said Abby Durfee Borden then and there instantly died.

And so the Jurors aforesaid, upon their oath aforesaid, do say, that [Lizzie Andrew Borden] did feloniously, wilfully and of her malice aforethought did kill and murder the said Abby Durfee Borden in manner and form aforesaid, then and there, against the peace of said Commonwealth, and contrary to the form of the statute in such case made and provided.

And the jurors on their oath, do further present that Lizzie Andrew Borden of Fall River in the County of Bristol, at Fall River in the County of Bristol, on the fourth day of August in the year eighteen hundred and ninety-two, in and upon one Andrew Jackson Borden, feloniously, wilfully and of her malice aforethought, an assault did make, and with a certain weapon, to wit, a sharp cutting instrument, the name and a more particular description of which is to the jurors unknown.

[Lizzie Andrew Borden] did feloniously, willfully

and of her malice aforethought did strike, cut, beat and bruise, in and upon the head of him, the said Andrew Jackson Borden, by the said striking, cutting, beating and bruising, in and upon the head of him, the said Andrew Jackson Borden, divers, to wit, ten mortal wounds, of which said mortal wounds the said Andrew Jackson Borden then and there instantly died.

And so the jurors upon their oath aforesaid, do say that the said Lizzie Andrew Borden, [murdered] the said Andrew Jackson Borden, in manner and form aforesaid, then and there feloniously, wilfully and of her malice aforethought did kill and murder; against the peace of said Commonwealth and contrary to the form of the statute in such case made and provided.

A true bill.

HENRY A. BODMAN,
Foreman of the Grand jury.

HOSEA M. KNOWLTON,
District Attorney.

For any defense attorney, it was an easy document to read: short. In Lizzie's case, she had two well-known and influential attorneys working for her: George Robinson, the former governor of Massachusetts, and Andrew Jennings, the F. Lee Bailey of his day. District Attorney Knowlton and Thomas Moody held first and second chairs at the prosecution table. The case would be tried before a three-judge panel.

In the New Bedford Courthouse on June 5, 1893, the trial of Lizzie Borden began. A jury of twelve men was selected.

During Moody's opening for the state, he made reference to the decedents. Suddenly theatrically, he exposed the skulls of Andrew and Abby Borden that had been skulking under a cloth at the defense table.

"They will be offered as evidence of the crimes!" Moody announced

"Objection!" Knowlton shouted, bolting out of his chair at the defense table.

Next to him, Miss Lizzie stared at her parents' heads. Miss Lizzie fainted, "sending a thrill of excitement through awe-struck spectators and causing unfeigned embarrassment and discomfiture to penetrate the ranks of counsel," according to one newspaper account.

Moody contended that Lizzie was the only one to have the motive and opportunity to commit the murders. He concluded by producing a worn-looking and dark-stained axe head that he claimed was the murder weapon.

After the prosecutor sat down, the defense slyly told the judge that they would preserve their opening statement until they presented their case. The prosecution then began their case by introducing several witnesses to essentially set the stage for what happened. Unless the jury bought the defense's "other guy" defense—"the other guy must have done it"— the jurors needed to understand where everyone was before the crime was committed, so that they could see that only one of a few could have done it.

The twenty-six year old maid and Irish immigrant Bridget Sullivan, whom the family had fondly referred to as "Maggie," gave her old employer a punch in the solar plexus when she testified that at the time of the murders, only she and Lizzie were in the house—she sleeping upstairs and Lizzie someplace else, where she did not know, since she was sleeping

Part of the prosecution's case rested on proving discord in

the family, specifically Lizzie's hatred of her stepmother. That would go to motive. Several witnesses would subsequently testify to antipathy between the two women who shared Andrew Borden. But the opinion of Sullivan, who was there every day, carried a special weight.

Sullivan was not a convincing prosecution witness. She sounded like a "whiner." On cross-examination, the legal eagle defense team got Sullivan to admit that in her two years of service to the family, she had never seen evidence of such problems.

"Everything was pleasant," she said. "Lizzie and her mother always spoke to each other."

The prosecution then presented witnesses, including Dr. Bowen, who first discovered and examined the bodies. The most brilliant testimony of the trial came from what would now be called a forensics expert, Professor Edward S. Wood, professor of chemistry at the Harvard Medical School. He was the prosecution's star witness in establishing their timeline of the crime.

The intention was to show that the stepmother was killed first and the father second. That meant the killer had to wait on the upper floor for a while before descending to finish the job. This is Wood's actual testimony under Mooney's patient questioning.

Q. Assuming, Professor, that the two persons whose stomachs you had under examination ate breakfast at the same table and time and partook of the same breakfast substantially, what difference in the time of their deaths should you say, from the examination of the stomachs now alone, would be indicated with reasonable certainty, assuming the digestion to have gone on normally?

A. Assuming the digestion to have gone on naturally in both

cases the difference would be somewhere in the neighborhood of an hour and a half more or less.

Q: Does digestion stop at death?

A. Well, it stops; yes sir. It stops so far as the expulsion of food
from the stomach is concerned. There is a sort of digestion that goes on after death in which the stomach wall
itself is partly digested.

Q. Was there anything of the kind here?

A. The membrane was a little bit softened, but not to any
extent.

Q. Is there anything in that circumstance to conflict with the
opinion you have given?

A. No sir, and it was included in my answer, that they had a
perfectly normal appearance, that being a post-mortem
change.

Q. And I understood your answer of an hour and a half as an
answer to my question, assuming the breakfast to be at the
same time and the process of digestion not interrupted, to
have been the difference to a reasonable certainty?

A. I didn't quite catch the whole of the question.

Q. Is that the difference that you fix to a reasonable certainty?

A. Not within narrow limits, but only approximately.

Q. Within what limits?

A. I should say within a half an hour one way or the other.

Q. Have you been present and heard the evidence in the case?

A. Yes sir.

Q. So far as relates to the condition of the bodies?

A. Yes sir.

Q. And the condition of the intestines?

A. Yes sir.

Q. And the various witnesses who have testified to the appearance of the bodies after they were discovered, and to the description of the intestines?

A. Yes sir.

Q. Taking all those facts as you have heard them, and also the examinations that you made yourself, what of them do you deem to be important in determining the time, the relative time, of the death of those two people?

A. The difference in the period of digestion, both stomach and intestinal, the drying of the blood, and the temperature of the body.

Q. And taking all those circumstances that you say you regard as important, all together, do you desire to modify in any way what you have already said as to the difference in time of death of the two people?

A. I should think that one corroborated the other, that they all tended to the same conclusion.

By far the most difficult task for the prosecution was getting beyond the lack of physical evidence to tie Lizzie directly to the crimes. The unanswered question hung over the proceedings like a rain cloud—if Lizzie had murdered her parents, why was her dress free of blood?

Alice Russell was called to the stand. She testified that Lizzie put a dress into the fire saying, "I am going to burn this old thing up; it is covered with paint." Russell's testimony implied that she burned the dress that contained the blood of her parents.

Russell also testified to Lizzie's ominous comments before the murders: including her statement, "that something is hanging over me—I cannot tell what it is," and "I feel afraid something is going to happen." Lizzie told Russell that "she wanted to go to sleep with one eye open half the time for fear somebody might burn the house down or hurt her father because he was so discourteous to people."

George Robinson leaped to his feet to cross-examine. Through some very clever questioning of Russell, he proceeded to show the jury that the person who really committed this crime would never do something as foolish as burning evidence. Such an action by a rational person would imply guilt.

Russell inadvertently gave Lizzie an alibi when she testified that Lizzie told her the morning of the murders that she had received a friend's note summoning her to her bedside; the friend was sick and needed Lizzie's assistance, which she readily gave that morning.

The defense also sought to blow holes in the state's proposed timeline, which they claimed had an eight to thirteen minute window between murders. Robinson showed the jury that for Lizzie to have committed the crime, she would have had to get rid of her bloodstained dress, wash herself free of any blood spatter, and dispose of the murder weapon. Robinson suggested the difficulty of washing blood off one's person, again, all within a maximum of thirteen minutes.

In fact, it was more than possible. The prosecution on rebuttal neglected to point out to the jury that the Borden home was so small that it only took seconds to get from room to room. Anyone on the inside planning the murder would have no problem carrying it out within that allotted time frame.

The prosecution pointed out on rebuttal that a search of the Borden premises never produced the note Lizzie claimed came from her sick friend. Nor did a police search turn up evidence of her "friend." Then the prosecution called the chemist, Eli Bence, to the stand.

Or tried to.

"I object," shouted Moody, and the jury was dismissed while the lawyers argued it out before the judges.

The prosecution wanted Bence to testify to his story that Lizzie had visited his drugstore and tried to buy some prussic acid. He had declined, saying she needed a doctor's prescription. She left without obtaining the drug. Such testimony would, of course, be extremely prejudicial to the defense, showing that on a previous occasion, Miss Lizzie had tried to obtain the necessary poison to kill her parents, and only by the luck of the law had been denied it.

The three judge panel denied the government's request to present the chemical and poison experts. The panel felt that it was just too prejudicial to the defense case. The prosecution immediately rested.

Throughout the trial, newspaper accounts kept readers apprised of the unseemly doings in the Massachusetts courtroom. Reporters looked at Robinson's cross-examinations with awe, while the state's case was shot through with holes, at least according to the press. What was clear was that the prosecution had a clear lack of physical evidence tying Lizzie to the crimes. They also had failed to prove an adequate motive.

The prosecution made it clear to the jury that Lizzie had a rotten relationship with her stepmother. That, plus the huge amount of money Lizzie and her sister inherited on their parent's death, should have been more than enough motive. Still, something hung in the air of the courtroom. It was the level of violence, of overkill, that the victims endured.

In 1892, people had never seen such violence before. A child killing her parents was an unheard of crime, let alone one who did it with an ax. Such a thing was unthinkable. To the repressed, provincial Victorians of 1890s Massachusetts, a rocket ship flying to the moon would be a more likely scenario.

Using the prosecution's own witnesses, defense attorneys Robinson and Moody had already begun to prove reasonable doubt. A later generation would have said of their strategy that the best defense is a good offense. They kept highlighting the contradictory testimony of the prosecution's own witnesses.

Everything seemed to break Lizzie's way, even the Constitution.

During the coroner's inquest, Lizzie had given contradictory and some said implausible testimony as to her actions on the day of the murders. The prosecution wanted to introduce that testimony as evidence of her lying, but the three-judge court wouldn't let them. The Massachusetts jurists made a decision that John Adams, the defender of the British at the Boston Massacre, would have been proud of.

The jurists decided that when Lizzie testified at the inquest, she was really under arrest, and therefore allowed an attorney. Testimony absent an attorney representing her was inadmissible because to deny her counsel when she was, in effect charged, would be to infringe her Fifth Amendment right to abstain from any self-incriminating statements. By seventy years, this legal decision presaged *Miranda v. Arizona*, which gave prisoners the right to counsel.

The defense had reserved its opening statement until now. Jennings went right for the heart:

May it please your Honors, Mr. Foreman and Gentlemen of the Jury: I want to make a personal allusion before referring directly to the case.

One of the victims of the murder charged in
this indictment was for many years my client and
my personal friend. I had known him since my
boyhood. I had known his oldest daughter for the
same length of time, and I want to say right here
and now, if I manifest more feeling than perhaps
you think necessary in making an opening statement for the defense in this case, you will ascribe it
to that cause. The counsel, Mr. Foreman and gentlemen, does not cease to be a man when he
becomes a lawyer.

Fact and fiction have furnished many extraordi-
nary examples of crime that have shocked the feelings and staggered the reason of men, but I think
no one of them has ever surpassed in its mystery
the case that you are now considering. The brutal
character of the wounds is only equaled by the
audacity, by the time and the place chosen, and,
Mr. Foreman and gentlemen, it needed but the
accusation of the youngest daughter of one of the
victims to make this the act, as it would seem to
most men, of an insane person or a fiend.

A young woman, thirty-two years of age, up to
that time of spotless character and reputation, who
had spent her life nearly in that immediate neighborhood, who had moved in and out of that old
house for twenty or twenty-one years, living there
with her father and with her stepmother and with
her sister—this crime that shocked the whole civilized world, Mr. Foreman and gentlemen, seemed

from the very first to be laid at her door by those
who represented the Government in the investigation of the case.

There was more windy prose, but Jennings had already
summed up his case: the other guy defense, in this case, the other
guy being "an insane person or a fiend." To prove it, Robinson
and Jennings summoned Uriah Kirby and Charles Gifford.

The two men testified that around 11 P.M. they saw a very
strange-looking man around the Borden residence. Dr. Benjamin Handy was called to the stand and told the jury that he
saw a sallow young man loitering near the Borden home at
about 10:30 A.M. the day of the murder.

With just those two witnesses, the defense had very neatly
offered up for the jury's consideration a second suspect in the
cases, even if he seemed rather incorporeal. Lizzie's sister,
Emma, was then called to the stand. Everyone was waiting to
hear what she had to say about her younger sister.

Emma testified that Lizzie and her father had a loving relationship. Emma claimed that Lizzie and her stepmother got
along. She almost seemed to be setting herself up as another
suspect when she told the jury that she, not Lizzie, bore lin-
gering resentment over a real estate transaction by her father
that gave her stepmother Abby control over a piece of family
property that was rightfully hers and Lizzie's.

Showing their contempt for the government's case by
calling no other witnesses to rebut the government's case or
show Miss Lizzie's high character, the defense then rested.
Jennings and Robinson summed up for the defense, pointing
out the obvious holes in the government's case and their
insistence on pinning the charges on poor, defenseless Lizzie
instead of going after the real killer, some fiend who was still
at large.

Hosiah Knowlton then "closed" for the prosecution case in his no-nonsense style. Presiding Judge Dewey then charged the jury, pointing out the differences between kinds of evidence and the weight to give them, particularly circumstantial evidence. He told the jury that the defendant's character counted greatly in weighing their decision.

It makes no difference what year it is: A lawyer never knows what a jury is going to do. They came back ninety minutes later. The court clerk turned to the jury foreman.

"What is your verdict?" the clerk asked.

"Not guilty," the foreman intoned.

In her excitement at being set free, Lizzie yelled, then collapsed into her chair, and then let out a second yell of pure joy, the likes of Jennings, Robinson, Emma, and other well-wishers crowded around her had never been heard.

Lizzie's head came up from where it had been buried in her sister's embrace.

"Now take me home. I want to go to the old place and go at once tonight," said Miss Lizzie. And so she did. Miss Lizzie went home to the house where her parents were murdered. Emma went with her. Commenting on the verdict, the *New York Times* said on its editorial page:

"It will be a certain relief to every right-minded man or woman who has followed the case to learn that the jury at New Bedford has not only acquitted Miss Lizzie Borden of the atrocious crime with which she was charged, but has done so with a promptness that was very significant."

The *Times* went on to say that the jury's verdict amounted to a "condemnation of the police authorities of Fall River who secured the indictment and have conducted the trial . . . [of the] vanity of ignorant and untrained men charged with the detection of crime, the usual inept and stupid and muddle-headed sort that such towns manage to get for themselves."

It was an indictment of small-town justice that the *Times* felt had led to an unjust prosecution.

Lizzie and Emma used their inheritance to buy a new house on the Hill, one of Fall River's best sections. Their new home was named Maplecroft. Emma lived there until 1905, when she moved out in middle age and got her own place. And Miss Lizzie?

For the rest of her life, Lizzie Borden was a patron of the arts. She associated closely with actors and dancers, theater people, who some of her class considered the lowest of the low. Lizzie loved being around them. But she always went home to Maplecroft, where she died in 1927 at the ripe old age of 67.

Lizzie Borden is buried in a plot in Fall River's Oak Grove Cemetery, which she shares with her father and mother. Her death put an end to her life but not to the mystery.

Did she really do it? Did Lizzie Borden really butcher her father and stepmother?

Let me ask you a question: Does a bear shit in the woods?

Of course she did! No one believes that defense crap of a shadowy man suddenly appearing on the scene and killing the Bordens. But while Lizzie was fast enough to get rid of the calico dress she was wearing when she murdered her parents, the one with the blood stains that she burned in front of Alice Russell, she wasn't smart enough to make the crime look like a robbery gone awry.

Beneath Andrew Borden's caved in skull cut to ribbons, his pockets bulged with greenbacks. Had Lizzie taken the money too, she would have committed the perfect crime. History would have said the Bordens were killed in the middle of a robbery, Lizzie would have gotten away with it, and I wouldn't be writing these words.

As to the specific defense suggestion that a "fiend" was abroad during midmorning in a bustling town like Fall River—that was the kind of curious plot one could absorb from Conan Doyle's Sherlock Holmes stories, which were popular at the time. What worked in fiction, though, didn't necessarily work in reality. A fiend abroad at midmorning in a bustling town like Fall River, and nobody sees anything strange? Not likely, not then.

The Fall River detectives had conducted a model of detection in any age. What they got wrong was the motive, greed always being the first one cops look to, next to sex, of course. The Fall River police figured Miss Lizzie had killed her parents for her inheritance. But why then, mutilate the victims after death?

Unfortunately, except for Dr. Wood's unimpeachable testimony as to times of death, there was nothing about the prosecution's case that wasn't circumstantially weak. The jury had no choice but to acquit on "reasonable doubt" if nothing more. Had it been present-day, on the prosdecution's list of expert witnesses would be one on parricide.

Whoever killed the Bordens engaged in what present-day criminologists describe as "overkill." The victims had continued to be assaulted by the blade after death. Absent any other indications of foul play, such overkill is characteristic of the crime of parricide, where a child kills a parent or parents. When a daughter kills a father, there is usually some history of sexual abuse.

During the Victorian era it was unthinkable that such behavior would even be discussed. But in cases where the female murderer lashes out at the father who has molested her and kills him when he is most vulnerable, usually asleep, it is actually an act of self-defense.

Lizzie Borden had been molested by her father, if not

physically, then certainly psychologically. Not only had Andrew Borden married the Wicked Witch of the West, he did nothing to stop the abuse the woman heaped on Lizzie. That much has been documented. Add to that Miss Lizzie's situation, being a spinster in Massachusetts in 1892, and it doesn't take Sigmund Freud to figure out she had quite a few problems.

With such a defense today, it is hard not to acknowledge that the outcome would be any different.

WHO KILLED MARY PHAGAN?

1914–1916—LEO FRANK

"The Ballad of Mary Phagan"

Little Mary Phagan
She left her home one day;
She went to the pencil-factory
To see the big parade.
She left her home at eleven
She kissed her mother good-by;
Not one time did the poor child think
That she was a-going to die.
Leo Frank he met her
With a brutish heart, we know;
He smiled, and said, "Little Mary,
You won't go home no more."

—as reproduced by F. B. Snyder in
The Journal of American Folk-Lore, 1918.

That there are numerous hate sites on the Internet that still argue the case against Leo Frank, though the crime actually occurred back in 1914, shows how the verdict of that long-ago jury still resonates today.

The story of who really killed Mary Phagan begins with an ex-Confederate Civil War general named Nathan Bedford Forrest. In the HBO cult favorite *Carnivale,* Forrest's grandson, Ben Hawkins, becomes the savior of mankind in the 1930s. It wasn't a far stretch.

Nathan Bedford Forrest was a brilliant general during a war that, considering the body count, found brilliance a rare commodity indeed. Besides Lee, the Confederates did have some good generals, but none was as brilliant a tactician as Forrest. In the wake of their defeat, ex-Confederate military men like Forrest were lost. Many, Forrest included, had been wealthy slavers and plantation owners who went bankrupt when the Reconstruction policies of the radical Republican Congress became law. In the South, hysteria was widespread that the black ex-slaves would finish John Brown's work and foment insurrection against the white majority.

To protect their communities from seeing anything like this become a reality, paramilitary vigilante organizations were born. Armed with post-Civil War–era Colt revolvers and Winchester repeating rifles, shotguns, Bowie knives, and strong hunks of rope, the vigilantes roamed the South. They wore anonymous white hoods with eye holes, and left blacks hanging from trees in a way strangely reminiscent of the Romans crucifying their mortal enemies.

The names of these vigilante organizations became legend, spoken in whispers—the White Brotherhood, the Order of the White Rose, the Constitutional Union Guards, and the Men of Justice were some of the better-known ones. But the biggest and most feared of all was the Ku Klux Klan. Eventually, the KKK, as it became known, integrated these other organizations to become a giant hate behemoth.

The Klan's reputation for terror was well earned. It needed to be respected if ever the government decided to combat it.

The Klan's success lay with its willingness to kill its perceived enemies, the black ex-slaves. The whippings and beatings the KKK administered to blacks indiscriminately throughout the South, their ability to lynch black men for the slightest suggestion of a racial infraction, enabled them to terrorize the populace and gain support from state and local governments. The popular sentiment arose that the KKK battled the Northern carpetbaggers as much as the encroaching black race, from which the still virginal Southern damsels needed to be defended.

Two years after the war ended, in April 1867 at Nashville, Tennessee, the Klan effectively incorporated itself by formally organizing. As the Grand Wizard of the Empire (gee, what famous movie "bad guy" does that remind you of?) they elected Nathan Bedford Forrest. The Grand Wizard would have ten assistants called Genii. No, none of them would be Barbara Eden.

Each former Confederate state was to be called a Realm. The Grand Dragon controlled the Realm, and used eight Hydras as staff. Under the Realm was a Dominion, which was formed from several state counties, or Provinces. The Dominion was controlled by the Grand Titan, assisted by six Furies. Ruling the Provinces were the Grand Giant and four Night Hawks. The most local level was the Den, governed by a Grand Cyclops with two Night Hawks as aides. Finally, members were called Ghouls.

I kid you not.

With so complicated an organizational structure, things didn't quite work out. After all, men attracted to hate organizations are not exactly the swiftest oars in the ocean in any age or ocean. Some of the Ghouls killed and terrorized indiscriminately—no surprise since many of them were unrepentant psychopathic killers the Union had stopped short of annihilating.

In 1869, General Forrest decided he could no longer have his good name associated with such a nonprofessional organization. To his everlasting credit, it should be remembered that Forrest resigned as Grand Wizard and ordered the Klan to disband. Unfortunately, his influence had waned considerably since the war. Few Dens listened, let alone Ghouls. The Klan gained political power throughout the South. Using force, it easily kept former black slaves from exercising their constitutional right to vote.

As a result, ex-Confederates exercised political control over state governments. It was, to coin a phrase, a dark time for the Republic. Just when it seemed like the hooded cowards of the Evil Empire were going to win, the Fifteenth Amendment to the Constitution was ratified on February 3, 1870.

It says:

> **Section 1.** *The right of citizens of the United States to vote shall not be denied or abridged by the United States or by any State on account of race, color, or previous condition of servitude.*
>
> **Section 2.** *The Congress shall have power to enforce this article by appropriate legislation.*

The idea of this amendment was to stop the former confederacy from using a former slave's color and previous servitude as a means of voting disenfranchisement. To put teeth into the amendment, Congress passed the first Force Bill on May 31, 1870. The Force Bill imposed heavy fines and federal imprisonment on anyone who used force, intimidation, or bribery to stop people from voting. Ultimate jurisdiction for enforcing the bill was placed under the executive branch.

The bill then proceeded to authorize the president to use "the land or naval forces" to make sure these rights were enforced. Going even further, for the first time, congressional elections were put under federal regulation. Interfering with them became a federal crime subject to stiff federal penalties. The following year, on February 28, 1871, a second "force bill" was passed to fill in the holes that the first one had ignored. But it wasn't until a few months later that Congress finally sounded the Klan's nineteenth century death knell.

On April 20, 1871, the Radical Republicans who controlled Congress did something the South *really* hated—they publicly rebuked the chivalrous knights of the KKK when they passed the third Force Bill. It made the organization and disposition of vigilante groups like the KKK a federal crime equivalent to sedition and would be dealt with accordingly.

What it meant was this: if you dressed up in a hood and went riding around the countryside terrorizing people in defense of the white race, you could be shot on sight by the occupying federal army. Considering that the Union had just won a bloody four year war on its brethren, it was a threat to be taken seriously. More so was the bill's even more controversial provision—at least in the South—that allowed the president to suspend habeas corpus in "lawless areas."

Now *that* was serious. It was one thing to outlaw vigilante white supremacist groups in pursuit of voting rights for the freed slaves. It was quite another to allow the president to suspend the most basic of Americna rights, guaranteed in the Constution's original text, that no citizen could be arrested and held without being charged in a court of law.

Despite opposition in the North as well as the South, the third Force Act worked: By century's end, the practical influence of the KKK was reduced to a few far-flung gangs. But there is a *je ne sais quoi* in the American culture that always looks for the other guy to blame. Those people who just like to hate, were looking for some new scapegoat in their pathetic attempt to justify their miserable lives.

On April 27, 1913, Newt Lee, a black night watchman at the National Pencil Factory in Atlanta, Georgia, discovered the blood-soaked body of 14-year-old Mary Phagan. Phagan had been a worker in the factory. Her job was to place metal tips on pencils. Georgia state law allowed minors as young as Phagan the opportunity not only to work, but to work full-time. She had been temporarily laid off in April because a shipment of metal tips had been late.

On Confederate Memorial Day, April 26, she had gone to the factory to collect $1.20 in back wages. She met with the factory manager, Leo Frank, in his office. Frank gave her the money, and she left. The next time anyone saw her, it was as a corpse covered by sawdust and dirt, so much dirt that detectives couldn't tell at first whether she was white or black. After looking a bit, these keen Sherlock Holmes types turned her over and rubbed the dirt off her face. They soon realized that her white cheeks had been cut and her eyes blacked, probably from battering, before death.

Bruises around her neck made it extremely likely she had been choked to death. The autopsy soon confirmed not only that, but that she had been choked with a piece of linen torn from her underwear. The killer had beaten her skull hard enough to crack it like a hard-boiled egg. The keen-eyed Atlanta sleuths found two notes on the floor where they couldn't be missed. The first said, "*Mam that negro hire down here did this i went to make water and he push me down that hole a long tall negro black that hoo it sase long sleam tall negro I wright while play with me.*"

The second note was equally unintelligible: "*he said he wood love me land down play like the night witch did it but that long tall black negro did buy his slef."*

Whoever had written the notes was uneducated, barely capable of putting a sentence together. Leo Frank had been an honors student at Cornell University. But being a master of Georgia African-American dialect seventy years before any such thing was acknowledged, was clearly beyond him in more ways than one. Frank couldn't have written the notes. The cops later chose to ignore this.

Since they had no other suspects, the cops decided to try and pin the murder on Lee, the black night watchman who found the body. But there was no case against Lee. If the cops wanted to hang him for the murder, they needed *something,* and they had nothing. They also knew it kept the public mollified if they had a black man in custody while they continued to "investigate."

Their suspicion next centered on the last person to see Phagan alive, Leo Frank. He happened to be a Jew. In the South of the early twentieth century, many people considered Jews to be a heretic "nation" of money-grubbing, hook-nosed, deceitful, vile maggots masquerading as human beings. Jews in the South reminded many who had been in the old Klan of the Northern carpetbaggers who exploited the South after the war. Leo Frank, however, was as far from a carpet-bagger as you could get.

He was a son of the South. Born in Cuero, Texas, in 1884, Frank's family moved when he was a child to the great Jewish community in Brooklyn, one of the five boroughs that comprise New York City. He attended Brooklyn public schools all the way through high school. In 1906, Frank graduated from Cornell University with a bachelor's degree in mechanical engineering and moved to Atlanta in 1907. His uncle owned the National Pencil Company and had hired him as the factory's new supervisor.

Over the next three years, Frank became a much-liked employer, respected for his fairness. In his personal life, Frank was an active member of Atlanta's Jewish community, the largest in the South. In 1910, Frank married Lucille Selig, daughter of a prominent Jewish family. In 1912, he became president of his local B'nai B'rith chapter. Frank had a good life; there had never been any bumps in the road until the cops came calling.

Cops love to see how people react under severe stress. To test Frank's reaction, they took him to the morgue, Pulling back the cover from Phagan's battered body, Frank's emotions betrayed him; he got nervous. Responding to police questioning, Frank claimed that he had paid the girl her back wages, but he never actually saw her leave the factory. Neither, apparently, did anyone else, except her murderer.

If ever a guy looked like a prime suspect it was Leo Frank. He was the perfect fall guy. Despite his birth, he was a true outsider in Southern society, a nebbishy looking man who controlled the fate of hundreds of good, Southern girls who worked for him. Despite no indication that Phagan had been sexually violated, newspapers speculated that she had been raped. All of this fanned the flames of anti-Semitism that had been growing in the United States ever since Jews had begun immigrating at the end of the nineteenth century.

Wherever they went throughout history, from their inception around 2000 B.C. to the present, Jews have excelled in business and the arts in indirect proportion to the population as a whole. As far as poor, uneducated Southerners were concerned, the only reason for this success was that they lied, cheated, murdered and some said, drank the blood of their littlest victims, an accusation known as a *blood libel*.

During the eighteen months prior to Mary Phagan's death, Atlanta had had a string of unsolved homicides. People were

tired of the fiend in their midst. They wanted action that trans-
lated into prosecution and execution. So Leo Frank, the last
man to see Mary Phagan alive, was arrested and charged with
her murder.

While the Atlanta police were making this arrest, they had a
third suspect, the best one, in their back pocket. They never
made it public that suspect number three was Jim Conley, a
black sweeper at the pencil factory with an extensive record of
petty theft and disorderly conduct. On May 1, his supervisor at
the factory caught him trying to rinse out a shirt in one of the
factory's sinks. The police later determined that the stains on
the shirt contained blood, then conveniently forgot about it.

The case against the two detained men went forward. On
May 8, 1913, a coroner's jury ordered Newt Lee and Leo
Frank to be charged with murder in the first degree. Found
guilty, they would be executed according to state statute. In
the aftermath of the indictment, the case went national.

Coast to coast, the telegraph wires burned up with coverage. Competing for scoops, newspapers covered every aspect
of the case. Soon, everyone was vying for the honor of solving
Mary Phagan's murder. Not one but two national detective
agencies, the Pinkertons and the Burns Detective Agency, vied
for the opportunity to investigate the case. Atlanta's police
chief released a statement that he had factual evidence that
would convict the girl's murderer. Upon being pressed to produce it, he demurred.

On May 18, the *Atlanta Constitution* finally broke the story
the police didn't want known—they had a third suspect, the
black man Jim Conley, in custody. Since his arrest, Conley had
been talking to the prosecutor, Hugh Dorsey. The prosecution's
entire case would eventually rest on Conley's broad shoulders.

Short and squat, the twenty-seven-year-old Conley would
go on to give police and prosecutors three different depositions.

Key details varied in each. In Conley's first deposition, given on May 24, he said that the day before the murder, Frank had called him into his office. Frank proceeded to dictate letters to Conley, during which Conley alleged that Frank muttered something like, "Why should I hang?"

This contradicted Conley's earlier verbal statements to police. In those statements, Conley claimed he was illiterate. If he was, how could he take down Frank's letters? Despite this inconsistency, the police were convinced that Conley was telling the truth, and that, therefore, Frank was guilty of Phagan's murder.

In a second sworn statement given four days later on May 28, Conley contradicted himself yet again when he stated that the letters had been dictated to him on the day of the murder. The next day, May 29, Conley offered new information: He claimed that he helped Frank carry Mary Phagan's body to the basement.

In this account, Frank called him into his office. The girl was already dead. Frank claimed she had fallen against a lathe in the machine shop and died. It took some convincing, but Conley eventually agreed to help Frank dump the body. Afterward, the two men went back to Frank's office where he dictated the letters found near the bodies.

Considering Frank's education, either Conley was the poorest note-taker in American criminal history, or he was a bald-faced liar. That same day, prosecutor Hugh Dorsey entered the grand jury room in Cobb County. He had told reporters beforehand that he was going to press for an indictment of Leo Frank and no one else. In fact, it took the Cobb County grand jury only ten minutes to indict Leo Frank on the charge of first-degree murder. If convicted, Frank faced death.

Newt Lee was set free. The state of Georgia then made Jim Conley a material witness against Leo Frank. He was placed in jail until the trial, in virtual isolation from anyone other than the police or Dorsey, and unavailable to questioning by the defense lawyers. As for the grand jury's other findings, the undertaker who embalmed the girl claimed there was evidence of sexual assault, but the county's own physician said there was insufficient evidence to come to that conclusion.

By May 28, handwriting samples from Frank, Lee, and Conley were released, along with a portion of the notes found near Phagan's body. The only handwriting that matched the notes was Conley's, who promptly changed his story yet again. Now, he said, he wrote the notes on the day of the murder on Frank's orders. He had fallen asleep while guarding Frank in his office. When he heard Frank's whistle, he came running up the stairs to his boss's office, where Frank latched onto Conley's stocky frame for support. That is when Frank asked Conley to write the notes and muttered the words, "Why should I hang?"

Conley then volunteered the one piece of information that would have broken the case open and seen the right man indicted: Before meeting with Frank, he had defecated into the elevator shaft. The official record of the case shows that the detectives took note. Dorsey then had Conley well-prepared for his appearance as the prosecution's star witness at trial.

On May 30, 1913, Dorsey had police take Conley back to the scene of the crime. Conley went over every detail—how he helped Frank load the girl's dead body into the elevator and how he took the elevator to the basement where he dumped it. Looking down into the elevator shaft, detectives saw the "dump" Conley had previously deposited there.

Intact.

The feces were intact. That, alone, made for a prima facie case that it was Jim Conley who killed Mary Phagan.

Conley had sworn to police that he had defecated in the shaft *earlier* in the evening, before the girl's body was found.

Later, at Frank's request, he had taken the elevator down to the *basement*, where he got off, dumped the body, and then shot back up again to meet with Frank in his office. If that were true, the elevator would have mashed the feces when it hit bottom, releasing its foul odor.

The human waste was still fresh and unmashed. Police and prosecutor either noticed this error and failed to report it or just never took note. The defense also failed to note this inconsistency at trial. On July 23, Jim Conley was brought in by Hugh Dorsey to go over his trial testimony one more time. Five days later, the case of *State of Georgia v. Leo Frank* went to trial.

Leo Frank's murder trial took place between July 28 and August 26, 1913. There was no direct testimony by prosecution witnesses that tied Frank to the crime. The best Hugh Dorsey could do was having character assassination witnesses testify, without evidence, that Frank was some sort of sexual deviant. The star witness, Jim Conley, testified on August 4 to yet another version of his oft-told tale.

This time, Conley claimed that Frank told him that he had killed the girl after she refused his sexual advances. Conley then helped Frank dispose of the body in the basement. When they returned to Frank's office, Frank said he would pay off Conley if he kept his mouth shut. According to Conley, the next thing Frank said was the ominous phrase, "Why should I hang?"

Frank then had Conley write the notes found near the body. On cross-examination by the defense, Conley admitted giving police several statements after he was discovered washing out the bloody shirt in the factory. He also admitted he had a police record. But despite being confused on some details, Conley stuck to the crux of his story.

The prosecution rested. When it was the defense's turn, they brought numerous witnesses to the stand to testify to

Frank's good character. Throughout the trial, thinly veiled anti-Semitic comments were elicited and published from various officials. The hope was that the character witnesses would show Frank as a person incapable of committing the crime for which he had been charged, in courtroom and in the court of public opinion.

On August 18, the nineteenth day of the trial, Leo Frank took the stand in his own defense. Testifying for four hours, he firmly told the jury that Jim Conley's story was nothing more than a tall tale. Frank claimed to have been in his office during the time the coroner fixed for the murder. He stuck to his story when Dorsey cross-examined him.

The summations brought the case's anti-Semitism to the forefront. Defense attorney Reuben Arnold stated during his closing that if Frank had not been a Jew, there would never have been a prosecution against him. Arnold claimed that the Leo Frank case was like the Dreyfus affair in France, where an army officer was tried, convicted, and sentenced for a crime he did not commit because he was a Jew.

Hugh Dorsey countered that it was the defense who introduced Frank's "Jewishness" into the case. "The word Jew never escaped our lips," Dorsey told the jury. "The Jews rise to heights sublime, but they also sink to the lowest depths of degradation!"

Without a trace of physical evidence to support it, Dorsey charged that Frank was a sexual deviant who masked these tendencies from his family and friends with a placid exterior. The defense countered that Conley was the murderer and had made a deal with the prosecution. He had testified against Frank to save his own neck.

Outside the courthouse, the crowd got ugly. They wanted to see the Northern Jew convicted. The newspapers encouraged Judge Roan to postpone giving the case to the jury until

Monday. They were afraid that deliberating on Saturday would lead to a weekend of rioting. The judge agreed. In the jury's presence, Roan met with the chief of police and the army commander of the local military barracks. Roan wanted to know about their ability to quell an uprising.

The defense later pointed out in its appeals that at that moment, the jury had clearly been led to believe that a verdict of not guilty would result in a riot. The federal government could easily have imposed the provisions of the Force Acts but President Wilson chose not to do it. To any except the most beknighted moron, Frank was being railroaded.

Reuben Arnold still had a closing to give. His back against the wall, the defense attorney came back Monday and courageously told the jury that Frank was the latest in a long line of Jews persecuted for their religious beliefs. Again, he exhorted the jury that Jim Conley was the true murderer.

Conley was not alone among prosecution witnesses to have an unsavory character. But if the truth came down to whom the jury believed, Jim Conley or Leo Frank . . . They came in four hours later, finding Leo Frank guilty of murder in the first degree. Frank and his lawyers, however, were not in the courtroom when the verdict was published.

Shouts of "hang the Jew!" had been heard over the courthouse grounds. Fearing mob violence if the verdict went Frank's way, Judge Roan had put him and his defense team in protective custody. When Frank and his lawyers were finally told of the verdict, they were shocked. They thought that they had at least established reasonable doubt. They had not counted on the fear, bigotry, and anti-Semitism of the post-Reconstruction South.

The next day, August 26, Judge Roan sentenced Leo Frank to hang for the murder of Mary Phagan. He set October 10 as the execution date. That date would subsequently be changed many times as Frank appealed the verdict and sentence to the Georgia Supreme Court. He lost. Frank appealed further, to no avail, through the federal court system until finally, he reached the Supreme Court. Suddenly, Frank had a very unlikely ally—the man who had sentenced him to death.

Judge Roan felt that Frank did not deserve death and that the death sentence should be commuted to life in prison. Also supporting Frank was Jim Conley's own lawyer, William M. Smith. He made the unusual public announcement that he believed his client, Conley, to be the murderer. Smith claimed that he had looked at all the evidence again and that it showed Conley's guilt, not Frank's. But as a matter of law, he had nothing new to offer.

During the time the Frank case was prosecuted, newspapers and magazines experienced a surge of investigative reporting. Frank's case was taken up by several prominent journalists on the national level who wrote a series of articles that concluded Frank was innocent. But where it really counted, in Georgia, the local press did not place much value in Smith's statement or the stories published about Frank in the newspapers and magazines coming out of the North.

Finally, Leo Frank got his day with the U.S. Supreme Court. Based upon his review of the facts of the case, Associate Justice Oliver Wendell Holmes would later write that Frank had been denied due process. Holmes noted that during the trial the judge and the defense lawyers, and possibly members of the jury, were threatened with lynching if Frank were found not guilty. Georgia Governor John Slaton had the National Guard prepared for possible rioting if Frank were found innocent. But Holmes and Justice Charles Evans Hughes were *dissenting* justices. The other seven, the majority, refused Frank's appeal.

Leo Frank's date of execution was set for June 22, 1915.

On May 31, Frank's attorneys filed a clemency appeal with

the Georgia Prison Commission in the hope of having his death sentence commuted. They denied the condemned man's appeal. That left the matter to one man: Governor John Slaton.

Governor Slaton had twenty days left in his term before he had to step down. A highly popular governor and before that a state legislator, he was a leading candidate for the U.S. Senate. The easy way out would be to leave the Frank problem to his successor, who would soon take office. But John Slaton was a man of honor.

Carefully, he reviewed the police reports, case files, and court record of the case. He took into account the dissenting votes of the U.S. Supreme Court and especially the recommendation for clemency from the trial judge. After reviewing the case fully, John Slaton believed Leo Frank was innocent. He further believed that, in time, his innocence would be proven.

Even more important than clearing Frank at the moment was saving his life. Slaton signed an executive order commuting the death sentence to life in prison. He ordered Frank transported immediately to Milledgeville Prison.

Relieved that he had been spared from death and fully expecting to be cleared, Leo Frank was transferred to Milledgeville. During the next two months, Tom Watson in his magazines *Watson's Magazine* and *The Jeffersonian* published openly anti-Semitic editorials that urged Georgia's citizens to take the law into their own hands and inflict frontier justice on Leo Frank, because the governor would not.

On July 18, a prisoner slashed Leo Frank's throat. Two other prisoners, by coincidence doctors, rushed to Frank's aid. They stopped the blood flow and stitched him up. A month later, just before midnight on August 16, 1915, twenty-five men from the Marietta area, driving in eight automobiles, pulled in at the Milledgeville Prison gates.

Marietta had become a shrine of sorts to Mary Phagan. She

was buried in a cemetery there. Her grave had become a lightning rod for the disaffected. They formed themselves into a group called the Knights of Mary Phagan.

Overpowering the two guards on duty at Milledgeville Prison, the Knights of Mary Phagan handcuffed the warden and the superintendent. They carried rope. Some would later claim that the lynch mob consisted of some of Marietta's finest citizens, including a clergyman and an ex-sheriff. Confronted in his cell, Frank calmly started to dress, and was told that he need not bother. Dressed only in prison shirt and pants, he was rushed out to a car and driven seven hours across the state.

It took all night, but as dawn broke, the lynch mob stopped at an oak grove outside of Marietta. Already there was a rope and a table for the condemned man to sit on, courtesy of Sheriff William Frey. The leaders tried to get Frank to confess to the murder of Mary Phagan. He calmly declined. Those in the group who were later interviewed said that his denials were convincing; many in the group decided he should not be lynched. The leaders, however, prevailed.

When asked if he had a last request, Frank asked to have his wedding ring returned to his wife. Once more, he was asked to confess. He said nothing. The table was set up under an oak tree. With Frank's hands shackled, he was led up onto the table. They threw a rope over a stout limb, and then tied a hangman's noose around his neck. The table was kicked out from under him, and Leo Frank was left hanging. The lynch mob quickly dispersed as Frank struggled against the rope until it strangled him to death.

News of the hanging quickly spread. A crowd gathered at the lynching site. Men, women, and children all came to view the Northern Jew hanging from the old oak tree. Photographers arrived and took shots as a festive group gathered around the body. Included in the pictures were members of the lynch mob who had come back to view their handiwork. The photographs were available as postcards in Marietta for many years afterward.

Some tore strips of cloth from Frank's clothes. Others snipped strands from the rope, making sure not to go too deep with their knives, lest the rope unwind and the corpse drop. Eventually, after some in the crowd made attempts to mutilate the body, it was cut down and taken into Atlanta. Even in death, Frank's rights were violated. Without family consent, officials decided to put the body on public view. With the police supervising the crowds, Georgia citizens came to view Frank's body.

Later that night, against Talmudic law, the undertaker embalmed him. Leo Frank's body was transported back to Brooklyn by his wife Lucille. He was buried at Mount Carmel Cemetery on August 18, 1915.

The case was not over.

Jim Conley was convicted of burglary in 1919. He served only one year of a 20-year sentence, the result of his "cooperation" in the Frank case. A gambling arrest followed in 1941 and then an arrest for being drunk and disorderly in 1947. After that, Jim Conley vanished from view until he died in his seventies in 1962. He never recanted his testimony.

To his grave, he claimed Leo Frank had killed Mary Phagan and ordered him to dispose of the body in the elevator shaft.

Who really killed Mary Phagan? And who were the members of the lynch party?

In 1982 an old man named Alonzo Mann came forth with the information that he had seen Jim Conley dragging Mary Phagan's body. Mann, then a thirteen-year-old office boy at the pencil factory, was told by Conley not to tell what he had seen, or Conley would kill him. Considering Conley had just murdered somebody, it was a threat to be taken seriously. The, Anti-Defamation League of B'nai B'rith then asked the Georgia Board of Pardons to grant Leo Frank a posthumous pardon. After first rejecting the application, they pardoned Leo Frank on March 11, 1986, more than seventy years after his lynching by the prominent citizens of Marietta, Georgia.

Jim Conley was the killer of Mary Phagan. He covered it up and blamed Frank. But Frank was Jewish, and the prosecution was anti-Semitic like much of the state at the time.

As a direct result of the Frank case, the Genii were let out of the bottle. All the hate that had been festering when the KKK was disbanded early in the century once again came to the surface. The hate mongering Knights of Mary Phagan gathered around a burning cross on the dark night of November 15, 1915, in Stone Mountain, Georgia.

This was the beginning of the rise of the Ku Klux Klan in the twentieth century. Mary Phagan was their first victim, Leo Frank their second, and John Slaton their third. To pay Slaton back for his support of Frank, the Klan galvanized his opposition. John Slaton never again held elective office.

The answer to the second question is a bit more complicated. The idfentities of those in the lynch mob was, for mahy years, a closely guarded secret. Except for some of the "bad guys," who had revisited the scene of crime, picnicked under Franks still hanging body and had their picture taken, the rest preferred anonymity.

Was Bruno Framed?

1934—Bruno Richard Hauptmann

No crime penetrated the twentieth-century American consciousness more than the kidnap/murder of Charles Lindbergh, Jr., or, as he came to be known, "The Lindbergh Kidnapping Baby." If there is any doubt about that, consider that the courthouse in New Jersey where the trial of Bruno Richard Hauptmann took place is now the scene of a long-running dinner theater reenactment of the trial in the actual courtroom.

The fact that Charles, Jr.'s daddy was Charles Lindbergh, the country's greatest contemporary hero, gives the case its timeless quality. Long after the case was adjudicated, over sixty years ago, historians still speculate:

Did he really do it?

Was the real killer, as alleged by the prosecution, Bruno Richard Hauptmann? Or was he part of some greater conspiracy? Perhaps someone wanted to pay Lindbergh back for a past slight? Or perhaps the truth is as simple as, "He didn't do it!"

In a time when most Americans had yet to even see an airplane, Lindbergh flew nonstop across the Atlantic and landed in one piece in Paris. Ironically, it was British Captain John

Alcock and Lieutenant Arthur Whitten Brown who made the first nonstop aerial crossing of the Atlantic on June 14,1919, from Newfoundland to Clifden, Ireland, in sixteen hours, and twenty-seven minutes.

Lindbergh trumped them.

On May 20, 1927, Lindbergh took just 33 1/2 hours to fly 1000 miles alone, from Roosevelt Field on Long Island to Orly Field in Paris. Were it just that simple, one aviator improving on another's record, Lindbergh would have become an historic footnote like Alock and Brown. Instead, in the eight years since Alcock and Brown's achievement, radio had become the premier communications medium. Technology and history had merged at a point where one could effect the other.

Lindbergh's flight captured the imagination of the American public. People listened anxiously at their radios across the country, united by this common experience of rooting for the man the emdia dubbed "the Lone Eagle." Now, all Lindbergh had to do was succeed and he would gain riches beyond his wildest dreams.

He did. After he landed safely in Parisw and came back to New York to a ticker tape parade, Charles Lindbergh became a god who did not dwell on earth. After that, he could name his price and perhaps his penance.

The century's first true superstar, Lindbergh had gone from mail pilot to international hero literally overnight. Everything any man would ever want, he got—fortune, fame, and most importantly his wife, Anne, a beautiful, intelligent, and talented woman. When his son came along, he had everything, and people admired him for it. He was ripe for a fall and the media that had put him up there would be equally diligent when covering his emotional downfall.

In one moment, the idol of millions would turn human, and his grief would make him even more popular.

The Lindbergh Baby Kidnapping Case began on March 1, 1932, the proverbial dark and rainy night. The scene was Hopewell, New Jersey, a wealthy New York suburb. The child's nurse, Betty Gow, checked on the sleeping toddler at 8 P.M. When she came in two hours later to check again, Gow found his crib empty. On this night a father's the worst nightmare happened.

Even though it was his son's life at stake, Lindbergh did not lose his cool. Investigating outside, Lindbergh saw a home-made extension ladder propped against the side of the house under the Charles, Jr.'s bedroom window. Nearby was a small white envelope. Lindbergh opened it.

Dear Sir!

Have 50,000$ redy 2500$ in 20$ bills 1500$ in 10$ bills and 1000$ in 5$ bills. After 2-2 days we will inform you were to deliver the Mony. We warn you for making anyding public or for notify the polise the child is in gute [sic] care. Indication for all letters are singnature [sic] and 3 holes.

When police arrived, they examined the ladder more closely and noted that one rung had been previously repaired, while the side rails of the middle section were split. Detectives figured that the weight of the child, plus the kidnapper's, was more than the ladder could handle. Thus, the broken rails.

The cops also found a chisel and what seemed like the best clue of all: large footprints leading away from the house toward the southeast.

In one of the gargantuan mistakes that still dog the history of the New Jersey State Police, detectives failed to measure those footprints so they could be used as evidence against any subsequent suspects.

It didn't take long for word of the kidnapping to blaze through the radio airwaves. Next morning, headlines splashed on front pages from coast to coast the terrible story and Lindbergh's ordeal. This was at a time when the kidnapping, let alone murder of a child, were unheard of and rare acts of human depravity. Good reasons, then, for people to follow the case like a big game of human roulette—what filmmaker Billy Wilder would later call *The Big Carnival*. That's what it was at the Lindberghs—a carnival.

Unable to control the flow of news coming out about the case, newsmen, gawkers, and hawkers all gathered at the Lindbergh estate for every morsel of information the living legend gave to the wretched press and, in turn, to their public. This was the biggest story going, and the press was determined to report everything about it to a public that sympathized intensely with the Lindberghs and quickly lusted for the blood of the kidnapper . . . or kidnappers.

The organization assigned the duty of tracking down the kidnapper and returning the baby unharmed to Col. Lindbergh was the New Jersey State Police. Its commander was a Jersey native, H. Norman Schwartzkopf. Unfortunately, Schwartzkopf was a soldier who had made the mistake of thinking he was also a detective. The only contemporary detective with whom he might be compared is Barney Fife.

Born in 1896, Schwartzkopf was a graduate of West Point. He saw action in Europe during the First World War. In 1918 when the war ended, Schwartzkopf's superiors gave him an interesting job. He became the military police chief of an occupied German town. It was good training for his future endeavor.

Schwartzkopf stayed in the military until 1921, when he

resigned his commission to return home to Newark, New Jersey. Just at that time, New Jersey's governor Edwards had decided to establish a state police force. He needed someone to command it. When the resumé of the recently discharged H. Norman Schwartzkopf, twenty-five years old, came across his desk, he looked perfect for the job.

Schwartzkopf was an apolitical candidate and made no bones about it. Following the tradition of army officers, he had never voted, preferring to remain politically neutral as was the wont of the military. He knew little or nothing about Jersey politics. That wasn't too surprising since he'd been away in the military for almost a decade.

Schwartzkopf was exactly what the governor wanted: a good dependable soldier. He gave Schwartzkopf the title of "colonel" and a mandate to build a state police force to Schwartzkopf's personal specifications.

The new police czar's idea was to train his troopers according to the army's Non-Commissioned Officers Manual. Never mind that being a cop required a completely different mentality from being a soldier. Being a cop meant dealing with people. Soldiers don't have to deal. There was also no instruction on how to interview subjects properly or conduct a kidnapping investigation for that first class of state police troopers, or for the many to follow.

On December 5, 1921, when they graduated, the first group of state troopers, eighty-one out of the original class drove their Harley-Davidsons from the Jersey Shore to the state capital in Trenton. Ironically, George Washington had captured the Trenton garrison from Hessian mercenaries in a surprise, *creative* attack in the winter of 1776. Washington became one of our greatest presidents precisely because he knew what worked in the military and what didn't in civilian life.

No matter the age, police officers need an appreciation of

the gray area between *true* crime and simply making a mistake, between criminals and amateurs. In true military style, there was no such thing as a gray area for Schwartzkopf. Things were either black or white. The ability to deduce, to think creatively, was suppressed in the New Jersey State police, which is how footprints at the Lindbergh crime scene did not get processed.

After his son was kidnapped, Lindbergh once again exhibited the kind of courage that had led him to his fame. Lindbergh took one look at who was in charge and told Schwartzkopf to lay off. He'd negotiate with the kidnappers himself. He would brook no official interference. He requested that no one be arrested until the ransom was paid and the baby was home safe.

This was Charles Lindbergh speaking! You think Schwartzkopf or any dumb immigrant's son was going to tell him what to do?! You may argue the merit, but the method was brilliant. With the same unerring instinct that brought him to Orly Field in Paris, Lindbergh honed in on getting his message out by manipulating the media that had made him.

Lindbergh and his wife Anne went live on both NBC radio networks Red and Blue (Blue would later be sold for $8 Million in August, 1943, later becoming ABC-TV), coast to coast, talking directly to the kidnapper. They said that they would keep quiet on any arrangements made—read meaning, paying ransom—that would bring their toddler back safely.

On March 4, two days after the baby was snatched, Lindbergh received the first note from the kidnapper.

"Don't by afraid about the baby. Two ladys keeping care of it day and night." The Lindberghs were warned to keep the cops "out of the cace." A later note would tell Lindbergh where to deliver the money.

Unless the kidnapper was doing it deliberately, he had

trouble with syntax and spelling, indicating he might be someone who was an immigrant and not familiar with the language. Schwartzkopf was between the proverbial rock and a hard place. With Lindbergh in charge, no one listened to him, at least for now. He might have come to that conclusion and made a statement to the press. Instead, he said nothing, and the press labeled him ineffectual.

The focus of the case soon shifted to the Bronx, New York, where a retired principal, seventy-two-year-old John Condon, wrote a letter to the *Bronx Home News* newspaper. In it, he offered the kidnappers $1,000 of his own money and promised "to go anywhere, alone, to give the kidnappers the extra money and promise never to utter his name to any person."

The following day, Condon found a letter in his mailbox, apparently from the kidnapper, asking him to "get mony from Mr. Lindbergh." He was told to await further instructions. Condon called Lindbergh and told him of the letter. Lindbergh told Condon to come out to his estate in Hopewell to discuss it. At the meeting that followed, Lindbergh became convinced that the kidnapper was using Condon as an intermediary. He gave Condon some of the baby's favorite toys to help identify him. He told Condon to place a "Money is ready" note in the *New York American*. Lindbergh had received instructions from the kidnapper on how to contact him.

On March 12, the doorbell at Condon's Decatur Avenue apartment rang. Opening the door, he saw a man who handed him a letter. The man said that another man, in a brown topcoat and brown felt hat, had stopped the taxi he was driving and asked him to deliver the letter to a Decatur Avenue address.

Right there, police should have known they were dealing with a true amateur. Not only was the kidnapper relying on a human being he didn't know to further his plot, he had obviously entered Condon's neighborhood. If the messenger had been immediately interviewed by a police artist, who were already in use at the time, police might have come away with a sketch of the suspect much earlier in the investigation than they eventually did.

The letter was from the kidnapper. He instructed Condon to take a car to a place close to an empty hot dog stand, near which he'd find a note explaining where to go next. He was to be at that location in "3\4 of a houer." Condon went to the empty hot dog stand, which was across the street from a cemetery, and found the next note: "follow the fence from the cemetery direction to 233rd Street. I will meet you."

Condon walked toward the cemetery gate. Inside the cemetery, a figure deep in shadows signaled him. Condon walked over to him. The man had a handkerchief over his nose and mouth.

"Did you [get] my note?" the man asked. Speaking with a clearly identifiable German accent with improper syntax, the man asked if Condon had the money. Condon replied that he could not bring the money until he saw the baby.

The German suddenly jerked his head around, as though he had heard something suspicious. As a kidnapper, he had good reason to be jumpy. Maybe Lindbergh hadn't listened? He spotted another man outside the cemetery. Maybe it was an undercover cop waiting to pinch him? The German turned and ran. The plucky teacher from the Bronx gave chase . . . and Condon overtook him.

Here's how stupid the German was. He *was* the kidnapper. And when the time came to communicate directly with Lindbergh's man to collect the ransom, he gets so paranoid that he runs at the moment of cashing in. Getting the point, *finally*, that if the cops were really there they would have arrested him already at the point of more than several guns, the German slowed. He and Condon sit down peacefully on a bench near some graves.

The man called himself "John." Condon told the man that he had nothing to fear; no one would hurt him. But the man feared retribution.

"What if the baby is dead?" he asked. "Would I burn if the baby is dead?"

Condon didn't get it. Why was he being asked to deliver a ransom if the baby was dead?

"The baby is not dead," John said, realizing his mistake but not fast enough. "Tell the Colonel not to worry. The baby is all right. Tell Colonel Lindbergh the baby is on a boat."

John said he would soon send Condon the baby's sleeping suit for positive identification. Sure enough, a few days later Condon received a package. Inside was the sleeping suit worn by Charles, Jr., on the night of his disappearance, positively identified by Lindbergh himself.

On Tuesday, March 31, Condon received a new note from John demanding that the ransom be ready by Saturday evening. Internal Revenue Service (IRS) officers helped put the $50,000 ransom in marked gold notes. If anyone tried to pass them, they would be a dead giveaway because gold notes were about to be taken out of circulation.

On Saturday evening, a message was delivered to Condon. It was John, telling him where to drop the ransom. Lindbergh had decided to guard his money and bring his child home alive. Together, he and Condon drove to a flower shop. Under a table outside, they found another note that directed them to a cemetery across the street. The kidnapper seemed to have a thing for cemeteries.

Lindbergh stayed at the flower shop across the street to spy on the action. The last thing he wanted to do now was spook the kidnapper, just when he was so close to getting Charles,

Jr., back. Across the street in the cemetery, Lindbergh could see Condon meet the man he described as John again.

"Hey doctor!" the German called.

After some negotiation, John handed over a note: "You will find the Boad [boat] between Horseneck Beach and gay Head near Elizabeth Island." Charles, Jr., was on board a ship called the *Nelly*. Condon handed over the ransom. The men parted and went their separate ways.

It had been an exceptionally civilized proceeding in contract negotiation by exceptionally civilized men. It was also, up to then—point the finger wherever you want—the absolutely most stupid kidnapping negotiation in American criminal history. Donald E. Westlake couldn't write anything funnier. And Westlake could write as fiction what happened next in reality.

Next morning, May 12, 1932, at dawn, the great pilot Lindbergh once again flew along the Atlantic Coast. This time, he wasn't on his way to Europe. He was searching for a boat called *Nelly*. Only the desperation of a father avoiding inevitable grief explained this wild goose chase. Of course, Lindbergh found nothing.

At a little after 3:00 P.M. the same day, a truck driver named William Allen stopped just north of the small village of Mount Rose, New Jersey. He needed to relieve himself. As he walked about seventy-five feet off the road to find a private place, he looked down to see, amid the leaves and earth, a shallow grave. You couldn't miss it: a small boy's head and foot stuck up out of the ground. It was soon identified as Charles Lindbergh, Jr.

From that point on, Schwartzkopf and his state police, which had taken hits from the press for their failure to arrest a suspect, took over completely.

Autopsy results strongly suggested that the child had died

from a blow to the head. From the level of decomposition, he had been dead for over two months, which suggested that he had died close to the day of the kidnapping. It was unclear how the blow was inflicted. Detectives developed a theory that as the kidnapper was climbing down with the baby, his foot slipped.

In one of criminal history's stupidest accidents, the kidnapper, the German, dropped Charles, Jr. The toddler fell to the ground and hit his head, *smack,* and died instantly. Now the kidnapper had a body he needed to dispose of. In some way, he transported the body to the dump site where he dug the shallow grave, which was later discovered by the truck driver.

As crazy as it sounded, the New Jersey cops had probably gotten it right. The kidnapper's bizarre actions could be now be seen another way—the desperate act of an extremely desperate man making it up as he went along.

Charles, Jr., had actually died *moments after* he was kidnapped. The kidnapper had gone through with the kidnapping hoax to collect the ransom. Now, finally, the detectives theorized that this was not the work of a professional criminal, who would have delivered the child unharmed in order gto collect his ransom and, most importantly, avoid being executed The death penalty was in wide use in most states for homicides, including New Jersey, as it is today.

The investigation bogged down. Schwartzkopf's Kops had failed to develop a network of informants that might have pitched in. The most they had was a sketch from Condon of what John looked like. With the muffler over his face, he bore an uncanny resemblance to radio's *The Shadow.* The question was, did he have two automatics underneath his coat like The Shadow did? Was he a killer?

A year later, police had no suspects. If the guy was stupid enough, to spend the marked gold notes—please God!—that would lead them right to him. Once again, the kidnapper showed his lack of professionalism. Yes, he was stupid enough.

At the end of 1932 and into 1933, the marked gold notes began to appear in circulation across New York City's five boroughs. Narrowing it down, cops realized that a concentration of the marked notes had been passed in Yorkville, a neighborhood of German immigrants on the Upper East Side of Manhattan.

Pounding the pavement, detectives were asking Yorkville merchants about anyone who might have been passing the notes. The first big break came in November 27, 1933, when a cashier at a movie house in Yorkville recalled taking a gold note for a movie from a guy who matched Condon's description of John. The cops now had a location the suspect had been seen in, but unfortunately, no suspect.

The case dragged on for nine more months. In September 1934, the head teller of a Bronx bank spotted a marked gold note with "4U-13-14-N.Y." penciled in the margin. The teller figured the notation was for a license plate, penciled in by a gas station attendant. Detectives checked, finally finding the attendant who wrote the notation at an upper Manhattan service station.

The attendant recalled the gold note. It came from an average-sized man with a German accent. He'd been driving a blue Dodge. Looking down at the note, the attendant told the man, "You don't see many of those anymore."

"No, I have only about one hundred left," the man replied and drove away. The conversation felt strange, so the attendant wrote down the car's license plate number.

The New York City Police placed a long distance telephone call to the New York State Department of Motor Vehicles in the state capital of Albany, 120 miles north of New York City. There, state employees compared, by hand, their records to the license plate number given them by the New York cops. It took a few hours, but they came up with a match.

The car in question, the one the attendant had gassed up, belonged to a thirty-five-year-old Bronx carpenter and German immigrant. His named was Bruno Richard Hauptmann.

The next morning, Hauptmann was arrested leaving his home in his blue Dodge. He had a marked $20.00 gold note on him. A search of Hauptmann's garage uncovered more than $13,000 in marked gold notes. Hauptmann claimed the money belonged to Isidor Fitsch, a German friend. Unfortunately, his friend Fitsch was not around to corroborate his alibi. He had gone back to Germany and died from tuberculosis only a few months after reaching his beloved fatherland.

However, Fitsch had left his belongings with Hauptmann. Upon discovering the notes among Fitsch's stuff, Hauptmann decided to spend some of the money. He had kept the discovery from his wife, Anna. Not surprisingly, Hauptmann became the prime suspect. While it was common during this era to coax answers out of suspects by force, there were cops smart enough to use other, less brutal methods, though just as effective in eliciting the truth.

Nevertheless, Hauptmann was given the third degree—interrogation under hot blinding lights with cops shouting questions, pushing, and shoving. He was put in lineups for Condon and other witnesses to identify. He gave handwriting samples to compare to the kidnappers' notes. As for the phantom Fitsch, all the detectives found was alliteration. No immigration record existed for an "Isidor Fitsch."

Physical evidence was a different story. Cops had the notes and a sawed-off board they found in Hauptmann's attic. Investigators deduced that Hauptmann had used some of this wood to repair the ladder, the one found outside Charles, Jr.'s bedroom the night he was kidnapped.

As for Hauptmann himself, he was married with children. According to neighbors, he was a withdrawn, hardworking man. On September 24, 1934, this hard working married man with children, Bruno Richard Hauptmann, was charged in federal court with extorting $50,000 from Charles Lindbergh and was held without bail. Two weeks later, in the Hunterdon County Courthouse in Flemington, New Jersey, the 23-member grand jury voted unanimously to indict Hauptmann on first-degree murder charges. The federal government, which only had Hauptmann, on one extortion charge, agreed to step aside and let New Jersey try him on the more serious charge.

Trial was set for January 2, 1935.

Before it even occurred, newspapers labeled it "the trial of the century," and with good reason. While previous "trials of the century" included millionaire Harry K. Thaw's 1906 trial for killing Stanford White, neither that or any since had the cachet of "Lucky Lindy." That was "the Lone Eagle's" other nickname, the one an adoring public gave him after his nonstop flight across the Atlantic. It was expected that Lucky Lindy would testify for the prosecution. Never before or since had such a celebrity testified in a federal trial. The trial would take place in the town of Flemington, the Hunterdon County seat. All eyes waited on Lindbergh.

The vultures gathered.

Vendors descended on Flemington, hawking miniature kidnap ladders and locks (supposedly) of Charles, Jr.'s hair even before the trial started. Over a thousand reporters gathered, including Walter Winchell and Damon Runyon, and thousands more of the curious, like radio comedian Jack Benny. The New Jersey attorney general, David Wilentz, had personally decided to prosecute. It was expected to be quite a spectacle.

Opening arguments began as scheduled on January 2, 1935. Wilentz outlined the state's case:

Hauptmann kidnapped the child. The ladder broke under the additional weight of the baby. Hauptmann dropped the child, who died on impact. Hauptmann quickly buried the body. Cruelly acting as if Charles, Jr. was still alive, he extorted the ransom.

Finishing his opening statement, Wilentz told the jury, "I will ask you to impose the death penalty for the crime." Edward J. Reilly, Hauptmann's attorney, then rose to his feet. Reilly argued that his client was innocent.

"The state's case is nothing more than circumstantial evidence, weak at best. Once you have heard all the evidence, you will have no choice but to find the defendant not guilty," he confidently told the jury.

It sounded as though Reilly might have something up his sleeve. Or maybe, it was just empty.

The prosecution didn't wait long and called their star witness. Dressed in a rumpled gray suit and blue tie, Charles Lindbergh took the stand. In open court, Lindbergh identified Hauptmann's voice as the one he heard talking to Condon in the cemetery.

A voice identification of the suspect, from the demi-God who made history's first solo transatlantic plane flight, was devastating testimony indeed. Would even one lowly juror doubt Lucky Lindy? What Reilly should have done was challenge Lindbergh's recollection on a dark, stressful night when he was an appreciable distance away from the man he had just identified as his son's kidnapper. There was little hope he could get Hauptmann off, but if he oculd could establish reasonable doubt, raise questions in the jury's mind about how the crimes were committed, he might get them to convict on a lesser charge, thus avoiding the electric chair.

Betty Gow, a Scottish maid who was the last person in the house to see Charles, Jr. before he was snatched, took the stand for the prosecution. On cross-examination, Reilly's tactic was to provide an alternate theory of the crime and the perpetrators. Reilly implied that Gow and accomplices—supposedly the disgruntled hunters—were in on the crime, which, of course, she denied. After testifying, Gow fainted while walking back to her chair in the courtroom.

The prosecution introduced evidence that Hauptmann had had a criminal record in Germany, including a conviction for a "second story job" using a ladder. Next, state trooper Corporal Joseph Wolf took the stand. Wolf described seeing a large footprint in the mud near ladder marks by the nursery window. He estimated the footprint to be larger than size nine. On cross-examination, Reilly rightly ridiculed Wolf for not measuring the footprint, and for not knowing whether the print came from a left or right shoe.

A second trooper who testified identified a ladder in the courtroom as the one he had discovered on the night of the kidnapping outside the Lindbergh home. Then came an eighty-seven-year-old area resident, Amandus Hochmuth, with particularly incriminating testimony. Hochmuth testified that Hauptmann, whom he later picked out of a lineup, was at the wheel of a car that drove by his home the day of the crime. In the car was a ladder.

Condon came to the stand and positively identified Hauptmann as John, the man to whom Condon gave the ransom money. On cross-examination, Reilly pointed out that Condon had failed previously to identify the defendant in a lineup. Condon skirted the question.

Colonel Norman Schwartzkopf testified on January 10. He said that the state police had gotten handwriting specimens from the defendant to compare with the ransom notes.

Handwriting expert John Tyrell, who had previously testified at the Leopold and Loeb trial, then testified that Hauptmann had, beyond doubt, written the notes. Clark Sellers, a second handwriting expert who testified, said, "He [Hauptmann] might as well have signed the notes with his own name."

Medical testimony followed about the child's cause of death from a fractured skull. Rather than testify that the child had died from a blow to the head sustained when he fell from Hauptmann's grasp—as detectives surmised—the coroner was more general in his testimony. He told the jury that "the blow [that caused the fracture] was struck *prior* to the death of the child." In the jury's mind, "prior to death" could also mean that Hauptmann had struck the child that deadly blow first to control him, then lost control of the situation and dropped him. Lindbergh listened to all the testimony, and was emotionally shaken.

Following testimony from police about Hauptmann's passing of the gold notes, Wilentz called a balding forty-seven-year-old xylotomist (wood expert) from Madison, Wisconsin, named Arthur Koehler. He identified the repaired boards in the kidnapper's ladder as having come from the wood in Hauptmann's apartment.

The prosecution rested. They had presented an exceptionally strong circumstantial case. Reilly's defense was to expand on what he had implied with Gow's cross earlier, an alternative theory of the crime.

Reilly tried to establish that neighbors were upset over Lindbergh's decision not to allow them to hunt on his property. They were the ones who had kidnapped and killed the toddler for revenge. Reilly also implied Lindbergh was negligent in not checking on the backgrounds of his servants. Any of them might have been involved in the kidnapping too.

Then he called Hauptmann to the stand to proclaim his innocence.

Speaking in halting English, Hauptmann attempted to elicit the jury's sympathy. He testified about his s struggle to make it in America financially. He vehemently denied kidnapping Charles Jr., and asserted again that the gold notes that he passed were not his, but had come from his deceased friend Isidor Fitsch's stash, which he had left with him before returning to Germany.

On cross-examination, Wilentz tried to show how the poor spelling in the notes was consistent with Hauptmann's problems spelling in English. For two days on the stand, Hauptmann stood up under Wilentz's caustic questioning. Among other things, Wilentz asked Hauptmann why Condon's phone number was found in Hauptmann's closet; how it was that a missing board in his attic matched the wood that had repaired the ladder; and, most importantly, how it was that the more than $13,000 in marked ransom money happened to be found in his apartment. Hauptmann's answers were vague, unconvincing.

During a break in the proceedings, people gathered in small crowds outside the courthouse. Watching intently from the visitor's gallery, Jack Benny quipped, "What Bruno needs is a good second act."

Hauptmann tried. He had witnesses, including his wife, testify that he was someplace else on the night of the kidnapping. After his alibi witnesses testified, Reilly rested the case.

During closing statements, Wilentz told the jury that after reviewing the facts of the case, they would find Hauptmann was "either the filthiest, vilest snake that ever crawled through the grass, or he is entitled to an acquittal." Of course, the prosecutor made it clear how he felt, describing the defendant as "the lowest animal in the animal kingdom," and "public enemy number one of this world."

Reilly told the jury that it was an inside job. The Lindbergh Baby Kidnapping was a conspiracy involving Condon and

Fitsch, among others. Unfortunately, like most conspiracy theorists, he could offer no evidence to support his theory. After Judge Thomas Trenchard's final instructions, the jury retired to deliberate at 11:21 A.M. on February 13. Eleven hours and seven minutes later, at 10:28 P.M., the bell in the courtroom rang, indicating that the jury had reached a verdict.

Judge, prosecutor, defense attorney, and defendant took their places in the courtroom. The jury filed in. Jury foreman Charles Walton stood to announce the verdict:

"We find the defendant, Bruno Richard Hauptmann, guilty of murder in the first degree."

Judge Trenchard asked Hauptmann to stand.

"The sentence of the court is that you suffer death at the time and place, and in the manner specified by law," the judge said, banged down his gavel, and the proceeding ended.

Next day, two reporters talked to Hauptmann in jail. They asked him if he was afraid to go to "the chair."

"You can imagine how I feel when I think of my wife and child," Hauptmann replied, "but I have no fear for myself because I know that I am innocent. If I have to go to the chair in the end, I will go like a man, and like an innocent man."

Hauptmann subsequently lost all his appeals to higher courts. Hauptmann's advisers tried to persuade him to confess, figuring that if he took responsibility, his sentence would be commuted. Hauptmann refused and continued to declare his innocence.

On April 3, 1936, at 8:44 P.M., Bruno Richard Hauptmann was strapped into New Jersey's electric chair and 2,000 volts of electricity were sent through his body. He died quickly. His corpse was released to his widow.

The case itself should have died there, but Lindbergh's celebrity and the public's thirst for salacious details of the rich, famous, and dead, caused the case to live on.

• • •

In the wake of his execution, doubts still lingered about Hauptmann's guilt. Many a pundit speculated that the crime had to be a conspiracy. The kidnapping, in this version, was just too difficult for an immigrant like Hauptmann to pull off. He must have been framed by someone a lot smarter than he was.

Was Bruno framed? No credible evidence has ever been presented to prove this theory, which nevertheless survives to this day. Did Bruno Richard Hauptmann kidnap and kill the Lindbergh baby? Yes, he did, and all by his lonesome.

Did Hauptmann kill Charles, Jr. intentionally, or was it an accident as the prosecution claimed? The law at the time did not make a differentiation regarding intent. If the child died while Hauptmann was in the commission of felony kidnapping, which he clearly was, that made him guilty of murder. Hauptmann was a failed second story man who thought he was smart enough to pull off the crime of the century. He wasn't.

After Charles, Jr.'s murder, Lindbergh and his wife Anne had more children. The youngest, Reeve Lindbergh, related in a 1999 interview how the murder effected her family.

"This happened before any of the rest of the children were born. We had no direct connection to it. The way we were impacted was by how we were brought up: completely removed from the famous parts of my parents' lives. We had no direct contact with the event, but felt it in how we were protected. They were very careful with us. They tried to give us normal, but private lives."

In her book *Under a Wing*, Lindbergh, an established author in her own right, writes that she thinks her brother's death was an accident.

"I think we have always felt that the intent was never to kill the child, and that the ladder broke when the man who was holding the child was coming down. That's pretty well borne out in the evidence. I never think of it as a murder but as a negligent homicide."

As to how the kidnapping eaffected her mother and father, Lindbergh says in the 1999 interview, "The focus on my parents was so great that the kidnapping became a kind of sensation that to a certain extent was dehumanized. It's like the Princess Diana phenomenon."

When asked about Hauptmann's guilt or innocence, Lindbergh answered, "The evidence is very strong in favor of his involvement. But the question is, 'Was anyone else involved?'"

On careful review of the evidence, the answer is unequivacably "no." The case is closed but not the story.

In 1936, the American military attaché in Berlin asked Lindbergh to report on the state of Germany's military aviation program. While in Germany, Lindbergh and his wife attended the Summer Olympic games as the special guests of Field Marshal Hermann Goering, the head of the *Luftwaffe*. Lindbergh was impressed by the German state-of-the-art bombers, and munitions factories, but most of all by the Germans' vitality as a people.

Lindbergh believed Germany was Europe's power and no one could beat them. "The organized vitality of Germany was what most impressed me: the unceasing activity of the people, and the convinced dictatorial direction to create the new factories, airfields, and research laboratories . . . ," Lindbergh wrote in his book *Autobiography of Values*.

Acting for the Fuhrer, in October 1938, Goering presented Lindbergh the Service Cross of the German Eagle for his contributions to aviation. Lindbergh like many in the world had access to news reports coming out of Europe of German persecution of Jews. When pictures appeared in newspapers of Lindbergh wearing his German award, many Americans recoiled in horror.

The Lone Eagle supporting the Nazis? Confirming Reeve Lindbergh's assessment of her father's character, he saw nothing wrong with the medal and just considered it one of many.

Lindbergh and his family came back to the U.S. in 1939. The Lone Eagle threw himself into isolationist politics. He delivered a radio address urging Americans to stay neutral, criticizing President Roosevelt for believing the Nazis could be fought and stopped. How naïve FDR was! Lindbergh had seen with his own eyes the strength of the German people.

"These wars in Europe are not wars in which our civilization is defending itself against some Asiatic intruder . . . This is not a question of banding together to defend the white race against foreign invasion," Lindbergh broadcast.

In a subsequent article in the right-leaning *Reader's Digest*, Lindbergh wrote, "Our civilization depends on a Western wall of race and arms which can hold back . . . the infiltration of inferior blood."

On September 11, 1941, in Des Moines, Iowa, Charles Lindbergh gave a speech in support of the America First movement, which was trying to keep the U.S. out of the war in Europe. Proving that he could be just as stupid as the man who killed his son, Lindbergh told the crowd that it was time to "name names."

"The three most important groups who have been pressing this country toward war are the British, the Jewish, and the Roosevelt Administration."

The Jews, of course, were the worst.

"Instead of agitating for war, Jews in this country should be opposing it in every way, for they will be the first to feel its consequences. Their greatest danger to this country lies in their large ownership and influence in our motion pictures, our press, our radio and our government."

The fallout from the speech was enormous. Branded an anti-Semite by friends and foes alike, he lost all commercial and civic endorsements and ties. Lindbergh had resigned his military commission in 1939. When the war began on December 7, 1941, asked for it back.

"You can't have an officer leading men who thinks we're licked before we start," said FDR in rejecting Lindbergh's application."

Lindbergh did defense consulting work during World War II for Henry Ford, who in addition to inventing the automobile, had made public his own anti-Semitic views. By the end of 1945, with the war over and the Nazi atrocities having been publicly exposed, Lindbergh finally realized something he hadn't earlier. He started thinking about what he called power.

"History is full of its misuse. There is no better example than Nazi Germany. Power without moral force to guide it invariably ends in the destruction of the people who wield it. Power . . . must be backed by morality . . . " he said in a 1945 speech.

What he really meant is history is full of the misue of power because of a lack of moral compass. Ironically, the first man to fly across the Atlantic Ocean alone himself lacked a moral compass to give his post-flight life a true direction. Historian William O'Neill expressed the views of many citizens when he ventured, that "In promoting appeasement and military unpreparedness, Lindbergh damaged his country to a greater degree than any other private citizen in modern times. That he meant well makes no difference."

A Bullet for Pretty Boy

1934—Charles Arthur Floyd, aka "Pretty Boy"

The failure of the FBI to anticipate the 9/11 conspiracy and the slaughter that followed has been well documented by the 9/11 commission. What haven't been exposed are more specific instances of the Bureau's abuse of its power and outright lying to protect its squeaky clean image. Nowhere is this more evident than in the Bureau's account of what became known as the "Kansas City Massacre" and the man the Bureau said led it: Pretty Boy Floyd.

Did he really do it? Was Pretty Boy Floyd part of the Kansas City Massacre?

Charles Arthur Floyd was born on February 3, 1904, in Georgia. He was the fourth of eight children born to Walter Lee Floyd and his wife Minnie Echols. As a boy, Charley was well-liked by his brothers and sisters. Easygoing, with a good sense of humor, he liked to play pranks on his siblings. His parents were Baptists who took their brood to church every Sunday.

In 1911, Walter Floyd packed up his family and moved to Sequoia County, in Oklahoma's Cookson Hills, where he became a tenant farmer. The area had changed little since it was Indian Territory patrolled by federal marshals. It was still lush and overgrown, a perfect place to hide out if the law happened to be after you.

People in the Cookson Hills watched out for each other. Many brewed moonshine or corn liquor. It was just something to help the family pay the bills. No one looked at it as anything illegal.

Charley and his brothers peddled their father's moonshine to make extra money for the family, but in 1915, Walter finally got out of the business. He uprooted his family a second time and moved to a farm in Akins, where he opened a general store. Charley, like most children, quit school after the sixth grade to help his father in his store and on their farm.

The worst that can be said of Floyd's parents is that they were too busy scraping along to give their son direction in life. But environment, more than anything, appears to have been the more determining factor in Floyd's career choice. Beer was perennially the most popular and cheapest alcoholic beverage kids had access to; Charley formed a liking for a local brew called Choctaw Beer. Everyone began calling Charley "Choc."

With no direction, Choc drifted through his early teens. His most serious crime before he was fifteen was stealing a box of cookies from J. H. Harkrider's store in Sallislaw. He was caught and immediately confessed, for which he was let off with a warning. Four years later when he was nineteen, he sought adventure on the road. Choc joined up with a crew of migrant farm workers.

The migrants farmed their way through Oklahoma and Kansas; some of them were honest folk, some on the lam from the law, others drifters who needed the money.

Choc loved the migrant life. An impressionable, likable teenager, he enjoyed listening to these men who bragged about their criminal experiences. They never hesitated to fight over something large or small, and they fought dirty when they had to. To Choc, they made crime seem like an idyllic, fun-filled life. His older sister Ruth would later claim that these men "changed his way of thinking and doing."

After the harvesting season, Choc returned to the Cookson Hills, and became a bum. He frequented the town's billiard and music halls. Getting bored, Choc and his friend Harold Franks broke in and held up the local post office. Their robbery netted them $3.50, all in dimes. Choc took the coins. He and Franks were soon arrested on a federal warrant. Choc had "knocked over" federal property.

Because Akins was so close a close community, it did not surprise anyone when witnesses to the robbery failed to show in court. The town was giving Choc a break. Without eyewitnesses, the case didn't hold up anyway. The judge had no choice but to set Choc and his friend free with a severe rebuke. After his release, Choc went straight for a few years. A handsome young man with dark brown wavy hair, dimples, and an easy smile, Choc was also intelligent, aggressive, and courageous. They were the perfect attributes for a captain of industry or an outlaw.

In early 1924 when Choc was twenty and she was sixteen, he married a local girl, Ruby Hargraves. They bought a small house in Akins and soon had a son that they named Charles Dempsey Floyd, the middle name after the popular heavyweight champion. A good father and husband, Choc worked in the cotton fields to make a living. But the work was hard.

Choc knew from the men he'd worked with as a migrant farm worker that there were easier ways to make money. Befriending nineteen-year-old petty thief John Hilderbrand, Choc left wife, child, and home in 1925, and with Hilderbrand headed for St. Louis, where they hoped to make their fortune. They did; within a month, they had held up half a dozen groceries and service stations. Their take was a paltry $565, but the work was fast, thrilling, and easy.

In September Hildebrand's buddy Joe Hlavatry called with a tip. Kroger's Food Store was expecting a large payroll during the late morning of Friday, September 11, 1925. Choc got ready. That morning, he, Hilderbrand, and Hlavatry stole a Caddy roadster in the alley next to the Kroger building in downtown St. Louis.

At a few minutes before 1 P.M., an armored truck drove up to Kroger's loading dock. As Choc and his men watched, a guard came out of the armored car and began to unload canvas bags of money. When the truck was emptied, the robbers entered the office building. From long trench coats, Choc and his men drew revolvers. They went straight to the cashier's office. Keeping the guards and the bank employees covered, Choc and Hlavatry grabbed the money sacks. Without firing a shot, the three left as quickly as they had come.

The inexperienced thieves bought a new Studebaker and proceeded to flash it around Fort Smith, Arkansas. Suspicious of the bums and their new vehicle, police stopped them. Hilderbrand and Hlavatry confessed to the robbery and named Choc Floyd as an accomplice. All three were charged with highway robbery on September 16, 1925.

Newspapermen found something interesting about the three holdup men, especially the way they went about the robbery professionally, without hurting anyone, in contrast to their apparent naiveté in spending money that they should have kept hidden.

In one such article, Kroger's payroll master referred to Choc as "a mere boy—a *pretty boy* with apple cheeks." The name stuck. "Choc" Floyd became "Pretty Boy" Floyd. Choc himself hated the new nickname and winced every time he read it in print. He pleaded guilty to highway robbery, and was sentenced to four years in the state pen in Jefferson City, Missouri.

Floyd's time behind bars hardened his resolved to remain

free the next time he engaged in a criminal enterprise. But unlike John Dillinger, who literally had criminal tutors behind bars, Floyd wasn't into any of that. He just wanted to serve his time quietly, which he did, and get out.

Released in 1929, he returned to the road and spent the next two years making a name for himself as a modern-day highwayman. Primarily a loner, he was twice arrested on suspicion of highway robbery. In fact, Choc had actually stopped cars and proceeded to rob the occupants. However, he didn't steal the cars, so the crime of carjacking would have to wait for another era.

On May 20, 1930, Choc's luck seemed to run out when he was arrested in Toledo, Ohio, on a bank robbery charge. The third time was the charm; the charge stuck. Convicted, Choc was sentenced to a maximum of fifteen years at the state penitentiary in Columbus, Ohio. Having been behind bars once, Choc was not about to repeat the experience. Manacled and heavily guarded, Choc was determined to escape when he boarded a train in Toledo that would take him to Columbus and prison.

During the ride, Choc talked his guards into taking off the handcuffs; he needed his hands, he claimed, so he could go to the bathroom. With his hand on his holstered Colt automatic, a guard took Choc to the bathroom. He waited outside while Floyd did his business inside. Inside, Choc got busy.

There was one window, on the far wall. It faced the tracks. He didn't hesitate for a second. Choc broke the bathroom window and jumped out into the night, landing on his feet and rolling away from the track, into the darkness.

After a while, the guard began to wonder why Floyd hadn't come out. He tried to get in, but the door was locked. After pounding on it and calling Floyd's name fruitlessly, he smashed it in, only to find nothing more than a broken window. As for Pretty Boy Floyd, he was long gone.

At the next station, the engineer coasted in with a squealing of brakes. Alighting, he informed the station manager who informed the police. Search parties were sent out and came back with nothing. For the state of Ohio, the whole affair was terribly embarrassing.

Choc made headlines for days after his dramatic escape:

> "PRETTY BOY" ESCAPES TRAIN TO PRISON
> FLOYD ESCAPES INTO NIGHT
> GUARDS SURPRISED—"PRETTY BOY" ESCAPES

Returning to Kansas City to hide out, Choc hooked up with William Miller, a fellow escaped con. As an outlaw, Miller was more established than Choc. He, too, had a nickname, "Billy, the Baby-Faced Killer." Miller had robbed and killed for some of Kansas City's top criminal combines.

The two decided to engage in highway robbery outside the city. First, though, Choc had an old score to settle. Choc had a longstanding feud with the Ash brothers, William and Wallace. Through the criminal grapevine, Choc had been informed that the Ashes had told the police he was back in town. This violated the unwritten code of the criminal world that you didn't rat on anyone.

By the time Floyd and Miller left Kansas City, the Ashes had been shot dead and left in a ditch outside the city. The cops figured it was Floyd, who they knew hated the Ashes, but they didn't care. If one criminal eliminated another, it saved the state the cost of a trial and execution.

Miller and Floyd were a short-lived dynamic duo. After robbing two banks of a combined total of $3,000, the men took their wives shopping in Toledo. A salesgirl in Uhlman's Clothing Store recognized Choc from wanted posters. Police were called, and the building was surrounded by cops. When the Floyds and Millers came out of the store with their wives, Police Chief Galliher ordered them to surrender. The two wanted men pulled guns.

Bullets flew in every direction; bystanders hit the ground. The outlaws were firing at the cops as they made their way down the street to their getaway car. A patrolman who had been using a police car for cover, saw that Floyd was almost at his vehicle. He came out from hiding and began firing in the open. Choc pumped bullets at him, inflicting a mortal wound to the cop's stomach. Miller, too, went down with a mortal wound, his to the chest.

Choc could hear the bullets ricocheting off his rear fenders as he drove an erratic course over sidewalks, through alleys, and down a one-way street the wrong way until he had outdistanced the pursuit. He headed out of Ohio, determined never to return. He headed for home, the Cookson Hills of Oklahoma. Once back home, 1931 would turn out to be the pivotal year in Choc's career.

The Depression was newly underway. Farms were failing literally by the minute. Economic conditions worsened every day. It was a national catastrophe as more and more farms in Oklahoma, Arkansas, and the rest of the midwestern states turned into what history called the Dust Bowl. Families that had occupied and, in many instances, farmed property for many generations were forced off their ancestral homes when banks foreclosed mortgages that couldn't be paid.

This was as perfect a breeding ground for legend as America would ever have. With a 24 percent unemployment rate, and government and private industry not responding to the working man, it was the perfect environment for a folk hero to emerge. Poverty, homelessness, starvation—these were the coin of the realm in America. And it was in these kinds of economic and social situations that crime has always thrived.

What separated Choc from his contemporaries, people like the ruthless John Dillinger and the maniacal Bonnie and Clyde was, quite simply, Choc Floyd's perception of economic and social conditions. Floyd saw that *everyone* was suffering from the Depression, except for the big guys. Choc became obsessed with striking at the heart of this perversity while attempting to save the people he had grown up with.

Perhaps this is the only time in American criminal history that the name Pretty Boy Floyd and the word "philanthropist" have been used together. Choc knew that if the Cookson Hills were going to be his hideout, he'd have to take care of the people of the area, whom he would count on not to betray him. People had nothing, and they would be beholden to him. Besides, it gave him pleasure to help his people out.

Choc decided it was time to rob the places where the money really was—the banks. He recruited George Birdwell, a middle-aged small-time thief he had known since childhood. Birdwell's job was to serve as lookout and help Choc to carry the goods. Between 1931 and 1932, Choc Floyd and Birdwell held up fifty-one banks in Oklahoma, a record that still stands. Choc used the same MO (modus operandi) for each robbery.

First, Birdwell would case the bank. He was looking at the physical layout, especially where the vault was; how many guards there were; what kind of alarm system the bank utilized; and how many employees needed to be covered.

Second, the day of the robbery, Birdwell would park the getaway car close to the bank. Wearing hats with brims pulled low and long trench coats, the two would enter the bank calmly, pull their firepower from under their coats, and proceed about their business.

Both Birdwell and Choc favored Thompson submachine guns. Choc would remove the butt stock of his. The modifications made the gun easy to conceal under his trench coat. Then, instead of the usual ammo cylinder he would install a twenty-round clip. As the robbery progressed, Choc would leap over the counter and gather up the cash from the cash drawers. If someone tipped off the cops or sounded an alarm, Choc and Birdwell would use a bank employee as hostage until they were out of harm's way. Then and only then would the hostage be released unharmed.

Not surprisingly, by the end of 1931 bank insurance rates doubled. Bankers put pressure on Governor "Alfalfa Bill" Murray to use the National Guard to catch Pretty Boy Floyd. Alfalfa Bill's response: "National Guard? As long as he stays down there where he's at [Cookson Hills] and is protected the way he is by those people, he will continue to rob banks— National Guard or not!"

Stories made the rounds of Choc's beneficence in helping out struggling farmers, widows, anyone who needed financial help. Choc was respectful of the people who sheltered him, earning their undying love and respect. Choc's reputation as "the Robin Hood of Crime" grew. The bankers, though, hated Pretty Boy Floyd's guts. The Oklahoma Bankers Association put up a $6,000 reward for the capture of Pretty Boy Floyd, dead or alive.

It made no difference. By 1932, Choc was regularly being reported in places where he had never been. He was a phantom, who came out of the morning mist, robbed a bank, and then faded back into the Cookson Hills until his funds ran low. The local, county, and state cops kept up a steady diet of Floyd search parties, to no avail, of course. Alfalfa Bill was right. As long as Choc stayed in the Cookson Hills, no one could touch him.

"On the morning of June 17, 1933, there occurred in front of the Union Railway Station in Kansas City, Missouri, one of the most brutal, premeditated mass murders recorded in the annals of American law enforcement. The killings, which took the lives of four peace officers and their prisoner, are now known as "'the Kansas City Massacre.'"

So begins the FBI file on "the Kansas City Massacre."

Choc Floyd was not a killer by nature. Up until 1932, he had only killed once, in an extreme instance, when police had cornered him. For Floyd, killing was the exception, not the rule. That's why the next chapter in Choc Floyd's life makes no sense whatsoever, unless of course, it never happened.

The way the FBI tells it, Floyd, working with outlaws Vernon Miller and Adam Richetti, tried to free Frank Nash. Nash was another outlaw and was being taken to the maximum security United States Penitentiary in Leavenworth, Kansas. Nash had originally been sentenced on March 1, 1924, at Oklahoma City for assaulting a mailman. He escaped prison in 1930. The Bureau of Investigation (the FBI's predecessor) began an immediate search for Nash. Tracked by federal agents to Eureka Springs, Arkansas, on June 16, 1933, Nash was captured there by the FBI while partaking of the therapeutic waters.

The FBI's investigation had disclosed what they claimed was a criminal conspiracy among the underworld's most powerful gangsters to rescue Nash before he could get to federal prison. Among the men involved in this conspiracy was Pretty Boy Floyd. On the morning of June 17, 1933, the file continues, Miller, Adam Richetti, and Pretty Boy Floyd drove to the Union Railway Station in a Chevy sedan. They took up positions in front of the train station and waited.

When Nash arrived, he was escorted by FBI Special Agent Raymond J. Caffrey, Otto Reed, the chief of Police of McAlester, Oklahoma; Kansas City police officers W. J. Grooms and Frank Hermanson, and two other FBI agents.

Removed from the train in manacles, Nash was duck-walked to Caffrey's waiting automobile, where he was placed in the front passenger seat. The two other FBI agents and Otto Reed took up the rear. Grooms and Hermanson took up positions around the car. Just as Agent Caffrey approached the driver's-side door of his auto from the front, he heard someone shout, "Up! Up!"

Caffrey looked up to see three masked men. Armed with machine guns, they had snuck up on the agent's blind side. "An instant later, the voice of one of the gunmen was heard to say 'Let 'em have it.' Immediately a fusillade of gunfire came from the weapons of the attackers. Shots were fired from the front and from all sides of Agent Caffrey's car."

Caught in the crossfire, Grooms and Hermanson were instantly killed. In the car, Otto Reed fell dead from multiple bullet wounds. "One of the FBI agents was severely wounded by bullets which entered his back and was [subsequently] confined to bed for several months," The FBI file continues. Caffrey was killed by a bullet that passed directly through his head as he stood beside the car.

As for the intended beneficiary, Frank Nash, "a misdirected gunshot entered his skull, thereby defeating the very purposes of the conspiracy to gain his freedom."

It was the local newspaper, the *Kansas City Star*, that first called it "the Kansas City Massacre." The story and the name made the front pages coast to coast. Radio journalists reported the story in stentorian tones. As for the FBI, they made sure to play up Floyd's part in the massacre. He was, they said, just as guilty as the other two of the slaughter.

Unfortunately, the FBI had no evidence of Floyd's involvement, because he wasn't there.

Up to the time of the massacre, Choc had only killed once, in self-defense. A robber by trade, his modus operandi was always the same—get in, get the goods, get out, and don't fire unless in self-defense. Not only did the FBI know this, they also knew that except for Birdwell, Floyd always worked alone. Yes, he knew Richetti, but he didn't know Miller or Nash. The FBI's idea that Floyd would put his life on the line for a gangster was ridiculous.

"[T]he FBI account is based more on speculation, perhaps even perjury. Survivors could not initially identify Floyd or Richetti to give the Bureau the excuse it needed to go after Floyd, the first bandit to make national news," write William Helmer with Rick Mattix in their 1998 book, *Public Enemies*.

Why then would the FBI blame him for something he didn't do, knowing full well that the evidence pointed to his innocence? Because Choc had become a folk hero. Songs were being written about the Robin Hood of Oklahoma outlaws. Floyd's ability to rob banks in Oklahoma with impunity, his success at embarrassing everyone, especially Director Hoover, who had pledged to rid the country of such outlaws, was almost as though he was painting a big red bullseye on his back.

Whether he was involved or not, Floyd now had FBI agents gunning for him. FBI Director J. Edgar Hoover wanted him dead or alive. Choc knew that the best thing he could do was get the hell out of the Midwest. Instead of heading back to the Cookson Hills, which were crawling with G-men, he did what no one expected and headed east. Using assumed names, Floyd, Richetti, and their wives moved into an apartment building in Buffalo, New York, in 1934. They kept a very low profile which was just as well because the Buffalo winter was miserably cold..

Back in Washington, Hoover was hot for their capture. He used the Kansas City Massacre as the rationale to lobby for increased FBI involvement, specifically passage of the 1934

Fugitive Felons Act, which made it a federal crime to avoid prosecution by stepping across state lines. That meant that the capture of fugitives like Floyd came under the Bureau's aegis.

The legislation passed Congress. As a result, Hoover created the bureau's "Public Enemies" list that would go on to become legendary. Choc hit number one on that first list, followed by the bank-robbing Hoosier, John Dillinger.

After seven months of isolation during Buffalo's frigid winter, Choc had had enough. He and Richetti went back to the Cookson Hills. While visiting his family there, Choc read of Bonnie and Clyde's bloody demise. Discovering that Hoover was targeting him next, he did not seem to care. Instead of leaving his life of crime, Choc kept going.

Like Bonnie Parker, Choc seemed to have a portent of his own death. He made it a point to see his family one last time. In a segment of the A&E TV series *Biography*, Glendon Floyd, Choc's nephew, recalled his last visit with "Uncle Charley."

"The last time I saw my uncle he was coming down an old dirt road, and I was probably about 8 years old. I got close to him and I was looking at him. He was grinning. He was in an old straw hat and overalls and a silk undershirt. That was my uncle."

Soon after, Choc joined Dillinger's gang, taking part in the holdup of the Merchants National Bank in South Bend, Indiana, on June 30, 1934. Afterward, Choc seemed to change his mind about his life. The FBI was intent on getting him. The G-men were looking for him everywhere. He decided to flee the country with his family, and go south of the border to Mexico.

On the way to the Cookson Hills to pick up his family, Choc and Richetti's auto hit a telephone pole in fog at the junction of Interstate 7 and the Pennsylvania Railroad tracks in Ohio. Although no one was hurt, the cops that came to investigate found themselves facing automatic weapons, with Floyd and Richetti's itchy fingers on the triggers.

Richetti took off into the brush. The lawmen eventually captured and disarmed him. Richetti was soon questioned. It made no difference that he gave a phony moniker. The Feds knew who he was . . . and his associate. Choc had escaped, shooting his way out, injuring one lawman in the foot.

Choc Floyd took to the forest. But this was a forest in Ohio; it wasn't the Cookson Hills. He had no idea where he was but he knew that he couldn't count on the locals for support. What had he done for them? He was just another outlaw. Choc Floyd was in hostile territory; his enemy was relentless. If he was to survive, he needed to get out pronto.

The dragnet closed in. In Washington, Hoover was informed of Richetti's capture and Floyd's escape. This time, Hoover figured he had him. Hoover responded by sending his most trusted agent, Melvin Purvis, from his Chicago office. Arriving in East Liverpool, Ohio, Purvis put together a posse of federal and local lawmen. Two days after getting into the field, Purvis got his first break.

A man wearing a pin-striped suit, which fit the clothing part of Choc's description, was seen near the Bell schoolhouse, ten miles from East Liverpool. Purvis rooted out a farmer who admitted that a man in a pin-striped suit, hungry and begging for food, had shown up at his door. He identified Choc from a mug shot.

Choc knew the cops were closing in; their pursuit had run him to ground. Trapped in Ohio, on unfamiliar ground, he didn't know which way to go. Wet from a heavy rain, tired, and hungry, Choc found a farmhouse on the edge of a cornfield. It was down a path that a sign identified as "Spruceville Road." A middle-aged woman wearing a striped house dress and white apron answered his knock.

"I'm the Widow Conkle," she said.

"I'm hungry and lost, Ma'am. Could you give me something to eat?"

The Widow Conkle saw an attractive, smiling young man
in his thirties, wearing a pin-striped suit that had seen better
days. The story he gave to explain his bedraggled presence was
that while hunting, he had gotten drunk and been separated
from his friends.

Conkle invited him in. While she cooked up fried pork
chops, rice, and potatoes, Choc washed up at the pump outside When he came inside, the Widow Conkle served him
what would turn out to be his last meal. About 4 P.M.,
Conkle's brother drove over to visit. Choc asked him for a lift
to the closest bus line. The brother agreed to drive him to
Clarkson, the next town over.

Choc had just gotten into the brother's car when he spotted
two sleek-looking, black autos coming quickly down
Spruceville Road. Choc had no idea who was inside, but he
rightly guessed it was police. Jumping out of the car, Choc
hightailed it for the cover of the woods, about two hundred
yards distant, through open field. As he ran, he pulled his .45
automatic from his belt.

The G-men got out of their cars and gave pursuit.
According to the FBI, the lawmen shouted at Choc to sur-
render, but the outlaw kept running. Chester Smith, a World
War I sharpshooter, was one of the local men in Purvis's posse.
He brought his rifle up and fired once. Smith had meant to
wound and not kill; in that he was successful.

The bullet hit Choc's right arm. The impact forced him to
the ground. But he got to his feet quickly and ran again
toward the cover of the forest.

"Surrender," Purvis shouted. Floyd didn't, and this time, the
G-man told his men to halt and fire a salvo. Choc went down

in a hail of bullets. Purvis was the first to reach the dying outlaw.

"Were you at Kansas City?" Purvis asked.

"My name is Charles Arthur Floyd," he replied. Choc died a moment later.

It is here that the FBI account differs sharply with the eyewitness account of Chester Smith, the sniper who first brought Floyd down. In Helmer and Mattix's *Public Enemies,* they quote Smith's 1974 account of Floyd's death, which is far different from the official FBI version that resides in Floyd's file.

Smith claimed that after he shot Choc in the arm, Floyd got up to run again. Smith wounded him a second time, again not fatally. Choc had made it to the cornfield, where he fell, still very much alive. Advancing to the cornfield, Smith picked up Choc's .45 automatic, which he had dropped while running. Now he was unarmed.

FBI agents and local cops made a circle around the wounded outlaw. As he said in the official account, Purvis asked Choc if he was involved in the Kansas City Massacre. But instead of merely giving his name, what Choc really said was, "I wouldn't tell you son of a bitch nothing!"

Purvis turned to an agent holding a submachine gun.

"Shoot into him," he said.

Smith watched the agent turn his weapon on Floyd. Setting it to "single shot" for increased accuracy, he fired into Choc's body.

When Purvis went over to the farmhouse to use the phone, Smith thought he was going to call an ambulance. Instead, Purvis called Washington to tell Hoover that Pretty Boy Floyd was dead. He wasn't, but he was critically wounded. Smith helped carry Choc to the roadside, where he soon died.

The body was taken to a funeral home in East Liverpool,

where plans for its disposal were made. Smith claimed that he waited over forty years to tell his story because he was reluctant to challenge the FBI's official story of the killing. By 1974, however, most of the men involved in Floyd's death were dead themselves. Smith saw no purpose in continuing to keep silent about the truth.

Did Pretty Boy Floyd really do it? Was he part of the Kansas City Massacre execution team?

No, he wasn't. The FBI is lying. The evidence shows conclusively that Choc Floyd was someplace else when the massacre occurred; there is also no evidence that he had any involvement with the men the FBI identified as his compadres. Considering that the executioners were masked, the FBI would have to show conclusive proof to say that Floyd was there. They have not.

Did Purvis have Choc Floyd executed as Smith charges? There is no reason to doubt Smith's account or motives, while there is every reason to doubt the official FBI version. Purvis's style was not to give any criminal a chance, even one who eschewed lethal force. He followed the same methodology when he shot John Dillinger the next year in an alley behind the Biograph Theatre in Chicago without giving the outlaw a chance to surrender.

Purvis later committed suicide in 1959 with the same gun he used to shoot Dillinger. While Purvis is largely forgotten today, and Hoover is ridiculed both for his professional and personal life, long before his body was even cold, Woody Guthrie had begun to think about a way of immortalizing Pretty Boy Floyd.

Throughout the 1930's, Guthrie wrote a series of ballads about the Depression era outlaws. He depicted them as populist heroes, but none more so than Choc. "The Ballad of

Pretty Boy Floyd," written in 1939, contains this lyric which touches at the heart of the popularity of Floyd and his ilk:

> *"And as through your life you travel,*
> *Yes, as through your life you roam,*
> *You won't never see an outlaw*
> *Drive a family from their home."*

THE ATOMIC SPIES?

1954—ETHEL AND JULIUS ROSENBERG

With the history-making atomic destruction of Hiroshima and Nagasaki in 1945, the United States emerged as the world's first superpower. Twenty-eight years into the Communist regime, the Soviet Union could not let the Americans maintain that superiority.

Russia believed that America had designs on the Soviet Republic, including the Iron Curtain countries of Eastern Europe. To keep the balance of power, and prevent the Americans from implementing their "plan," the Soviets needed the secret of the atomic and later the hydrogen bomb. Only by being equal with the United States on a nuclear level could Russia ever hope to feel safe.

The Soviets understood the value of enemy intelligence. In April, 1943 the USSR established its secret intelligence service, the NKGB, later changing its name in March 1946 to the MGB. Another name change followed in March 1953 to MVD, finally settling in March 1954 on its best-known acronym: the KGB.

One thing that was consistent throughout this period was that regardless of what it was called, the Soviet secret police was entrusted with the job of recruiting traitors to help unlock the nuclear secrets of "the bomb." One of those traitors was Klaus Fuchs, a British physicist who worked on the

Manhattan Project that developed the atomic bomb. On several occasions in 1945, Fuchs met with a Soviet agent named "Raymond" and gave him key information about the design of the world's first nuclear weapon. Fuchs, however, did not realize that the Americans were hot on his trail.

American spies intercepted coded cables from the Soviet consulate in the United States to the KGB in Russia. U.S. cryptanalysts successfully deciphered the cables. One of them was a report Fuchs wrote on how the bomb's development was progressing. Picked up for questioning, Fuchs was confronted with the evidence against him and confessed. He told the G-men about his meetings with "Raymond."

Three months passed until the FBI identified "Raymond" as mild-mannered chemist Harry Gold. It was Gold, as "Raymond," who got the top-secret information for the atomic bomb from Fuchs and passed it to the Russians. But had Fuchs been at the top of the chain of traitors, or was there someone above him?

By 1950, authorities had begun to focus on a soldier at Los Alamos, New Mexico, who, Gold said, had paid him $500 for information about the implosion lens for the atomic bomb. Gold didn't know the soldier's real name but he thought that the soldier's wife "may have been Ruth." He also remembered that the soldier came from New York City.

Two days later, FBI agents showed Gold a picture of a man Gold positively identified as the soldier who paid him the $500. The name of the man in the picture was David Greenglass. Brought in for questioning by the G-men, Greenglass quickly admitted that he was the Los Alamos soldier who bought the information from Gold. But it was what he now added that became part of history. He said that his wife, Ruth, and his brother-in-law, Julius Rosenberg, were part of the spy ring that worked for the Soviets.

• • •

By the time he was sixteen, Julius Rosenberg was a passionate member of the City College of New York's (CCNY) Young Communist League. The son of Polish Jewish immigrants, he had grown up on Manhattan's Lower East Side. He met his future wife, Ethel, at a union fundraising party.

Graduating from CCNY with a degree in engineering, Rosenberg began work as a civilian employee for the army's signal corps in 1940. According to Greenglass, late in 1943 he began talking to his brother-in-law Julius Rosenberg about espionage. Then, shortly after their initial conversation, Rosenberg dropped his Communist Party affiliation. Greenglass claimed Rosenberg did this to keep a lower profile. Once Rosenberg began working for the Soviets, the last thing he needed was the extra scrutiny a Communist Party affiliation would afford him.

In 1944, Greenglass said, Rosenberg approached his sister Ruth, and asked if his brother-in-law, Greenglass, would give him notes on Manhattan Project research. Greenglass said yes. For the next year, he fed Rosenberg information, sometimes directly, sometimes through intermediaries, about the high-explosive lens mold being developed at Los Alamos for the atomic bomb.

On June 16, 1950, FBI agents went to Brooklyn, New York, where Rosenberg lived with his wife and two boys. Taken in for questioning, Rosenberg was confronted with Greenglass's charges.

"Bring him here—I'll call him a liar to his face!" Rosenberg told the G-men.

They responded by releasing him but Rosenberg knew the government was just toying with him. It was a matter of time until he was arrested again and this time charged. This was the height of the Red Scare of the 1950s, when many Americans like Senator Eugene McCarthy thought they could smell a "Commie" under every rock.

Realizing he needed help, Rosenberg engaged the services of prominent defense attorney, Emmanuel Bloch.

By mid-July 1950, Greenglass and wife Ruth had given the FBI additional information about Rosenberg's guilt. A warrant was issued. The FBI found their way back to Brooklyn. In full view of his two young sons, Rosenberg was cuffed by the G-men. As he was hustled out of his apartment, a team entered to search for incriminating evidence.

With Julius Rosenberg now in custody, the FBI turned its attention to Ethel, his wife. Who would know her better, the Bureau knew, than her own family? Once again, they turned to Brother David and sister-in-law Ruth. The Greenglasses told the FBI that Ethel was present during certain conversations regarding Julius's spying activities. They also claimed she typed information for Julius, which later found its way into Russian hands.

The government was in a bind. As far as hard evidence, there was nothing other than the charges of her brother and sister-in-law. The case was circumstantial and exceedingly weak. Even if she was involved in the spy ring, it had to be on the periphery. Despite that, the FBI charged her with spying. FBI director Hoover explained his actions.

"There is no question" that "if Julius Rosenberg would furnish details of his extensive espionage activities, it would be possible to proceed against other individuals. [P]roceeding against his wife might serve as a lever in this matter," Hoover stated.

Following through on Director Hoover's "suggestion," G-men arrested Ethel on August 11, 1950. She, too, was denied bail and she, too, denied any involvement in an atomic conspiracy. But with Ethel in custody, Hoover now had his lever. Making certain that he knew Ethel was in custody, Hoover had Julius Rosenberg questioned again.

Once again, Rosenberg continued to deny any involvement in passing secrets to the Russians. There was nobody for him to roll over on; he was innocent. There was no conspiracy. It was all in the government's mind. Not only was Rosenberg more adamant than ever that he was innocent, the government now had to prosecute Ethel or else release her and face public ridicule.

Hoover couldn't and wouldn't do that. Back off and suddenly drop the charges on Ethel? How would that look, especially to Julius Rosenberg, whom they were definitely going to face in court? Searching for any information that would help with the prosecutions, FBI agents questioned all of the Rosenbergs' associates and friends. Fearful of prosecution themselves, some left the country rather than face FBI scrutiny, including Morton Sobell, a friend of the Rosenbergs. He found shelter in Mexico but not for long.

During this roundup, a Rosenberg acquaintance, Max Flitcher, told the FBI that Rosenberg had tried unsuccessfully to recruit him to work for the Soviets in 1944. He also described a meeting with his friend Morton Sobell, in which Flitcher was supposed to serve as a go-between. Sobell would give him a can of film that he was supposed to turn over to Rosenberg.

Sobell was extradited from Mexico and turned over to the FBI. He was put on trial with the Rosenbergs in Eastern Federal District Court in Brooklyn, New York, on March 6, 1951. The charge was conspiracy to commit espionage, a violation of the Espionage Act of 1917.

During his opening statement, U.S. Attorney Irving Saypol told the jury that the defendants "have committed the most serious crime which can be committed against the people of this country." They had conspired to provide the Soviet Union with "the weapons the Soviet Union could use to destroy us." It was a capital crime, punishable by death.

In his opening statement, defense attorney Bloch declared the defendants innocent. He urged the jury to give his clients "a fair shake in the American way," and not to "be influenced by any bias or prejudice or hysteria." He was referring not just to the "Red Scare," but the fact that all of the members of the so-called atomic conspiracy were Jewish. The last thing Bloch wanted was for anti-Semitism to influence the outcome of this case as it did Leo Frank's.

Saypol then began his case by calling Max Flitcher to the stand. Flitcher covered his relationship with Sobell, including a car ride the two took together in 1948 to a mysterious location where they delivered a can of film containing defense secrets to Julius Rosenberg.

Next to the stand was twenty-nine-year-old David Greenglass, who testified that he had passed sketches of the high-explosive A-bomb lens mold to Julius Rosenberg. Greenglass's testimony was cut short when the prosecution called Walter Koski to the stand. An Atomic Energy Commission physicist, he explained how the sketches Greenglass passed could help the enemy develop an atomic bomb.

It was a brilliant strategy.

The prosecution had now shown the jury, in layman's terms, the true importance of the sketches: if the Soviets had the bomb, like America they would be capable of wholesale annihilation. The implication was that the people responsible for that betrayal, the Rosenbergs and Sobell, were guilty as charged.

Saypol then called David Greenglass to continue his incriminating testimony. He told the jury the arcane details of spying. There were secret meetings on shadowy streets with dim figures in dark cars. A Jell-O box was cut in half so the two pieces could be used by Soviet agents as identification. Notes were burned in a frying pan. Finally, Greenglass recalled, he felt the FBI closing in and contemplated an escape to Russia. The FBI caught him before he could flee.

Ruth Greenglass testified that she was approached by her brother Julius to act as an intermediary. Julius wanted her to see if David would give him progress reports on the Manhattan Project. When David agreed, Julius told her how to handle a courier from Albuquerque. Soon, Harry Gold was knocking on her door. In his hand was half a Jell-O box that indicated who he was.

Ruth Greenglass's piece of testimony damned Ethel. She claimed to be present when Ethel Rosenberg typed up some of her brother David Greenglass's notes from the Manhattan Project.

Called to the stand, Harry Gold testified that he had numerous meetings with Anatoli Yakovlev, head of the Soviet delegation to the United Nations and the KGB's chief of U.S. spy operations. During a 1945 meeting in particular, he remembered being in a Manhattan bar when Yakovlev gave him a piece of onionskin paper with the name "Greenglass" and an Albuquerque address typed on it.

Gold's orders were to go to New Mexico, locate the typed address, and announce to the person who opened the door, "I come from Julius." Gold went on to say that Greenglass provided him with handwritten notes and sketches relevant to the development of the atomic bomb.

Most trials with large public impact have something unexpected. In the Rosenberg case, that was Elizabeth Bentley. Bentley had been labeled "the Red Spy Queen" by the press when she marched to the stand at the trial. An attractive former spy for the Soviets, Bentley had switched to the capitalist side in 1945.

With a flair for publicity, Bentley had written books about her experiences in the spy game and made money. She testified that she was the intermediary who set up the contact between Julius Rosenberg and Jacob Golos, chief of the KGB's American operations until his death in 1943. She said that five or six times she got early morning calls from some man identifying himself as "Julius." Julius used her as an intermediary in setting up meetings with Gold.

And then, the prosecution rested.

The entire country followed the story through radio and newspapers. The few who had televisions watched the evening newscasts for word on what happened that day.

No matter how dramatic the testimony sounded, it was pretty damning stuff. If all the prosecution testimony was to be believed, Julius Rosenberg was the driving force to get the information on the development of the atomic bomb into the hands of the Soviet Union. That would make him the most infamous spy in U.S. history. His infamy would place him right up there with Benedict Arnold, the greatest traitor of them all. Sobell and Ethel Rosenberg, however, appeared to be at the fringes of the spy ring at best.

The defense's only chance to obtain acquittal and save the defendants' lives was to show reasonable doubt. Emmanuel Bloch needed to show that one or more prosecution witnesses were lying. The defense decided that the Rosenbergs and Sobell were their own best witnesses. It was a risky tactic.

If the jury didn't believe the defendants, the case was over; they would be convicted and die. Even if the jury did believe them on direct testimony, on cross, when the prosecution got its chance, it would attack the defendants with no mercy. Sobell, wisely, declined to testify. The Rosenbergs marched into the breach.

Taking the stand, Julius Rosenberg forcefully testified that he was a man of modest means who lived an ordinary life, far from the super spy the prosecution was attempting to show he was. As for actually being a spy, Rosenberg said that was preposterous. He denied ever having anything to do with the prosecution witnesses who had implicated him.

Rosenberg testified that he never received information from Greenglass about the lens mold or anything else, for that matter. He knew nothing of cut-up Jell-O boxes. His brother-in-law was a liar. What he did know was that in 1950, Greenglass approached *him* for money to leave the United States because he feared the FBI was closing in on him.

Ethel Rosenberg's testimony supported Julius's version of events—she knew nothing and said nothing. She never directly denied the one piece of evidence that damned her—typing up Julius's spy notes. The defense had her testify dispassionately instead of emotionally, as an innocent caught in a spy game maze. But by making her into a taciturn woman instead of a *victimized* woman, she seemed more independent, more self-assured, more capable of committing espionage.

On rebuttal, the prosecution called photographer Ben Schneider to the stand. The operator of a small photo shop near the Brooklyn courthouse, Schneider testified that the Rosenberg family came to his store in June 1950. They wanted three dozen passport-type photos. Rosenberg said they were planning a trip to France, where they had inherited property.

Schneider was a good witness. He said that he remembered the Rosenbergs, because it was an unusually large order and they had two boys who were difficult to control. Details like that were what swayed a jury. It would later be revealed that the FBI found Schneider through a jailhouse informer named Jerome Tartakow. Tartakow had been Julius's chess partner and confidante ever since his incarceration eight months earlier.

The month-long trial ended with passionate summations

from both sides. After being charged by the judge, the eleven-man, one-woman jury retired to their deliberations. Reaction was swift: eleven to one for conviction. Several hours went by, trying to convince the lone holdout who was concerned about how Ethel's execution would affect her family.

When the jury told the judge they were ready, they reentered the courtroom silently. The judge asked if they had reached a verdict. The jury foreman delivered a verdict of guilty for all three defendants. At sentencing, Judge Irving Kaufman characterized the defendants crimes as "worse than murder." He blamed them for the 50,000 American soldiers killed during the Korean War.

Sobell got thirty years. The Rosenbergs were sentenced to death. Ethel Rosenberg would be the first woman in almost a century to be executed by the federal government. The last was Mary Surratt, who was convicted of aiding in the murder plot to kill President Lincoln and was hanged in 1865.

Over the next two years, the Rosenbergs became poster children for the abolishment of capital punishment. From their cells at Sing Sing Prison in Ossining, New York, they read about what was happening on the outside. Holding aloft signs that read, "Don't Kill My Mommy and Daddy," sons Robert and Michael marched at rallies staged to protest their convictions as part of the Red Scare.

With celebrities speaking out for them, the Rosenbergs appealed their death sentences. Defense attorney Emmanuel Bloch took his case through the court system. At each turn-down, he appealed to a higher court until he reached the top. Needing a majority of five Supreme Court justices to stay the execution, Bloch pleaded his case and got four.

The execution proceeded as ordered.

Shortly after 8 P.M. on June 19, 1953, Julius Rosenberg was strapped into the electric chair at Sing Sing Prison. When the switch was thrown, two thousand volts of electricity shot into his body. The prison lights dimmed as Julius Rosenberg's heart stopped. A judge pronounced him dead, his lifeless body was lifted out of the chair, onto a gurney, and wheeled out.

Ethel followed her guards into the room. She sat down in the chair. It was warm. The execution hood was put over her head, the straps tightened, and a fifty-seven-second cycle of two thousand volts of electricity jerked her body upright in the chair. Presumed dead, she was unstrapped from the chair before a physician could check her.

Whoops.

A physician put his stethoscope to Ethel's chest; she was still alive. Back they dragged the unconscious woman, face still covered by the death mask, strapped her into the electric chair, and this time gave her two more cycles of 2,000 volts. That did the job.

There was a funeral at the I.J. Morris Funeral Chapel in the Flatbush neioghborhood of Brooklyn. With the interring of the Rosenbergs, it was done, or so most thought.

Did they really do it?

Were Julius and Ethel Rosenberg spies who passed the secret of the atomic bomb to the Soviets?

The prosecution's case against both Rosenbergs was circumstantial. Ethel's conviction in particular, based as it was on the self-serving testimony of the Greenglasses, seemed more an acquiescence to the political conditions of the time rather than based on hard evidence.

It was impossible until recently to state categorically one way or the other that the Rosenbergs were either "innocent" or "guilty." What finally happened to reveal the truth was the effectiveness of the United States pressure under President Ronald Reagan in the 1980s to force the Soviet Union to "keep up with the Jones's."

Reagan's defense buildup during his tenure as president bankrupted the Soviets in their efforts to keep up with the West's wealthiest nation. After the Soviet Union fell in the early 1990s and the country converted to democracy and capitalism, the Rosenbergs were not forgotten, least of all by the one man in the KGB who knew them best. He was now free to talk.

In 1997, during interviews with the *New York Times* and the *Washington Post,* and in a PBS documentary, Alexander Feklisov, eighty-three, revealed himself as Julius Rosenberg's contact in the KGB. He told his interviewers that he had not received permission from the KGB's successor, the Russian Foreign Intelligence Service, to go public. Rather, he felt an allegiance to the Rosenbergs and a desire to set the record straight for history.

Feklisov claimed that Julius Rosenberg handed over American military secrets to the Soviets, but he never handed over anything of substance about the atomic bomb. Meeting with him between 1943 and 1946, Feklisov told the *Post* that Rosenberg helped organize an industrial espionage ring in the United States that brought the Soviets top secret information on American electronics.

"I would say that he gave us important information, but in the field of electronics; they provided us information with different kind of radars," Feklisov said in the PBS documentary.

He wears his sympathy for the Rosenbergs, however, on his sleeve.

"Julius was a great sympathizer of the Soviet Union. There were others who also believed in communism, but were unwilling to fight. Julius was a true revolutionary, who was willing to sacrifice himself for his beliefs."

Despite this attempt to make Rosenberg into a hero, Feklisov confirmed the heart of the government's case against him. Feklisov confirmed that Julius stole A-Bomb details and that he, Feklisov, had received a sketch of a "lens mold." Feklisov described the latter as "a childish scribble—it was meaningless."

Feklisov was not an engineer, and therefore unqualified to make such a judgment. But by confirming the theft, he was also confirming that Julius Rosenberg had been guilty as charged.

As for Ethel, "She had nothing to do with this—she was completely innocent. I think she knew, but for that you don't kill people," he said.

An old Communist, Feklisov's comment is a little too self-serving, considering the terrorist tactics his agency used to control the Soviet people and spy on other nations. The real question was not the punishment the Rosenbergs received, but were they guilty as charged?

Clearly, Julius was.

Julius Rosenberg turned over secrets about the atomic bomb to an enemy country. Whether what he turned over was important enough to give the Soviets everything they needed to make the bomb is a judgment best left up to engineers without any political ideology. Despite trying to downplay the importance of the information Rosenberg gave him, Feklisov knew that Julius Rosenberg was a traitor. Julius Rosenberg was guilty of the overt act of spying for the Soviets.

As for Ethel, if she did know what her husband was doing and typed up his notes anyway, then she was certainly guilty of aiding and abetting a capital crime, which itself could be punishable by death, depending upon the death penalty statutes in force at the time. But in Ethel's case, the government cleared erred.

Regardless of guilt, no one should have two thousand volts of electricity shot through them, or in Ethel's case 6,000, because of weak, circumstantial evidence. The government needs to do a better job of proving its case before it executes someone on such flimsy evidence. Ethel Rosenberg should have been judged not guilty on "reasonable doubt" alone.

Shame on the U.S. Supreme Court for not commuting Ethel Rosenberg's death sentence.

The remaining question in the case, of course, is the government's use of the death penalty. That the death penalty doesn't work, that it is barbaric and a colossal waste of money is not the issue. While many Americans made their feelings known in pro-Rosenberg rallies, the government was well within its rights by statute to carry out the executions. The death penalty was in force at the time of their crimes, and the Rosenbergs received due process.

A bigger question is, if Feklisov felt so strongly that the Rosenbergs hadn't given the Soviets anything worth the death penalty, why did he let it happen? Feklisov noted in the PBS interview the large international groundswell for mercy.

In the United States, organization after organization argued for their innocence and demanded that the verdicts be set aside. Feklisov seemed to be saying what could he do, a lowly KGB agent, that an international ambassador could not? In that, he is right.

In the 1950s, no one would have believed Feklisov, even had his government allowed him to come forward and absolve the Rosenbergs of all charges. Being defended by a die-hard Communist like Feklisov would just serve to show how far down the traitor's road Julius Rosenberg had really gone.

In the end, one life was sacrificed for another on the altar of what FBI director Hoover called "the truth." We all know, now, what Hoover was doing over that altar.

THE MURDERED CIVIL RIGHTS WORKERS, PART I

1964—VICTOR RAY KILLEN

MISSISSIPPI, AUGUST 4, 1964

Special Agent Joe Sullivan of the FBI was supervising the digging. The blue flies swarmed over the large mound of dirt.

"Hold it," he yelled

The bulldozer halted.

Blue flies belong to a family of flies commonly called filth flies. They feed off everything from decaying human bodies to garbage. Since the bulldozer wasn't at the dump site to uncover a garbage dump, the blue flies sudden descent signaled the possibility that the FBI had finally, after 44 days, found the bodies of the three missing civil rights workers. Their names were Andrew Goodman, Michael Schwerner, and James Chaney.

Adjusting their rabbit ear antennas until they could clearly see the pictures of the missing three, families remained riveted to their TV sets for the latest news on the three. On the streets, afternoon tabloid newspapers splashed across their front pages the possibility that the missing civil rights workers had finally been found.

The reason the case was getting so much publicity was because Goodman and Schwerner were white. Only Chaney was black. Two missing *white* civil rights workers was news.

One missing *black* man was not, not in Mississippi, which had a long history of lynching blacks.

Sullivan had the FBI workers move in to dig by hand. He didn't want evidence destroyed by a backhoe's crass manner. Digging at a suspected crime scene is like archaeology—you dig carefully, not because you are afraid of damaging a million year old fossil but because you are afraid of damaging a body, which in itself would show evidence of a crime.

Like a boot.

A boot can be a direct indication that you have something significant, especially when it's attached to a foot, like the one Sullivan saw sticking out of the dirt. The agents worked carefully, sifting through the dirt by hand, uncovering it slowly, until they were looking at the body of Michael Schwerner.

Throughout the day, they excavated . . . slowly. Eventually, they came to Andrew Goodman and, finally, underneath him on the bottom, James Chaney. The first thing the cops thought was that the men were killed in reverse order of discovery. They theorized that Chaney was killed first and dumped in the dirt. Dirt was put over him, and then Goodman was killed, and finally Schwerner, with the same burial process being followed for each.

"We interrupt this program to bring you a special bulletin."

Throughout that day, the networks, ABC, NBC, and ABC kept putting their announcers with the most portentous deliveries at the mike to cut into regular shows with updates of the grisly discoveries. When the truth was finally confirmed by the FBI that all three men were dead, dumped into the earthen dam where thety had been found, Americans watched NBC's *Huntley-Brinkley Report,* CBS's *Evening News with Walter Cronkite,* and ABC's *Howard K. Smith Report.* With 99.9 percent of the viewing audience watching, the big story of the day was the three murdered civil rights workers, the two whites and the one "Negro."

Many white, middle-class Americans immediately wondered what the two white boys were doing with the black one in a place neither of them belonged in? The bigots in the country thought they were agitators, just looking for trouble that had found them. On the left, the liberals thought the three were martyrs to the cause of civil rights.

Like much of the history of crime in America, the answer was someplace in between.

The only word to describe Michael Schwerner, Andrew Goodman, and James Chaney's visit to Neshoba County, Mississippi, in the summer of 1964 to investigate a church burning would be "naïve," though some might say "stupid."

Schwerner was a field organizer for the Congress of Racial Equality (CORE), a prominent and respected civil rights organization. He had organized a black boycott of white-owned businesses in and around Meridian and gotten many of those same blacks to register to vote. The Ku Klux Klan not only hated Schwerner for it, they wanted him dead. In 1964 Mississippi, the Klan ruled.

The Imperial Wizard of the KKK in Mississippi was Sam Bowers. In secret communication with the KKK klaverns in Lauderdale and Neshoba counties, Bowers called for Schwerner's murder. He referred to him as "Jew Boy" or "Goatee," the latter because of the facial hair that Schwerner favored.

On Memorial Day 1964, Schwerner visited Longdale in rural Neshoba County, where he had a meeting with the elders of Mt. Zion Church. The discussion centered on the use of the church as a "Freedom School." Bowers's intelligence apparatus, which consisted of Ghouls throughout the state, had informed him that Schwerner wasn't finished in Longdale; he was coming back to create more trouble.

On June 16, 1964, ten members of Mt. Zion Church emerged from a long evening meeting at 10 P.M. to find their church surrounded by thirty men armed with shotguns, rifles, and revolvers. Their heads were hidden under the trademark white canvas hoods. Covering the front entrance and back entrances, the Klanners noted that every one of the ten people who had emerged from the church was a "nigger." There wasn't a white face among them. Bowers's intelligence regarding Schwerner had been wrong.

Frustrated that "Jew Boy" had not showed up where they expected him to, the KKK took some diesel fuel, spread it through the bottom floor of the church, and sent it up in a fire that blazed through the night as a strong message to anyone who would buck the KKK on their home ground. Then to drive the message home, they drove their fists and other weapons into the bodies of the ten "niggers."

At the moment of the beatings, "Jew Boy" Schwerner was in Oxford, Ohio, attending a three-day program sponsored by the National Council of Churches to train recruits for the Mississippi Summer. This was an attempt to get blacks to register to vote. Schwerner had arrived for the training accompanied by his top aide, James Chaney, a black citizen of Meridian. When they heard what had happened at Mt. Zion Church, Schwerner and Chaney decided to return to Mississippi and investigate. Schwerner in patrticular was determined to ferret out whoever was responsible for the church arson.

It was while attending the Oxford, Ohio, conference that Schwerner made the acquaintance of an idealistic Queens College student, Andrew Goodman. Schwerner asked the novice to accompany him and Chaney back to Meridian. Goodman agreed.

Armed only with principles, up against hundreds of years of hate and bigotry, the three civil rights workers drove their blue CORE-owned Ford station wagon down to Meridian, where they arrived on June 21. After a few hours respite, they were off again for Longdale. Before leaving, Schwerner told CORE worker Sue Brown that if the three didn't return by 4:30, she should put up the Bat Signal. And then, they were off.

Here, Schwerner's judgment should be seriously questioned. Longdale was known as a danger zone for civil rights workers. The Klan was especially powerful there. It was generally known that Neshoba County law enforcement was Klan-friendly. Sheriff Lawrence Rainey and his deputy Cecil Price liked to wear white robes and hoods in the dark. Publicly, they were never known to give blacks a break. If the three civil rights workers got into their jurisdiction, they were bound for trouble.

Schwerner knew he was going into danger. Otherwise why give Brown the last-minute instruction? Yet he chose to advance into what was, literally, a combat zone, with one of his "soldiers," Goodman, a civil rights novice.

By early afternoon, they were in Longdale, inspecting the Mt. Zion Church crime scene. The ruins of the church still smoldered. Some of the church members warned them that a group of whites was looking for them. Finally, Schwerner got the message. It was time to get out of town. Fast.

At 3:00 P.M., they headed back to Meridian and soon got to what in retrospect really was a metaphysical crossroads: Highway 491. A narrow clay road, Highway 491 was intersected by numerous dirt roads. They had traveled on 491 from Meridian. It was a good highway to spring an ambush on. It was also the most direct way home. However, there was an alternative.

Highway 16, a two-lane blacktop, passed west through

Philadelphia, the county seat, before heading out to Meridian. While it would take longer, there were a lot fewer hidden roads and cul-de-sacs from which the Klan could spring an ambush. Chaney turned west down Highway 16.

It was just a matter of coincidence. Proceeding east on the same road, about to collide into American criminal history, was Deputy Sheriff Cecil Price. Someplace outside of Philadelphia, Price spotted the well-known blue CORE station wagon heading his way. At the wheel was James Chaney.

"I've got a good one! George Raymond!" Price shouted into his CB radio.

He had misidentified Chaney as black civil rights leader George Raymond, a man the Mississippi Klan despised. Price slammed on the brakes, whipping his car around in the same motion. Then, when he had traction again, he slammed his foot on the accelerator. The big V-8 engine went from 0 to 60 in less than five seconds. Price flicked a switch on the dashboard.

The flashing red lights crowded his rear-view mirror. Whether or not Chaney could outrun the cop was never a question. He decided to obey the law and pulled the wagon over to the side of the road just inside Philadelphia's city line. Schwerner, Goodman, and Chaney were immediately arrested and taken into custody by Price, for alleged suspicion in the church arson.

Brought by Price to the Neshoba County Jail, they were briefly held behind bars while the deputy went off to converse with Neshoba County Klan Kleagle (Klan recruiter) Edgar Ray Killen. Price told Killen that not only did he have Schwerner in custody but one other white boy and a "nigger" as well.

Shortly after 10 P.M., Deputy Price came to the jail and told the jailer on duty, "Chaney wants to pay off—we'll let him pay off and release them all." That seemed to imply that Chaney was posting bail, which he could not have, because he had no

money and no assets. Price led them to the CORE wagon.
They went east out of Philadelphia on Highway 19. If the
three didn't know it already, they were being allowed to leave
in order to enter into a carefully staged trap.

According to three Klan members who turned state's evidence, Edgar Ray Killen had been busy that afternoon after
his conversation with Deputy Price.

An ordained Baptist minister, Killen counted many among
his flock, including one couple whose son would grow up to
become a state judge. In addition to his duties as a minister,
Killen had duties as the Klan Kleagle. He didn't think being a
man of the cloth in any way conflicted with his Klan duties.

During an afternoon meeting at the Longhorn Drive-In in
Meridian with upper echelon Klan members, and then a later
one at Akins's Mobile Homes with younger members who
would actually pull the trigger, the plan to kill the three was
outlined. Killen allegedly told the dozen or more Klanners
involved to buy rubber gloves—to avoid leaving clues—and to
be in Philadelphia by 8:15 P.M.

Killen gave the Klanners a drive-by tour of the Neshoba
County jail. He explained the three were about to be released
and what was expected to happen. Then, to establish his own
alibi, the wily preacher went off to a local funeral home to pay
his respects to a recently deceased uncle.

Like clockwork, Price stuck to the plan. He followed the
CORE wagon out of town, while two other cars filled with
Killen's Klanners drove out to intercept them. Soon Price caught
up with the three. Seeing Price's high performance Chevy sedan
in his rear view, Chaney sped up and tried to make a run for it.
Inexplicably, seconds later Chaney braked and pulled over.

"I thought you were going back to Meridian if we let you
out of jail." Price said.

Chaney responded that was exactly what they were doing

"You sure were taking the long way around," said the affable deputy. "Get out of the car."

If ever there was a chance to escape with their lives, this was it. Maybe it was the nonviolent tenets of the movement they belonged to, or maybe something else—a lethargic acceptance that comes to people condemned to death. Whatever it was, the three offered no resistance as they got into Deputy Price's car. Soon the cars with the two young Klanners arrived. The three-car procession then traveled down an unmarked dirt turnoff called Rock Cut Road.

Wayne Roberts, a twenty-six-year-old who had been dishonorably discharged from the Marines, was the executioner. He shot Schwerner first, Goodman second, and Chaney last at point-blank range; they never had a chance. The bodies were then taken to a dam site at the 253-acre Old Jolly Farm owned by Philadelphia businessman Olen Burrage. The bodies were thrown unceremoniously together in a depression at the dam site. A Caterpillar D-4 moved in, and the bodies were covered with tons of dirt, seemingly to lay buried there for centuries before being discovered.

At 12:30 A.M., worried CORE staffers in Meridian called John Doar, the Justice Department's prosecutor in Mississippi. Figuring the three to be dead, at approximately 6:00 A.M., Doar asked the FBI to investigate a possible violation of federal law: if the three civil rights workers were murdered, they would have been denied their civil rights. It was a revolutionary way to proceed with an investigation.

The FBI knew that even if the three were murdered and they got the killers dead to rights, they wouldn't get a conviction in a Mississippi state court. The state officially opposed integration. The prosecutors would have to get a conviction in federal court, where the penalty for violating somebody's civil rights was a prison sentence, as opposed to the state penalty for murder—death. Still, getting any sort of conviction in the case would be an achievement.

Meridian-based FBI agent John Proctor was assigned the case. In Neshoba County, Proctor tried to track down the three, talking to blacks, community leaders, and, of course, Sheriff Rainey and Deputy Price. An Alabama native, Proctor seemed like a good ole boy. After interviewing Price, the deputy felt so comfortable that he slapped Proctor on the back.

"Hell, John," he said, "let's have a drink," and pulled some moonshine in a bottle out of the trunk of his high performance Chevy.

The next day, June 23, ten special agents and Harry Maynor, Proctor's New Orleans–based supervisor, arrived to assist in the investigation, which the FBI code-named MIBURN (for "Mississippi Burning"). Proctor soon received a tip that a smoke-infested ruin of a car had been spotted in exceedingly rural northeast Neshoba County.

When he got to the scene, Proctor was met by Joe Sullivan, the FBI's Major Case Inspector. Together, they viewed the burned-out wreckage of the blue CORE station wagon. The FBI kept searching for the bodies, following dead lead after dead lead. By June 25, President Johnson had assigned the U.S. Navy to assist in the search.

Trucks full of sailors arrived in Neshoba County and were soon sent into the snake-infested swamps and woods. FBI Director J. Edgar Hoover announced the opening of the FBI's first office, ever, in Mississippi. Unfortunately, none of this meant success; the three remained missing. Sullivan speculated that the case "would ultimately be solved by conducting an *investigation* rather than a *search*."

By differentiating between a luck-filled search versus an intellect-driven investigation, Sullivan was bringing the case closer to conclusion. But the Feds soon found out when questioning county locals that they would get little or no cooperation; everyone was either scared of the Klan or agreed with their methods. Therefore, the FBI relied on informants, Klan members who were turning state's evidence to avoid lengthy prison terms.

It was through one of these informants that the FBI found out about the location of the bodies at the dam site on Old Jolly Farm. John Proctor shrewdly decided to invite Deputy Price to the dam site to help with body removal. He wanted to see what the cop's reaction was.

"Price picked up a shovel and dug right in, and gave no indication whatsoever that any of it bothered him," Proctor would say later.

To a detective, there is perhaps nothing better than an observant pathologist. Unfortunately, that did not exist in the case of the murdered civil rights workers.

Dr. William Featherston, the Jackson pathologist who conducted the autopsies, believed that any damage done to the bodies was done by the bulldozers at the scene. He confirmed his opinion in a subsequent interview with *The Clarion-Ledger* in which Featherston said, "Apparently a lot of damage done to Chaney's body occurred when the scoop caught his body. . . . He was the last one to be buried. He was the one who suffered most of the injury due to disinterment."

Dr. David Spain believed that was garbage. A private New York City pathologist brought in by family members to conduct a second autopsy, Spain discovered that Chaney had been beaten extensively before his death.

"It was obvious to any first-year medical student that this boy had been beaten to a pulp," Spain wrote in *Mississippi Eyewitness*. He detailed other injuries to Chaney not included in the autopsy report—a broken jaw and a crushed right shoulder.

The state of Mississippi, and Dr. Featherston, not only chose to ignore Dr. Spain's expert opinion. Featherston obtained state assistance in filing an ethics complaint against Spain with the College of American Pathologists. Featherston's complaint said that since he was the pathologist of record, Spain had no right to conduct a second autopsy, despite the fact that the family of the deceased had requested it.

The secret of why Chaney may have been treated differently can be found in the long-sealed records of the Mississippi Sovereignty Commission, a segregationist spy agency overseen by Mississippi's governor from 1956 to 1973.

> "James Chaney, the colored member of this group, is alleged to have broke (sic) away from the group of men that were holding them captive," commission investigator Andy Hopkins wrote in his Jan. 26, 1965, report for the Sovereignty Commission's files. "Shortly after he made the break, he was shot at several times by several different people but was struck by only three bullets, each of which was alleged to have been fired from a different firearm."

For the next four months, the FBI worked their Klan informants, extracting as much information as possible on who did what and when in preparation for federal indictments. Finally on December 4, 1964, a team of federal agents swooped down on Neshoba and Lauderdale Counties. The Feds arrested nineteen men for using state law (Price) to deprive the three, Schwerner, Chaney, and Goodman, of their civil rights. Six days later, a federal commissioner dismissed the charges.

The Justice Department appealed to federal court. On February 24, 1965, Federal Judge William Harold Cox, a segregationist, threw all the indictments out save the two against

Rainey and Price. The case finally wound its way to the Supreme Court. In March 1966, the Warren Court overruled Cox and reinstated the indictments.

The trial in *United State v. Cecil Price et al.* began on October 7, 1967, in the Meridian courtroom of Judge William Cox. Cox was a segregationist and a constant thorn in Chief Prosecutor John Doar's side. It was the latter's job to enforce federal civil rights laws in Mississippi. Cox felt it was his job to oppose federal intervention and uphold state rights, including state-sanctioned segregation.

Defense attorneys used their peremptory challenges to remove all twelve potential black jurors from the jury pool. Seated was an all-white jury of seven men and five women, ranging in ages from thirty-four to sixty-seven. One of them had been a member of the KKK "a couple of years ago." When Doar challenged for cause, Cox denied the challenge and seated the juror. To anyone watching, it was clear that justice for the dead civil rights workers might be a long time coming.

The heart of the government's case consisted of the testimony of the three Klan informants, Wallace Miller, Delmar Dennis, and James Jordan. Miller provided perspective, describing how the Lauderdale Klavern was organized. Then he testified to conversations he'd had with Kleagle Edgar Ray Killen and Exalted Cyclops [the boss] Frank Herndon about the June 21 "operation" in Neshoba County.

The next piece of the prosecution's case came together when Delmar Dennis, a paid FBI informant, implicated Sam Bowers, Imperial Wizard and founder of the White Knights of the KKK of Mississippi, in the murder conspiracy.

"It was the first time that Christians had planned and carried out the execution of a Jew," Dennis quoted Bowers, who said this only after Schwerner, Goodman, and Chaney were killed. Dennis went on to relate a Klan meeting on the property of Klan member Clayton Lewis, Philadelphia, Mississippi's mayor.

"Is Mr. Lewis in the courtroom?" Doar asked.

Dennis pointed to Clayton Lewis, who was, at that moment, sitting at the defense table. Lewis was one of the defendants' twelve-attorney defense team. If it wasn't clear up to that point how pervasive the Klan presence was in Mississippi, the government was driving that point home. Now, just like the heavyweight champion Cassius Clay, the government went for the knock-out punch—James Jordan, an eyewitness to the killings.

Jordan, however, had a weak constitution. Fearing a Klan assassination, he was heavily guarded by G-men with drawn guns. Before he even got to court, the stress got to him. He was briefly hospitalized for hyperventilating. The next time he tried to get into court, he collapsed and was carried out of the courtroom on a stretcher. Finally, the third time was the charm—Jordan made it to the witness stand, health intact.

Under direct examination, Jordan described the events of June 21 and the early morning of June 22, starting from the Klan gathering to discuss the job in Meridian, through the actual executions and the burial of the bodies under tons of dirt at Old Jolly Farm. Afterwards, one black woman collapsed in sobs and had to be carried from the courtroom.

The Reverend Charles Johnson, a civil rights activist, gave direct testimony as to his relationship with Schwerner. During cross-examination, Defense Attorney Laurel Weir asked Johnson if he had tried to "get young Negro males to sign a pledge to rape a white woman once a week during the hot summer of 1964."

"Highly improper," said Judge Cox from the bench.

"The question was passed to me in writing," Weir admitted.

"Who wrote it?" the judge asked.

The courtroom was silent. Finally, a defense attorney answered that the author of the note was "Brother Killen," referring to the defendant Edgar Ray Killen.

The medical examiner, Dr. William Featherston, took the stand. His testimony was brief and to the point. Schwerner had apparently been killed by a shot through the heart. So had Goodman. Featherston explained he had to say "apparently" because the bodies had been buried forty-four days, making his examination more difficult.

"You do not know for sure whether or not any of these bullets actually penetrated the hearts, do you?" defense lawyer Travis Buckley asked.

"No, sir," Featherston replied.

"And having made no detailed examination you do not know as a matter of fact whether or not sodium cyanide or some other similar alien which would induce death by poisoning was present in those tracts, would you?" Buckley asked.

"No, sir," Featherston replied. "I also don't know if they were hit by lightning, bit by a rattlesnake or maybe by some other cause of death."

The government rested, and the defense took over with a group of alibi and character witnesses who, to Northern observers, seemed right out of James Dickey's *Deliverance*. These "citizens" testified that the defendants were all good men, who always told the truth and had good reputations, one and all. As to their whereabouts on the night in question, how could there be any doubt where they were, after Uncle Eb, Aunt Violet, and yes, even Beaver Cleaver testified, under oath, that they had been everyplace from hospitals to, in Killen's case, a funeral home, when the three were murdered?

The defense rested. In his closing to the jury on October

18, John Doar tried. "This was a calculated, cold-blooded plot. Three men, hardly more than boys, were its victims."

Doar pointed at Deputy Price at the defense table. He summed up his case: "Price used the machinery of law, his office, his power, his authority, his badge, his uniform, his jail, his police car, his police gun, he used them all to take, to hold, to capture and kill. What I and the other lawyers say today will soon be forgotten, but what you twelve do here today will long be remembered."

It was quite beautiful, and haunting. As for the defense, its closing was a reiteration of its opening. Every one of the defendants was someplace else, and numerous witnesses had supported that contention. These men were wonderful human beings and a credit to the human race. The judge then charged the jury.

A day later, the jury had still not reached a verdict and felt they were deadlocked. The judge brought the jury into the courtroom and gave them the "Allen charge," an intimidating bit of legal rhetoric that amounted to "get your asses back into that jury room and reach a verdict." The idea was to avoid a mistrial and having to do the whole thing all over again. Sometimes it works, sometimes it doesn't.

On the morning of October 12, 1967, it worked. The jury returned with its verdict. Seven of the defendants were convicted of denying the Chaney, Goodman, and Schwerner their civil rights by killing them. The convicted included Deputy Sheriff Cecil Price, Imperial Wizard Sam Bowers, and trigger man Wayne Roberts. Eight others were acquitted, including Exalted Cyclops Frank Herndon, Olen Burrage, who owned the burial site, and Sheriff Lawrence Rainey.

The jury was "hung" on the charges against three other defendants, including Klan recruiter and minister "Brother" Edgar Ray Killen. It had, however, been close—eleven members of the jury had voted to convict Killen. Were it not for that lone holdout, he would have gone to federal prison too.

During sentencing on December 29, Judge Cox gave each of the defendants an average of six years in federal prison. Cox said after sentencing, "They killed one nigger, one Jew, and a white man—I gave them all what I thought they deserved."

Let it not be said that Cox was a jurist who minced words.

Murder has a way of rippling through generations. It makes no difference how it happens. When someone is murdered, people survive—the husbands, wives, brothers, aunts, uncles, sons, and daughters of the dead. Just their mere presence on earth cries out for justice when their loved ones have not been given the law's full protections, even in death.

By the end of the century, their names had all but been forgotten. But the martyrdom the KKK and their adherents so feared did indeed take place. As the century was approaching its close and the new millennium its beginning, forces were at work to bring the importance of the civil rights struggle to the attention of future generations. The vehicle for that interest was the law, and an increased interest in American society to see justice done in what have become known as "cold cases."

The murders of the three civil rights workers fell into that category.

All it would take would be another twenty-nine years for it to finally be brought to resolution.

John Wilkes Booth in the morgue at Enid, 11 days after his death. (Library of Congress).

FRANK LESLIE'S
ILLUSTRATED
WEEKLY

NEW YORK, JUNE 29, 1893.　　[PRICE, 10 CENTS.

THE BORDEN MURDER TRIAL.

A SCENE IN THE COURT-ROOM BEFORE THE ACQUITTAL—LIZZIE BORDEN, THE ACCUSED, AND HER COUNSEL, EX-GOVERNOR ROBINSON.
DRAWN ON THE SPOT BY B. WEST CLINEDINST.—[SEE PAGE 417.]

The Borden murder trial—A scene in the courtroom before the acquittal:
Lizzie Borden, the accused, and her counsel, ex-Governor Robinson.
Drawn on the spot by B. West Clinedinst for *Frank Leslie's Illustrated Weekly*
(Library of Congress).

Charles Lindbergh on the witness stand during the trial of Bruno Richard Hauptmann. *World-Telegram* staff photo. *New York World-Telegram* and the *Sun Newspaper* Photograph Collection (Library of Congress).

Dr. Samuel Mudd, full-length portrait, seated, facing front. *New York World-Telegram* and the *Sun Newspaper* Photograph Collection (Library of Congress).

Julius and Ethel Rosenberg, separated by heavy wire screen, as they leave the U.S. Court House after being found guilty by a jury. *World Telegram* photo by Roger Higgins. *New York World-Telegram* and the *Sun Newspaper* Photograph Collection (Library of Congress).

THE BOSTON STRANGLER

1962–1966 ALBERT DE SALVO

Here is the story of the Strangler, yet untold,
The man who claims he murdered thirteen women,
young and old.
The elusive Strangler, there he goes,
Where his wanderlust sends him, no one knows
He struck within the light of day,
Leaving not one clue astray.
Young and old, their lips are sealed,
Their secret of death never revealed.
Even though he is sick in mind,
He's much too clever for the police to find.
To reveal his secret will bring him fame,
But burden his family with unwanted shame.
Today he sits in a prison cell,
Deep inside only a secret he can tell.
People everywhere are still in doubt,
Is the Strangler in prison or roaming about?

—Albert DeSalvo

To Americans, serial killing is far from being a new type of crime. The first known serial killers in American history were the infamous Harp cousins, Big Harp and Little Harp, who terrorized and killed along the Natchez Trace and Cave in the Rock, Ohio, from 1790 to1800.

The ninettenth century brought the Bloody Benders of Kansas and H. H. Holmes, aka Herman Mudgett. In the twentieth century, serial killing didn't see an uptick in public perception until the strange case of the Boston Strangler. He was, arguably, the first American serial killer of the twentieth century to terrorize a whole city—Boston.

Boston's residents read of his exploits in newspaper headlines smeared with red ink that looked like dried blood on the newsprint. But it wasn't just newspapers that trailed the Strangler, picking at the scraps of bodies he left behind. Television in the early 1960s was just beginning to feel its oats. It had become the premier communications medium after a short infancy. Wherever you were in the United States, local and national broadcasts captivated viewers with the Strangler's exploits. The panic he exploited just added to his allure.

The Strangler was the media's first superstar killer. Lost in the media maelstrom, was a human face on the proceedings. Or, the police conclusion that there was more than one person committing the crimes. It had started this way.

BOSTON, JUNE 14, 1962

There is an underclass that exists in America, of people who live well above the artificially set poverty line, but cannot afford to own a house. To them, the promise of Jefferson's Declaration of Independence has yet to be met. Some of them live in the Back Bay neighborhood of Boston. In the 1960s, the residents were predominantly renters.

Anna Slesers belonged to this group. She was a petite, fifty-five-year-old divorcee who looked years younger. An émigré from Latvia, she had a son and daughter. Settling in a small third floor apartment in the Back Bay, Slesers and her kids took up residence at 77 Gainsborough Street. It was one in a row of brick town houses that some real estate speculators had subdivided into small apartments.

Anna made her living, $60.00 a week, as a seamstress. She lived in a third floor walkup in Back Bay with her son on the third floor of the building. On the evening of June 14, 1962, her kids weren't around although son Juris was due soon. He was supposed to take his mother to a Latvian memorial service.

Anna had finished her dinner and figured she had enough time to take a bath before Juris got there. During her bath, she turned on the radio and listened to the opera *Tristan und Isolde*.

Just before seven o'clock, son Juris knocked on his mother's door. When there was no answer to his repeated knocks, he got worried Enough to throw his shoulder at the door. A second time, it cracked the lock, and the door flew open. No one was in the living room. Going through the apartment, he found his mother in the bathroom. The cord from her robe was tied around her throat. He thought it was suicide.

Juris called his sister in Maryland to tell her what had happened. He also called the police. Responding were homicide detectives James Mellon and John Driscoll. Mellon in particular would always remember finding that first body. From Gerold Frank's classic work of true crime, *The Boston Strangler:*

> She lay outstretched, a fragile-appearing woman with brown bobbed hair and thin mouth, lying on her back on a gray runner. She wore a blue taffeta housecoat . . . from shoulders down she was nude. She lay grotesquely, her head a few feet from the open bathroom door, her left leg stretched straight toward him, the other flung wide, almost at right angles, and bent at the knee so that she was grossly exposed . . ."

The Strangler had tied the blue cloth belt of her housecoat around her neck. He'd knotted it tightly, its ends turned up like a bow, and tied it under her chin like a bonnet. That much was obvious. But so much was missed by those first-responding detectives simply because serial killing was a relatively rare crime in the twentieth century, and no one on the planet had been trained to track down serial killers. There was no such thing as a profiler.

A good, contemporary profiler or criminologist might have looked at the crime scene and then, considering what happened next, have formed certain opinions as to the type of individual who would commit this kind of crime. No matter how much voodoo the profiler engaged in, it was better than what the police then had on the assailant, which was nothing. Things didn't get much better.

Between June 1962 and January 1964, thirteen women in the Boston area were strangled:

The victims:

14 June 1962:	Anna Slesers, 55
28 June 1962:	Mary Mullen, 85
30 June 1962:	Nina Nichols, 68
30 June 1962:	Helen Blake, 65
21 August 1962:	Ida Irga, 75
30 August 1962:	Jane Sullivan, 67
5 December 1962:	Sophie Clark, 20
31 December 1962:	Patricia Bissette, 23
9 March 1963:	Mary Brown, 69
6 May 1963:	Beverly Samans, 23
8 September 1963:	Evelyn Corbin, 58
23 November 1963:	Joann Graff, 23
4 January 1964:	Mary Sullivan, 19

What terrified the public was that these were not prostitutes, drug addicts, or other types of criminals whose lifestyles would take them close to the grave anyway. These were predominantly established, middle-aged, and in some cases elderly victims. It was a society that as yet could not comprehend innocent women being the victim of one killer, killing over a period of time—the very definition of what has come to be known as serial killing.

As for the Boston police, they did not believe the murders were the work of one strangler but at least two. The public, however, influenced by the media, felt that all the victims were the work of that one, lone fiend, "the Boston Strangler." All that was necessary was to put a face on the fiend. But which one?

Then suddenly, the murders stopped. Eleven months after the murders ceased, Albert DeSalvo was arrested on a completely different charge and readily confessed to being the Boston Strangler.

Albert DeSalvo was born in Chelsea, Massachusetts, to Frank and Charlotte DeSalvo on September 3, 1931. Albert never had a chance from the start. It was an accident of birth that Albert had an abusive father who beat his wife and kids frequently. Children in these kinds of situations find some way to act out.

Growing up, Albert was arrested on more than one occasion on assault and battery charges. His adolescence was filled with periods of inconsistency, times when he behaved well and times when he behaved badly. Eventually, Charlotte divorced Frank and remarried. She did all she could to give Albert a more normal life. From all contemporary accounts, they had a good relationship

When he was seventeen, Albert was drafted into the army in 1948. He enjoyed army life and was eventually promoted to

Specialist E-5, only to be busted back to private for failing to obey a superior's order. It was while he, like many Americans at the time, was stationed in West Germany that he met Irmgard Beck. She was a beautiful woman from a well-respected family. They fell in love and married.

In 1955, one year before he left the military, DeSalvo was arrested for fondling a young girl. The charge was eventually dropped. That same year, his first child Judy was born with congenital pelvic disease. It devastated the family. Irmgard didn't want to have another child like that. For fear of bringing another sick child into the world, she avoided sex with Albert at all costs.

By this time, DeSalvo had an insatiable sexual urge. It could not be satisfied. He needed sex at least five or six times, sometimes more a day. Since he couldn't obviously get it at home, he had to find it someplace else. His answer was burglary, which is today seen on the rap sheet of many a serial killer. Burglary is actually looked at by criminologists as a sexual crime because it involves an invasion of a person's privacy.

By 1960, DeSalvo had numerous arrests for burglary, and yet each time, received a suspended sentence. The system clearly was not working. In between his breaking and entering forays, he had managed to convince his wife to finally have sex with him. In 1960, son Michael was born without any congenital problems.

Strangely enough, while he engaged in his criminal activities, DeSalvo was gainfully employed. Construction maintenance worker, a teamster in a Boston shipyard, and a press operator at American Biltrite Rubber were all jobs held at one time or another. Because of his muscular build, no job involving physical strength was too much for him.

Albert DeSalvo was well-liked by the people who knew him. Wife Irmgard and son Michael loved him. His co-workers enjoyed being with him, and his boss had nothing but good things to say about him. But he was a thief; that much was certain. DeSalvo was also something else: a braggart. Albert liked to exaggerate his achievements. It made him feel like he was the winner, the guy on top. He was definitely a guy who talked too much. Most of the time, it was hot air. But in March 1961, his friends and family saw another side of Albert DeSalvo.

Cambridge police caught DeSalvo trying to break into a house. Brought in for questioning, he quickly confessed to the crime. He went further, claiming to be the infamous Measuring Man who talked his way into women's houses in order to take their vital statistics.

"I'm not good-looking, I'm not educated, but I was able to put something over on high-class people. They were all college kids and I never had anything in my life and I outsmarted them," he told the police about his Measuring Man antics.

Once again, the system did not work. Since Albert had that regular job and was his family's sole support, the judge took pity on him and gave him only eighteen months behind bars. He was released in April, 1962. The Boston stranglings began two months later with the first victim, Anna Slesers. It would take two more years before Albert came to the attention of police again, this time in a very big way.

On Oct. 27, 1964, Albert DeSalvo broke into a Boston home and surprised a young, newly married woman sleeping in her bed. Putting a knife to her throat he said, "Not a sound or I'll kill you." Stuffing underwear in her mouth, he staked her out on the bed, arms and legs tied to the four corners. Then Albert proceeded to kiss and fondle her.

That was it. There was no rape, no strangling, no murder. After getting instructions from the victim on the best way to leave, he told her, "You be quiet for ten minutes." Apologizing for his atrocious behavior, he left her lying there. Eventually, she got free and called the police. When questioned, her description of her assailant to the police sketch artist matched the Measuring Man uncannily.

Brought in for questioning, DeSalvo was placed in an interrogation room with a two-way mirror at the far end. Standing behind it was the victim, who identified Albert as her assailant. The cops then placed Albert under arrest. Released on bail, he went home to relax, not realizing that police routinely sent mugshots of recently charged suspects over the wires to other venues, along with a description of the suspect's crimes and police record.

Cops down in Connecticut immediately made Albert as the Green Man, a sexual deviate who sported green work pants while assaulting women. Rearrested, newly charged with the Green Man assaults, he claimed to have broken into four hundred homes and committed numerous rapes, at least three hundred in New England. If he was to be believed, Albert DeSalvo had been a very busy man indeed with a very full life: father, friend, co-worker, thief, rapist, but was he a murderer?

Boston police did not think he could possibly be the Boston Strangler. To the trained eyes of the detectives on the case, Albert seemed more like a braggart than a murderer. The braggart was smart enough to have a pre-arraignment meeting with his attorney, Jon Asgiersson. Aware that a lengthy prison sentence for his current crime would leave his family without their breadwinner, Albert inquired of his attorney:

"What would you do if someone gave you the biggest story of the century?"

Asgiersson asked if he meant the Boston Strangler?

"Yes," DeSalvo answered.

"Are you mixed up in all of them, Albert? Did you do some of them?"

"All of them," Albert answered.

Albert wondered if maybe Asgiersson could sell the story and bring in some money for his family while he was going through the court system. DeSalvo knew that even if he wasn't charged as the Strangler, his current list of crimes would add up to almost certain conviction. It was doubtful he would ever see freedom again.

"If you knew the whole story you wouldn't believe it," he told one of the detectives. "It'll all come out. You'll find out."

At police request, the judge sent Albert DeSalvo to Bridge-water State Hospital for psychiatric evaluation. While they still didn't think he was the Strangler, they wanted a professional psychiatric evaluation. While at Bridgewater, Albert made the acquaintance of George Nasser, a convict with the IQ of Lex Luthor. He became Albert's confidante and convinced him that he not only should go ahead and admit to being the Strangler; maybe they could make some money at it. They could collect the reward for information leading to the arrest and conviction of the Strangler.

Nasser's attorney was the prominent defense specialist, F. Lee Bailey. When he visited Albert at Bridgewater, Albert told him, "I know I'm going to have to spend the rest of my life locked up somewhere. I just hope it's a hospital, and not a hole like this [Bridgewater]. But if I could tell my story to somebody who could write it, maybe I could make some money for my family."

This was before the Son of Sam Laws. In the wake of the famous serial killer case in New York City, many states, including New York, passed laws still on the books today that prevent lawbreakers from benefiting from their crimes.

Bailey's primary concern was keeping his client out of "the chair" while ascertaining the truth of his claims. He wasn't about to make a deal for an innocent man. The system, for a change, was about to work.

After he questioned DerSalvo personally, Bailey became convinced that simply on the breadth of detail, DeSalvo had to be the Strangler. In an unusual collaboration between adversaries, Bailey gave the Boston police access to DeSalvo, the absolute access to question him about the Strangler murders, as much as they wanted to assure themselves he was their man. And they did. They got more than fifty hours on tape with 2,000 transcription pages in which DeSalvo proved to the police that she had information on the victims and the crime scenes that only the killer would know.

There was one catch. None of it was admissible in court. Bailey had made that clear beforehand. Everyone knew DeSalvo wasn't getting out. The question was how to clear the homicides and serve justice without convicting DeSalvo for the Strangler Crimes, without his confession. The answer was supplied by Bailey who writes in his book *The Defense Never Rests* that he told the prosecutors, State Attorney general Edward Brooke, and District Attorney Bottomly:

"When I met Albert, there were enough indictments pending against him to pretty much ensure that he'd never be walking the streets again. Now, I've helped him disclose that he's committed multiple murder, it's a certainty he'll never be released. Show me some way to avoid the risk of execution— I'll run the risk of conviction, but not execution and you can have anything you want. I know damn well that neither of you really wants to see him killed. Tell me, is that asking too much?"

It wasn't. The state decided to try DeSalvo on four counts of breaking and entering and sexual assault charges relating to the Green Man crimes. Bailey tried to use an insanity or irresistible impulse defense to spare Albert prison. Found not guilty by reason of insanity he would be confined to a mental hospital for the rest of his life and get the help Bailey felt he needed.

Unfortunatelty, the jury didn't see things the defense lawyer's way. They convicted DeSalvo on all charges. The judge gave him life. And just like that the Boston Strangler was behind bars, justice was served, and the case ended.

Not really.

"My goal was to see the Strangler wind up in a hospital, where doctors could try to find out what made him kill. Society is deprived of a study that might help deter other mass killers who lived among us, waiting for the trigger to go off inside them," Bailey later wrote.

DeSalvo was stabbed to death by another inmate at the infirmary of Walpole State Prison, in November of 1973. Any opportunity to talk to him again was lost with his death.

Was Albert DeSalvo just a braggart, or was he really the Boston Strangler? Did he really do it?

Except for his confession there was no physical evidence to tie him directly to the stranglings. DNA testing was decades away. But remember what DeSalvo told his attorney in his initial confession? When asked if he was involved in the Strangler murders he claimed he did "all of them."

That's a lie.

At the request of the relatives of victim Mary Sullivan, who had doubts about DeSalvo's guilt and his claim to be the Strangler, both bodies were disinterred. Sullivan's was dug up in 2000 and DeSalvo's in 2001. DNA tests were performed on their corpses for comparison purposes. If DeSalvo had raped and strangled her as he claimed, he would have left a forensic footprint.

After extensive testing, Dr. James Starrs, professor of forensic science at George Washington University, announced at a crowded press conference on December 6, 2001, that none of the DNA found on Sullivan, including a semenlike substance, matched DeSalvo's.

"I'm not saying it exonerates Albert DeSalvo but it's strongly indicative of the fact that he was not the rape-murderer of Mary Sullivan," Professor Starrs said.

Was Albert DeSalvo the Boston Strangler? Yes, he was. One of them. He had too much accurate and unpublished information on many of the other killings to have simply read the stuff in a newspaper and memorized it.

But he was not the killer of Mary Sullivan, as Dr. Starr proved. That person could still be out there.

THE TWENTIETH HIJACKER

9/11/01—ZACHARIAS MOUSSAOUI, AKA "THE TWENTIETH HIJACKER"

The instructors at the Pan Am flight school near Minneapolis–St. Paul picked up the phone and called the FBI.

On the previous day, a swarthy man speaking poor English had shown up. He wanted to learn to fly a 747. It wasn't every day that swarthy men speaking poor English showed up asking that question. So the flight school called the FBI.

Taken into custody on an immigration violation on August 15, 2001, the man was identified as Zacharias Moussaoui, a member of the Al Qaeda band of terrorists. The government would eventually decide to charge him as the twentieth man in the 9/11 terrorist plot.

Moussaoui, along with the nineteen men who hijacked the four planes on September 11, 2001, had trained in American flight schools on 747 aircraft. Most of them were interested in only one thing—flying in the air. Takeoffs and landings seemed to be unimportant, which they would be if you were planning to hijack the planes in midair to execute a suicide mission.

Is Zacharias Moussaoui the twentieth hijacker? Was he going to be the twentieth man on one of the four planes that crashed on September 11th—as the federal government claims? Or, with apologies to Lee Majors, is he the fall guy? With no one else alive to blame, he's the most likely suspect.

To try and answer those questions and others, left in the wake of the attacks on the World Trade Center and the Pentagon by al Quaeda on September 11, 2001, Minnesota FBI agent Colleen Rowley wrote a controversial May 21, 2002, memo to FBI Director Robert Mueller:

> I have deep concerns that a delicate and subtle shading/skewing of facts by you and others at the highest levels of FBI management has occurred and is occurring. The term "cover up" would be too strong a characterization which is why I am attempting to carefully (and perhaps over laboriously) choose my words here. I base my concerns on my relatively small, peripheral but unique role in the Moussaoui investigation in the Minneapolis Division prior to, during and after September 11th and my analysis of the comments I have heard both inside the FBI (originating, I believe, from you and other high levels of management) as well as your Congressional testimony and public comments.

What was happening was unprecedented. A respected FBI agent was redressing her boss and the agency she loved. Even more, she sounded like she knew what she was talking about.

> I feel that certain facts, including the following, have, up to now, been omitted, downplayed, glossed over and/or mis-characterized in an effort to avoid or minimize personal and/or institutional embarrassment on the part of the FBI and/or perhaps even for improper political reasons. . . .
>
> 1) The Minneapolis agents who responded to the

call about Moussaoui's flight training identified him as a terrorist threat from a very early point. The decision to take him into custody on August 15, 2001, on the INS "overstay" charge was a deliberate one to counter that threat and was based on the agents' reasonable suspicions.

During the beginning of their investigation, the FBI found that Moussaoui's visa had expired. The INS had done nothing about it, but for the FBI, this lapse was a perfect way to detain him while building their case. Searching his personal possessions, the FBI found a laptop computer, two knives, fighting gloves, and shin guards. He seemed to be training for some sort of violent physical encounter.

"I'm a marketing consultant," Moussaoui claimed, but he was unemployed and had no employment record. Yet he had a $32,000 bank balance. According to his visa, he had made extensive trips to Afghanistan. Questioned about this, the FBI would later report, "He became extremely agitated, and he refused to discuss the matter further. Moussaoui was extremely evasive in many of his answers."

That same day, August 15, agents interviewed his roommate. The roommate told the FBI that Moussaoui believes it is "acceptable to kill civilians who harm Muslims." The roommate said that Moussaoui revered Muslim "martyrs, and that Moussaoui might be willing to act on his beliefs."

Agent Rowley's report continued:

> 2) As the Minneapolis agents' reasonable suspicions quickly ripened into probable cause, which, at the latest, occurred within days of Moussaoui's arrest when the French Intelligence Service confirmed his affiliations with radical fundamentalist Islamic

groups and activities connected to *Osama bin Laden,* they became desperate to search the computer lap top that had been taken from Moussaoui as well as conduct a more thorough search of his personal effects. The agents in particular believed that Moussaoui signaled he had something to hide in the way he refused to allow them to search his computer.

Rowley and the other agents didn't know what Moussaoui had on his hard drive, but they felt it had something to do with terrorist activities in the United States. They needed to establish just cause to search his computer. They were determined to get in.

3) The Minneapolis agents' initial thought was to obtain a criminal search warrant, but in order to do so, they needed to get FBI Headquarters' (FBI HQ's) approval in order to ask for Department of Justice approval to contact the United States Attorney's Office in Minnesota. Prior to and even after receipt of information provided by the French, FBI HQ personnel disputed with the Minneapolis agents the existence of probable cause to believe that a criminal violation had occurred/was occurring. As such, FBI HQ personnel refused to contact [DOJ] to attempt to get the authority.

While reasonable minds may differ as to whether probable cause existed prior to receipt of the French intelligence information, it was certainly established after that point and became even greater with successive, more detailed information from the French and other intelligence sources.

Nor did FBI HQ personnel do much to dis-
seminate the information about Moussaoui to
other appropriate intelligence/law enforcement
authorities. When, in a desperate 11th hour
measure to bypass the FBI HQ roadblock, the
Minneapolis Division undertook to directly notify
the CIA's Counter Terrorist Center (CTC), FBI
HQ personnel actually chastised the Minneapolis
agents for making the direct notification without
their approval!

The use of the exclamation point at the end of the paragraph emphasized FBI HQ's cupidity. Rowley was charging
that the FBI's reticence to share information between agencies, as well as the Bureau's own bureaucratic incompetence,
was partly responsible for what happened on 9/11. What is
really scary is her assertions that the FBI did little or nothing
to take the evidence of Moussaoui's combat training and
match it with similar intelligence coming out of the FBI's
Phoenix office, that Middle Eastern men, the ones who were
on the three flights on September 11, were enrolled in area
flight schools. These worthies' sole interest was in flying the jet
once it was aloft. They had no interest in learning how to take
off or land.

Gee, I wonder why? If I can ask this question without the
words "Special Agent" before my name, why couldn't the Feds?

The problem with chalking this all up to the "20–20
hindsight is perfect" problem is that this is not a case
of everyone in the FBI failing to appreciate the
potential consequences. It is obvious, from my first-
hand knowledge of the events and the detailed doc-
umentation that exists, that the agents in Minneapolis

who were closest to the action and in the best position to gauge the situation locally, did fully appreciate
the terrorist risk/danger posed by Moussaoui and
his possible co-conspirators even prior to September 11th.

Even without knowledge of the Phoenix communication (and any number of other additional
intelligence communications that FBI HQ personnel were privy to in their central coordination
roles), the Minneapolis agents appreciated the risk.
So I think it's very hard for the FBI to offer the
"20–20 hindsight" justification for its failure to act!

Even after the attacks had begun, the SSA [FBI
Supervisory Special Agent] in question was still
attempting to block the search of Moussaoui's
computer, characterizing the World Trade Center
attacks as a mere coincidence with Minneapolis's
prior suspicions about Moussaoui.

The level of bureaucratic incompetence was astonishing.
Even after the bombings, the government was still trying to
stop Moussaoui's computer from being searched.

Agent Rowley continued:

It's at least possible we could have gotten lucky and
uncovered one or two more of the terrorists in
flight training prior to Sept. 11. . . . There is at least
some chance that . . . may have limited the Sept.
11th attacks and resulting loss of life.

Then, Rowley really went for the bullseye.

The last official "fact" that I take issue with is not

really a fact, but an opinion, and a completely
unsupported opinion at that. In the day or two following September 11th, you, Director Mueller,
made the statement to the effect that if the FBI had
only had any advance warning of the attacks, we
(meaning the FBI), may have been able to take
some action to prevent the tragedy.

Ever dutiful, Rowley tried to let her boss know he was putting his foot into his mouth.

Fearing that this statement could easily come back
to haunt the FBI upon revelation of the information that had been developed pre-September 11th
about Moussaoui, I and others in the Minneapolis
Office, immediately sought to reach your office
through an assortment of higher level FBI HQ
contacts, in order to quickly make you aware of the
background of the Moussaoui investigation and
forewarn you so that your public statements could
be accordingly modified.

Finally when similar comments were made
weeks later, in Assistant Director Caruso's congressional testimony in response to the first public
leaks about Moussaoui, we faced the sad realization
that the remarks indicated someone, possibly with
your approval, had decided to circle the wagons at
FBI HQ in an apparent effort to protect the FBI
from embarrassment and the relevant FBI officials
from scrutiny.

Rowley was writing all this knowing full well she was
probably sacrificing her career. You don't say that your boss

was an arrogant bastard and the upper echelon personnel of
your employer were a uniform bunch of sons of bitches in
front of the world and expect to get away with it.

It made no difference. Rowley was a patriot. If a government was not functioning to serve the people, and functioning
well, it needed to be exposed and reformed.

> Although I agree that it's very doubtful that the full
> scope of the tragedy could have been prevented, it's
> at least possible we could have gotten lucky and
> uncovered one or two more of the terrorists in
> flight training prior to September 11th, just as
> Moussaoui was discovered, after making contact
> with his flight instructors.

Rowley acknowleged: "It is certainly not beyond the realm
of imagination to hypothesize that Moussaoui's fortuitous
arrest alone, even if he merely was the twentieth hijacker,
allowed the hero passengers of Flight 93 to overcome their
terrorist hijackers [four instead of the five on the other flights]
and thus spare more lives on the ground."

What Rowley said next hinted at perhaps the real truth of
Moussaoui's actual job in the United States. "And even greater
casualties, possibly of our nation's highest government officials, may have been prevented if Al Qaeda intended for
Moussaoui to pilot an entirely different aircraft."

Rowley was making a suggestion that a second terrorist
plot might have existed, with different personnel, including
Moussaoui: "There is, therefore, at least some chance that discovery of other terrorist pilots prior to September 11th may
have limited the September 11th attacks and resulting loss of
life."

That memo left the government in a tight spot. The public

was thirsting for blood. A Gallup survey three weeks after the attack showed that 68 percent of those surveyed favored the death penalty for Moussaoui. While conventional wisdom might say that the further away from 9/11 things got, the less the public thirsted for blood, that was not the case.

A continent away, the French government asked Attorney General John Ashcroft not to seek the death penalty against Moussaoui, a French citizen.

"We do not accept the death penalty," stated French Justice Minister Marylise Lebranchu. She also stated that the French government had offered their consular services to Moussaoui, which he refused. She didn't have to add that along with every other member of the European Union, France had condemned the death penalty.

As Moussaoui languished in federal prison, the government put together their case against him. They were determined to prove he was the twentieth hijacker. As to the issue of death, at a White House press briefing on March 19, 2002, the following exchange took place between a reporter and Presidential Press Secretary Ari Fleischer:

Q. I want to ask one another question. This has to do with Zacharias Moussaoui who is going to be—I don't know if he's going to be asked for the death sentence or not, by the Justice Department, there are some versions that that might be the case. He seems to be the only surviving member of the terrorist group that took over the plane, at least that is the accusation. Would the President back a death penalty request by the Justice Department for Zacharias Moussaoui if he's found guilty of the charges?

MR. FLEISCHER: That's not a determination the President makes. The matters of justice, matters of the charges that should be brought in courts of law are matters that the

President delegates to the professionals and the Department of Justice to decide. I can share with you that when the President made the determination that Mr. Moussaoui would not be tried in a military tribunal, that he would indeed be tried in a civilian court, he was aware of the possibility that one of the charges [that] could be brought included a death penalty. But this was a decision made by the professionals at the Attorney General's office. The President is not involved in that process.

The reporter failed to do his follow-up. In his first year in office, 2001, President George W. Bush had had his attorney general, John Ashcroft, resume executions of federal prisoners. The first of many executions to come occurred in June 2001 when Oklahoma City bomber Timothy McVeigh and drug-dealing murderer Juan Raul Garza were executed by lethal injection. McVeigh went first, becoming the first federal prisoner executed in thirty-nine years.

The government was certain Moussaoui was in on the 9/11 attacks. What did it matter what the French said or wanted? Most Americans looked at the French as two-timing, weak-kneed frogs.

While hanging no longer existed as a method of execution for federal crimes, the Bush administration was no less anxious to put Moussaoui to death by lethal injection. Attorney General John Ashcroft announced the government's intention to seek the death penalty against the French citizen.

Showing that his incarceration had done nothing to improve his command of the language, Moussaoui stated: "I came to the United States of America to be part, O.K., of a conspiracy to use airplane as a weapon of mass destruction, a statement of fact to strike the White House, but this conspiracy was a different conspiracy than 9/11."

Government investigators believed that meant a suicide attack on the White House. However, and most importantly, the government could present no evidence that Moussaoui had met the other September 11 hijackers.

The case dragged on. But as it did, another organization that would prove to be the best detectives yet, worked doggedly on the case. The National Commission on Terrorist Attacks on the United States held hearings in public and private throughout 2003 and 2004 in an effort to get at the truth of the conspiracy.

At their December 8, 2003, session, Stephen J. Schulhofer, the Robert B. McKay Professor of Law at New York University gave testimony. Professor McKay was also a member of the Century Foundation, a nonprofit, nonpartisan organization, founded in 1919, that conducts public policy research and analyses of economic, social, and foreign policy issues, including inequality, retirement security, election reform, media studies, homeland security, and international affairs.

He testified:

> In July 2001, officials at headquarters and else-where ignored a Phoenix field office request for an investigation of suspicious individuals [the eventual 9/11hijackers] seeking flight training. Testimony does not identify any specific reason for FBI inaction at that crucial juncture; it seems possible that no FBI official made a conscious decision on the matter at all. Whatever the explanation, the Bureau unquestionably had ample legal authority to pursue such an investigation.

As for Moussaoui, Professor Schulhofer continued:

In August 2001, FBI headquarters rejected a Minneapolis field office request to seek a FISA warrant
to search Zacharias Moussaoui's computer and
other personal effects, because headquarters officials apparently believed that FISA requirements
could not be satisfied. That belief was simply incorrect, and inexplicably so. FISA required (and would
still require) probable cause to believe that Moussaoui was associated with an international terrorist
group, but the French intelligence report on
Moussaoui easily satisfied the "common sense,
practical" probable cause standard.

Once again, Agent Rowley was being proven correct and
once again, reasonable doubt had surfaced over Moussaoui's
role in 9/11. Perhaps sensing that the government's case against
him was growing weaker by the minute, in March 2005, Moussaoui decided to cop a guilty plea in an effort to avoid the death
penalty. He would throw himself at the mercy of the presiding
judge Leonie Brinkema and hope that he wouldn't die.

The French government's response was swift:

STATEMENT MADE BY THE MINISTRY OF FOREIGN
AFFAIRS SPOKESPERSON

(excerpt)
(Paris, April 25, 2005)

We have learned of Zacharias Moussaoui's intention to plead guilty in federal court in Alexandria.

The French authorities recall that they cannot
intervene or interfere in a judicial procedure, neither abroad nor in France. It is up to Zacharias

Moussaoui's American attorneys to handle his
defense in the court in Alexandria or for our com-
patriot to defend himself if he refuses the assistance
of attorneys. We cannot compel him to accept the
services of attorneys nor prevent him from
pleading guilty if he has decided to do so.
We recall that after refusing the benefit of
French consular protection after his arrest on
August 16, 2001, in the United States, Zacharias
Moussaoui finally accepted our assistance and at his
request was visited by French consular authorities
on July 19, 2002. In spite of an offer by our consul
general in Washington, Zacharias Moussaoui has
however not renewed his request. French consular
representatives however are attending the hearings
and will continue to follow the judicial procedure
very closely.

Moussaoui, an eccentric personality, had a rocky relationship
with his attorneys. During the case, he hired and fired them,
and even represented himself, in every possible legal combination. But when he finally walked into federal court on April
23, 2005, he was accompanied by his attorney Alan Yamamoto.

With Federal District Judge Leonie Brinkema presiding,
Moussaoui told her that he had decided to plead guilty to the
six terrorism charges the government had lodged against him.
He knew he could face the death penalty. But Moussaoui told
the judge, he had nothing to do with the 9/11 conspiracy.
Instead, he had engaged in a *second* conspiracy to free Sheik
Omar El Ramein, a terrorist and prisoner in the super max-
imum security federal prison

In the statement of facts that accompanied the guilty plea,
Moussaoui acknowledged a personal relationship with Osama

bin Laden. The government claimed that bin Laden was very fond of the Moroccan-born Frenchman. Bin Laden, again according to the government, had selected Moussaoui to be a part of an attack on the United States.

According to Moussaoui, bin Laden urged him to "follow his dream," which makes bin Laden sound like a character from a Broadway musical. Despite his boss's hyperbole, Moussaoui's dream was simple—to become an Islamic martyr. He made clear that his was a completely different conspiracy from the 9/11 plot.

"I was being trained on a 747 to eventually use this plane to strike the White House," Moussaoui told Judge Brinkema. Without knowing it, he was alluding to the second plot that FBI Special Agent Rowley had speculated on in her memo to FBI director Robert Mueller, who in turn answers to Attorney General John Ashcroft.

Moussaoui told Brinkema that he hoped to avoid death. However, "I will be ready to deal with the consequences, whatever they may be. It can be that some people decide that I will spend my life in Florence, Colorado. It's possible."

That's the location of a maximum security federal prison with infamous inmates including the Theodore Kaczynski aka "The Unabomber," Richard Reid aka "the Shoe Bomber, and Oklahoma City bombing conspirator Terry Nichols.

In case he was executed, he wanted a Muslim professor of his acquaintance "to make sure that my body will be buried in a Muslim land." Otherwise, "I will be buried in Arkansas."

What was wrong with Arkansas? He then added more soberly, "I've come to understand that the course I've chosen will lead me potentially . . . to the gas chamber or the lethal injection."

Moussaoui had been getting good legal advice. He had previously tried to petition the court to call other federal prisoners, charged with terrorism, as defense witnesses. He was sure they would absolve him of responsibility in the 9/11 plot. But the government had demurred, backed up by the judge. Such access to the prisoners, either live in court, or access to their classified interrogations, could compromise national security in the war on terrorism, the government had said. The court had concurred.

The administration of President George W. Bush had also threatened a transfer of Moussaoui's case to a military tribunal, where he would have far fewer rights. In fact, at that very moment in another federal court, the family of Dr. Samuel Mudd was making the argument that a military tribunal had no right to try civilians. If they won, President Bush would never even have the option of calling a military tribunal to order.

Judge Brinkema didn't rattle. On October 2, 2003, she ruled that the government could not seek the death penalty against Moussaoui precisely because they disallowed his access to three captured al-Qaeda operatives. The defense maintained that their testimony would exonerate the defendant's involvement in the 9/11 conspiracy. Moussaoui subsequently helped the government out when he crossed up his attorneys with the "guilty" plea. That put the death penalty back on the table. There was, however, method to Moussaoui's seeming madness.

Moussaoui had picked up a little bit about the American criminal justice system. He had noticed that it allowed even the worst criminals an opportunity to plead their case in open court. Sure enough, Judge Brinkema told the defendant that such witnesses and testimony, that had been disallowed because of national security concerns previously, could be used as a mitigating factor in the penalty phase of his hearing before a jury.

At the prosecutor's table, Attorney General Albert Gonzalez

must have swallowed hard. That meant that now the man who had copped the strangest plea in U.S. criminal history, claiming to be part of the 9/11 conspiracy though he had just said in court that he was not, would get access to their secret records. Not only that. Gonzalez would have to convince twelve jurors to put Moussaoui in the death chamber. One holdout and it's life.

Brinkema scheduled the penalty phase of the trial for February 2006.

Did he really do it? Was Zacharias Moussaoui the twentieth hijacker? No, he wasn't. Was he involved in another plot to destroy the Whtie House? I take him at his word—he was.

The government never really had a conspiracy case against him for the 9/11 plot. One thing that emerged through the four-year ordeal of Moussaoui's case has been that he isn't the archetypal dedicated suicide terrorist. Instead, the picture that emerges is of a wily, albeit eccentric personality with a keen nose for survival—all of which still makes Moussaoui a bona fide terrorist, best kept behind bars for the rest of his life.

Will the jury sentence Zacharius Moussaoui to death? Personally, I wouldn't be a bit surprised if the Unabomber and the Shoe Bomber had some company.

Hero or Villain? Part 2

1868–2002—Dr. Samuel Mudd
1865–2005

President Jimmy Carter's involvement in the case of Dr. Samuel Mudd didn't occur until 1978. Plenty had to happen before that took place.

Mudd, O'Laughlen, and Spangler had been sentenced to hard labor and were immediately put in transit to their prison, the toughest and worst in the federal system in 1865. It wasn't Florence, Colorado, which hardly existed at the time. The prisoners were sent to the dreaded Fort Jefferson in the Dry Tortugas. A chain of islands seventy miles west of Key West in the Gulf of Mexico, the place was known as the American version of Devil's Island.

It was during Ponce De Leon's Florida explorations that he discovered the Dry Tortugas in 1513, so named because De Leon caught over a hundred sea turtles when he visited. *Tortugas* is "turtles," in Spanish. As for the adjective "dry," the chain didn't have any fresh water, making it dry. By the 1700s, it made no difference what you called the place. It had become home to a whole corporation of pirates who used the Dry Tortugas as a base to attack shipping in the Gulf of Mexico.

After the War of 1812, some brilliant generals in Washington thought up the idea of a group of forts from Maine to Florida that would provide one continuous defense of the

U.S. coastline. Fort Jefferson, in the Dry Tortugas, was built to protect the southern coastline and guard the commerce-laden approach to the Mississippi River. Fort Jefferson was supposed to be the greatest of the group, a huge brick monstrosity that looked impenetrable. But during the next fifty-odd years, it became obvious that the nature of war had changed, that the interior of the country as well as the coastlines needed to be protected as well—in some cases even more so.

With its isolation and parched climate the fort seemed ideal during the Civil War as a prison for deserters and other criminals. Never again would it be a fort with defense in mind. It became popularly known as a prison for the unredeemable. If the isolation, climate, or hard labor didn't kill you, the yellow fever would.

Yellow fever was one of the scourges of the nineteenth century. Up until 1900, when scientists discovered that it was spread by mosquitoes and that by eliminating mosquitoes you could eliminate the disease, there was no real way to fight it.

During the last few days of July 1865, the United States Navy steamship *Florida* tied up at Fort Jefferson's docks. The prisoners began to disembark. They moved like condemned men, languidly in the midsummer tropical heat, trudging to a six-meter high, six-sided, red brick building that took up most of the land on the mosquito-infested island. It was a place of no redemption, no hope.

The passengers walked over a small wooden bridge spanning a moat that encircled their destination: Fort Jefferson. Passing through a single door in a high wall, they came into a huge, dank interior. They were ordered by a guard to stop in front of a group of soldiers. When they did, an officer stepped forward with the same speech he gave every new load of arrivals. They were through being "passengers."

"You are now within the walls of the Fort Jefferson Military

Prison in the Dry Tortugas," the officer announced. "You men have been convicted and sentenced to serve your punishment here. No prisoner has ever successfully escaped from Fort Jefferson. No one will ever escape. It is more than two hundred kilometers across open ocean to the nearest occupied land."

The federal prisoners arriving that day included Spangler, O'Laughlen, and the thirty-two-year-old Dr. Samuel Mudd. Soon after they arrived, there was a yellow fever outbreak.

Prisoners showed the classic symptoms: jaundice or yellow skin, high fever, and black vomit. The doctors felt powerless. The only thing they could do was to try to lower the fever, keep the patients as comfortable as possible, and hope they pulled through. The disease, though, had an 85 percent mortality rate.

Within the prison, no death from the disease was felt more than that of the prison doctor. With him gone, there was no one present to help the patients, unless . . . Dr. Mudd moved into the vacuum left by the deceased physician.

Moving into the breach, Dr. Mudd treated the increasing number of men who became sick with yellow fever. Many of those who survived felt that they owed their lives to Dr. Mudd. Thus began the campaign to rehabilitate Dr. Samuel Mudd's reputation. Redemption had come to Fort Jefferson long before it came to Shawshank. The prisoners in Fort Jefferson who survived the yellow fever outbreak all wrote to President Johnson, requesting that Doctor Mudd be pardoned because of the lives he had saved.

AFFIDAVIT CONCERNING CERTAIN STATEMENTS
MADE BY DR. SAM'L A. MUDD, SINCE HIS TRIAL.

CAMP FRY, WASHINGTON, D.C.
August 22, 1865.

BRIG.-GEN. JOSEPH HOLT,
Judge Advocate General, U. S. A.:

SIR—I am in receipt of your communication of this date, in which you request information as regards the truthfulness of certain statements and confessions reported to have been made by Dr. Mudd while under my charge, *en route* to the Dry Tortugas.

In reply, I have the honor to state that my duties required me to be constantly with the prisoners, and during a conversation with Dr. Mudd, on the 22nd of July, he confessed that he knew Booth when he came to his house with Herold, on the morning after the assassination of the President; that he had known Booth for some time, but was afraid to tell of his having been at his home on the 15th of April, fearing that his own and the lives of his family would be endangered thereby.

He also confessed that he was with Booth at the National Hotel on the evening referred to by Weichmann in his testimony; that he came to Washington on that occasion to meet Booth by appointment, who wished to be introduced to John Surratt; that when he and Booth were going to Mrs. Surratt's house to see John Surratt, they met, on Seventh street, [where] John Surratt was introduced to Booth, and they had a conversation of a private nature.

Dr. Mudd had with him a printed copy of the testimony pertaining to his trial. Upon a number of occasions, he referred to same. I will also state that this confession was voluntary, and made without solicitation, threat or promise, and was made after the destination of the prisoners was communicated to them, which communication affected Dr. Mudd more than the rest. He frequently exclaimed, "Oh, there is now no hope for me," or, "I cannot live in such a place."

Please acknowledge the receipt of this letter.

I am, General, very respectfully,
Your obedient servant,
GEORGE W. DUTTON,
Capt. Co. C. 10th Reg't V. R. C. com'dg Guard.

Sworn and acknowledged at Washington, D. C., this 23rd August, 1865, before me.

G.C. THOMAS,
Notary Public.

If Captain Dutton was to be believed, upon hearing his destination was the Dry Tortugas, where he was convinced he would die, Mudd confessed to everything the prosecution had alleged in their indictment. In making his decision on whether to pardon him or not, President Johnson had access to this document. Whether he read it or not is unclear.

Simultaneous to this campaign to have himself exonerated by the president, Dr. Mudd had also filed a habeas corpus petition in the United States District Court for the Southern District of Florida. He argued that the Hunter Commission (the name given the military commission that tried him) lacked jurisdiction over him.

On September 9, 1868, Judge Thomas Jefferson Boynton denied Dr. Mudd's petition, finding that President Lincoln "was assassinated not from private animosity nor any other reason than a desire to impair the effectiveness of military operations and enable the rebellion to establish itself into a government. . . . It was not Mr. Lincoln who was assassinated, but the commander-in-chief of the Army for military reasons."

Mudd appealed the denial of his habeas corpus petition to the Supreme Court. On February 8, 1869, however, President Andrew Johnson fully and unconditionally pardoned Dr. Mudd and released him from prison because of his service in battling the yellow fever epidemic. The Supreme Court then dismissed as moot Dr. Mudd's appeal of the district court's denial of habeas corpus relief because Dr. Mudd was no longer incarcerated.

Now a free man, Dr. Samuel Mudd returned to Maryland, where, in 1876, he was elected to the state legislature. Mudd died of pneumonia in 1883 at the age of forty-eight. That should have been the end of the story—a slow fade-out with history left to judge whether Mudd was guilty or not. But in 1901, Dr. Mudd's grandson, Richard Mudd, was born in Washington, D.C. As he got older, Richard discovered his family legacy. Becoming a physician himself, Dr. Richard Mudd devoted his life to clearing his grandfather and the family name.

One hundred and eleven years after President Abraham Lincoln was assassinated, in 1976, seventy-five-year-old Dr. Richard Mudd filed an application with the Army Board for Correction of Military Records ("ABCMR"), a civilian board set up pursuant to 10 U.S.C. §1552, to make recommendations to the Secretary of the Army regarding the correction of army records.

Dr. Richard Mudd sought to have the ABCMR correct the record of his grandfather and to declare him innocent. Dr.

Mudd asserted two errors: (1) that the Hunter Commission lacked jurisdiction to try Dr. Mudd, and (2) that Dr. Mudd was not in fact guilty of the offense with which he was charged.

It takes a while for things to get done in the army. Simultaneously, Dr. Richard Mudd petitioned President Jimmy Carter to pardon his grandfather.

The president's White House Counsel at the time was Bob Lipshutz. Patrice Apodaca, a member of Lipshutz's staff, wrote a memo to Lipshutz regarding Dr. Mudd's petition to the president. The full text of the memo can be found in Appendix III. It contains this operative paragraph:

> In addition, there was no evidence that during the Civil War, Dr. Mudd established a presence in any Confederate state or entered into any relationship with Confederate officers that could bind him to act on their orders. To the extent that any substance can be attached to the charges against Dr. Mudd, his acts should have been characterized as political rather than as acts of war which could provide a basis for military jurisdiction.

The memo left out the evidence presented to the Hunter Commission. Nowhere in the Apodaca memo is there any mention of the sworn eyewitness testimony of the ex-slaves, who saw Mudd in communication with known Confederate spies. Nor is there any mention made of the "white" eyewitness accounts on at least two occasions of Mudd's meetings with Booth.

In response to Dr. Mudd's petition to pardon his grandfather, President Carter wrote the following:

July 24, 1979

To Dr. Richard Mudd:

"I am aware of your efforts to clear the name of your grandfather Dr. Samuel Alexander Mudd, who set the broken leg of President Lincoln's assassin, John Wilkes Booth, and who was himself convicted as a conspirator in the assassination. Your persistence in these efforts, extending over more than half a century, is a tribute to your sense of familial love and dedication and is a credit to the great principles upon which our nation was founded.

Your petition and the petitions submitted to me on behalf of your grandfather by numerous members of Congress, several state legislatures, historians and private citizens have been exhaustively considered by my staff over the past two years. Regrettably, I am advised that the findings of guilt and the sentence of the military commission that tried Dr. Mudd in 1865 are binding and conclusive judgments, and that there is no authority under law by which I, as President, could set aside his conviction. All legal authority vested in the President to act in this case was exercised when President Andrew Johnson granted Dr. Mudd a full and unconditional pardon on February 8, 1869.

Nevertheless, I want to express my personal opinion that the declarations made by President Johnson in pardoning Dr. Mudd substantially discredit the validity of the military commission's judgment.

While a pardon is considered a statement of forgiveness and not innocence, the Johnson pardon goes beyond a mere absolution of the crimes for which Dr. Mudd was convicted. The pardon states that Dr. Mudd's guilt was limited to aiding the escape of President Lincoln's assassins and did not involve any other participation or complicity in the assassination plot itself—the crime for which Dr. Mudd was actually convicted. But President Johnson went on to express his doubt concerning even Dr. Mudd's criminal guilt of aiding Lincoln's assassins in their escape by stating:

". . . it is represented to me by intelligent and respectable members of the medical profession that the circumstances of the surgical aid to the escaping of the assassin and the imputed conceal-ment of his flight are deserving of a lenient con-struction, as within the obligations of professional duty and, thus, inadequate evidence of a guilty sympathy with the crime or the criminal;

And . . . in other respects the evidence, imputing such guilty sympathy or purpose of aid in defeat of justice, leaves room for uncertainty as to the true measure and nature of the complicity of the said Samuel A. Mudd in the attempted escape of said assassins. . . ."

A careful reading of the information provided to me about this case led to my personal agreement with the findings of President Johnson. I am hopeful that these conclusions will be given widespread circula-tion which will restore dignity to your grandfather's name and clear the Mudd family name of any nega-tive connotation or implied lack of honor.

Sincerely,

Jimmy Carter

Suspecting that President Carter had not seen all the evidence, I decided to contact him. I called the Carter Institute.

"You're in luck," said one of the president's staff. "The president is in town for the week."

I faxed over my questions regarding what the president had and had not seen when he wrote this letter.

A week later, I opened my mailbox to see a simple white letter-size envelope. My name and address was in the middle of the front. In the upper right hand corner where the stamp should have been, it said in script, "Jimmy Carter Postage and Fees Paid." I remembered that ex-presidents are among the few who have franking privileges.

I turned it over to open it and saw the return address "one Copenhill, Atlanta, Georgia 30307." That was the Institute's address. I figured it was just the Carter Institute acknowledging my query. I opened the letter and had to read it three times before I got it. I felt tingly all over.

> To Fred:
>
> Both the Attorney General and White House Legal Council [sic] assessed the issue, and I took their advice.
> I didn't check the evidence personally.
>
> Best Wishes,
>
> Jimmy C.

There is no evidence in the Carter Presidential Papers at the Carter Institute that the Attorney General or White House Counsel reviewed the transcript of the trial. It didn't make sense that a humanitarian like Jimmy Carter would ignore the testimony of former slaves.

He never saw it. The president's letter to Mudd might have read differently if his attorney general and White House counsel had gone back a little further in the federal archives, to which they had ready access, before briefing their boss.

While redress from the executive branch was nevertheless exhausted, there was still the military to consider. Dr. Richard Mudd continued his crusade to clear his grandfather. Finally, the ABCMR conducted a hearing, and found that Dr. Mudd never served in the military and continued to practice medicine during the Civil War.

At the time Lincoln was shot, Dr. Mudd was a civilian and a citizen of Maryland; Maryland was not a secessionist state, and the Hunter Commission had overruled all requests for a change in venue to the civilian courts in the District of Columbia "which were open and functioning."

The ABCMR unanimously concluded that the Hunter Commission "did not have jurisdiction to try [Dr. Mudd], and that in so doing denied him his due process rights, particularly his right to trial by a jury of his peers. This denial constituted such a gross infringement of his constitutionally protected rights that his conviction should be set aside. To fail to do so would be unjust."

The ABCMR therefore recommended that the Secretary of the Army order the Archivist of the United States to correct Dr. Mudd's record by showing that the conviction was set aside. History was about to be changed. Then, six months later, William D. Clark, Acting Assistant Secretary of the Army, denied the Board's recommendation and Dr. Richard Mudd's request.

Clark found that the precise issue which the ABCMR proposed to decide, the jurisdiction of the military commission over Dr. Mudd, was specifically addressed at the time in two separate habeas corpus proceedings, one before the Chief Justice of the Supreme Court, the other before a U.S. District Court. There also was an opinion by the Attorney General of the United States. The effect of the action recommended by the ABCMR would be to overrule all those determinations.

Dr. Mudd requested reconsideration of Acting Assistant Secretary Clark's decision, and the army agreed to review it. On February 2, 1996, Sara Lister, Assistant Secretary of the Army, denied Dr. Mudd's request to vacate Dr. Samuel Mudd's conviction. Assistant Secretary Lister rested her decision in part on the fact that the authorities at the time, both the Attorney General and the district court that had ruled on the habeas petition, concluded that the Hunter Commission had jurisdiction. She also stated:

> Even if one could argue with hindsight that jurisdiction was improper, the appropriate time to make that challenge was 130 years ago within the confines of our judicial system. This was attempted by Dr. Mudd and he lost. His appeal of Judge Boynton's decision to the U.S. Supreme Court was not heard because of the pardon.
>
> At that time, he decided not to judicially challenge the jurisdiction again. For the sake of the law and history, his descendants must live with the ramifications of his decision.

Dr. Richard Mudd then challenged the army's denial of relief. And so, the Mudd Case entered the new millenium. In March 2000, the Secretary of the Army determined that Dr. Samuel Mudd was not wrongfully convicted. The Mudds next took the case into the court system.

In March 2001, Judge Paul L. Friedman of federal district court denied the Mudd family redress; Mudd's convictions stood. The Mudd family filed a notice of intent to appeal with the U.S. Court of Appeals in Washington, D.C., and subsequently requested several extensions before actually filing such an appeal.

On June 18, 2001, Justice Department lawyers filed a

"motion for summary affirmance," in effect asking the court to forgo briefs and oral arguments, and to decide the appeal; based on the "clearly correct" lower court record. However, a three-judge panel of the U.S. Court of Appeals for the District of Columbia denied the Justice Department's request for summary affirmance in December 2001. Entering into 2002, one hundred thirty-seven years after conviction, Dr. Mudd's case was, astonishingly, still alive in the federal courts.

In May 2002, the driving force behind the appeal, Mudd's grandson Dr. Richard D. Mudd, died at the venerable age of 101. Dr. Richard Mudd II, Richard's son and Samuel Mudd's great grandson, vowed to continue on and so he did.

In November 2002, the U.S. Court of Appeals for the District of Columbia denied the appeal of Judge Friedman's final decision for "want of standing." The court said that since Dr. Samuel Mudd was not a member of the military, neither he nor his descendants was allowed to petition to alter the military record.

The Mudds were running out of options. The Mudd family intended to appeal to the Supreme Court. To say that at this point fate took a hand is putting it mildly.

In February 2003, the U.S. Supreme Court announced that it would not hear the appeal of the 138-year-old conviction of Dr. Samuel Mudd for complicity in the assassination of President Lincoln. The reason? The lawyer for the Mudd family had missed the deadline for filing his brief.

And that was that. The legal appeals of Dr. Samuel Mudd reached an end. But the questions persisted.

Did Dr. Samuel Mudd know John Wilkes Booth? Of course he did. The evidence conclusively shows he met with him and for quite some time at each meeting.

Did Mudd recognize Booth when he came to him for aid? Of course he did! He knew Booth personally. If he hadn't, he probably would have recognized him anyway. In 1865, John Wilkes Booth was the most popular actor in America; everyone knew him, not only his visage but his voice. It is also beyond doubt that Mudd was a Southerner through and through who supported slavery and thought little or nothing of President Lincoln, and on more than one occasion had wished him dead.

The Mudd Family did the right thing by asking the courts to adjudicate whether or not the military commission that tried their forebear was constitutionally sound. It was a similar argument that would be brought to bear against President George W. Bush when he signed an Executive Order allowing a military commission to try any civilians, including Americans the government thought were allied with terrorist organizations, especially Al-Qaeda.

If Mudd had won on that point alone, then his lawsuit would have been surely worth it. Civilians shouldn't be tried by military when civilian courts exist to do the job. That makes the whole Lincoln Conspiracy Trial a sham, which it was. If the government wants to find a way to execute someone, it can.

That doesn't mean any of those found guilty were innocent. I believe they all were guilty, with the exception of Spangler, who was Booth's dupe. But the use of a military court tainted those verdicts for history.

It was by going further and challenging the evidence, that Dr. Richard Mudd made a huge mistake, because the evidence shows clearly that Dr. Samuel Mudd was guilty of aiding and abetting John Wilkes Booth in the conspiracy to murder President Abraham Lincoln.

By the way, to set the record straight: the expression "His name is Mud" does not derive from the case of Dr. Samuel Mudd. The phrase appeared first in print in 1820, 45 years before Lincoln's murder. It probably derives from eighteenth century English slang. The word "mud" was used as a synonym for "dope" or "dolt," which some of the Lincoln conspirators certainly were.

THE MURDERED CIVIL RIGHTS WORKERS, PART 2

2005—EDGAR RAY KILLEN

One of the controlling principals in U.S. criminal law is that murder is the one crime that has no statute of limitations.

Whether the state is Michigan, which has not had capital punishment since the nineteenth century, or Texas, where they have always had capital punishment, murder is the one crime that every single state agrees on in their criminal statutes: There's no statute of limitation on murder charges.

Why is the crime of murder held on so high a pedestal in our society when every other crime has a statute of limitations? Is the motive some antiquated idea of justice, or is it a real moral impulse on the part of the state to hold the guilty accountable? The answer, I think, is more personal.

Cold case squads are usually composed of cops and prosecutors, sometimes aided by victims' families, who want to see justice done. These men and women can best be compared to Nazi hunters like Simon Wiesenthal and Beate Klarsfeld. Like their predecessors, they are society's last line of offense against someone who is about to get away with murder by outlasting and outliving his pursuers. A conscious decision is made not to allow a bad guy to escape justice for a murder he committed in the past, simply because he is now old and frail.

If the bad guys happen to have committed what today

would be called a hate crime during the civil rights era, they're in trouble. There has been a concerted social and legal movement in the Southern states over the past decade to bring to justice those killers who murdered people during the civil rights struggle before the killers died.

For example, in 1994 the state of Mississippi convicted Byron de la Beckwith for the 1963 sniper killing of state NAACP leader Medgar Evers. The case, unfortunately, became a film in which de la Beckwith was played by a usually reliable James Woods as a cross between a hundred year old bald vampire and Pa Kettle.

In 2002, Alabama convicted Bobby Frank Cherry for killing four black girls in the notorious bombing of a Birmingham church in 1963. Mississippi was next.

By 2005, only two who allegedly participated in the conspiracy to kill Michael Schwerner, Andrew Goodman, and James Chaney were still alive—former deputy Price and "Brother" Edgar Ray Killen. Mississippi showed it was ready to face up to its past. With the relatives of all three urging him on, with the local paper the *Clarion Ledger* cheering him on, Mississippi Attorney General Jim Hood filed murder charges against Edgar Ray Killen. In their indictment, the state charged that Killen recruited the members of the Klan to kill the civil rights workers, and fingered them, that is, told the killers where their victims could be found.

Finally, a jury would be asked to strip away prejudice, both old and new, and take a hardedged look:

Did Edgar Ray Killen really do it?

Did he organize a murderous KKK mob that night so long ago in 1964, and set them on the path that led to the deaths of three young men who became martyrs to the civil rights struggle?

• • •

In the state of Mississippi, the person who plans the murder is as guilty as the person who carries it out. Conviction on a murder one charge carried a mandatory penalty of life in prison. To show the state meant business, the governor personally had State Attorney General Jim Hood and Neshoba County District Attorney Mark Duncan prosecute the defendant.

To say that Hood and Duncan were hoping for a conviction is putting it mildly. A murder conviction in the case of the slain civil rights workers, after forty-one years, would go along way toward wiping out the previous injustices both Hood and Duncan's offices had shown during the civil rights era. On the defense side, respected criminal defense attorney James McIntyre represented Killen.

The second trial of Edgar Ray Killen, eighty years old, began on June 15, 2005. Sidelined by a recent logging accident, Killen sat erect in a wheelchair, inhaling oxygen from a tube beneath his nostrils. No open flames would be allowed in court.

There was Killen all right; no mistaking his perpetual scowl. This time, he was on trial for murder.

Killen gave the proceedings the respect he felt it deserved. After Killen complained of high blood pressure, presiding Judge Marcus Gordon, who knew of Killen, politely excused him for the day. Judge Gordon would later observe that his parents had been members of Killen's church.

For observers close to the age of fifty and above, the trial was something never thought imaginable. A jury that included African Americans was about to hear evidence against a former leader of the Ku Klux Klan in the state of Mississippi. Times had changed so much that now the odds were *favoring* a conviction. If the prosecution did their job, they could gain the first murder conviction in one of the most significant unsolved triple homicides of the twentieth century.

If.

Schwerner's remarried widow, Rita Schwerner Bender, was one of the first to testify for the prosecution. Under Hood's patient questioning, Bender stripped away the years. Suddenly, Bender was talking of the civil rights struggle in Mississippi; and to everyone in that courtroom, it was 1964. They could feel the repeated harassment and threats the civil rights workers faced in Mississippi—all of which Bender, now a Seattle lawyer, outlined.

With an ache in her voice, Bender recalled how she and "Mickey" (Schwerner) were at a civil rights training session in Ohio in June 1964. That's where they found out that the Mount Zion United Methodist Church in Longdale had been burned to the ground by the Klan.

"They had to go back and see those people," Bender told the court. "You don't abandon people who have put themselves at risk." It was what Schwerner fervently believed.

What Bender did not testify to was that Schwerner, an experienced and dedicated activist, must have known how much the Klan hated him. How could he not? The Klan was the most powerful paramilitary force in the state. They were just looking for an opportunity to get "Jew Boy" Schwerner. Was it really necessary at that moment to put his life on the line and the lives of his two friends? Would it be clichéd to suggest that Nathan Hale would have agreed with their decision?

After Bender's testimony, the state introduced parts of the 1967 trial transcript, specifically accounts of the three Klan informants who had since died.

"Reverend Killen said they had three of the civil rights workers locked up, and we had to hurry and get there and were to pick them up and tear their butts up," Klan member James Jordan testified in 1967. Jordan had testified that after telling Klan members how to get the three and what to do with them, he was dropped at a nearby funeral home to attend a funeral.

That was how the prosecution claimed Killen established his alibi for the time of the killings.

Compelling and convincing testimony came from a former Meridian police officer and one-time Klansman named Joseph Hatcher. Hatcher testified that Killen told him where the three young men were buried.

Another witness, Mike Winstead, a convict serving a prison sentence, testified that after the state reopened the investigation, "My grandfather asked [Killen] if he had anything to do with those boys being killed, and he [Killen] said 'yes,' and he was 'proud of it.' "

The prosecution didn't hesitate to pull at the tear ducts too. Fannie Lee Chaney, James's mother in her eighties, cried throughout her time on the stand. Carolyn Goodman read in open court a postcard sent by her son Andrew a day after he had seen Mississippi for the first time, and hours before he would die:

> Dear Mom and Dad, I have arrived safely in Meridian, Mississippi. This is a wonderful town, and the weather is fine. I wish you were here. The people in this city are wonderful, and our reception was very good. All my love, Andy

With the prosecution resting, the defense opened and went about its business in the same way as the 1967 trial—character witnesses to show that Killen had nothing to do with planning the murders and that he wasn't anyplace near the murder site when the three were killed. Killen's brother and sister proceeded to testify that Killen was at a Father's Day celebration on the Sunday when he was supposed to have plotted the murders. He had numerous witnesses to verify he was at his uncle's funeral when the three were actually killed.

On Saturday, June 18, with the trial winding down, the Associated Press reported the following: "Attorney General Jim Hood told reporters after court recessed that prosecutors are asking the judge to allow the jury to consider a lesser charge of felony manslaughter in the case."

No explanation was offered but you didn't need Superman's X-ray vision to figure out what Hood was up to. If he failed to prove murder under the law as defined in Mississippi, Killen could be found not guilty by the jury on all three counts and walk. But a manslaughter conviction, for which the jury had to believe Killen caused the death of the three in some way, would carry a maximum of twenty years on each count. To an eighty-year-old man in failing health, even a conviction on one count meant death behind bars.

On Monday June 18, Harlan Majure, a former mayor of Philadelphia, Mississippi, testified that Killen was a "good man." When questioned about his view on the Klan, Majure testified that it "did a lot of good up here. . . . As far as I know it's a peaceful organization." Majure also testified that he saw Killen at the funeral home the evening the three civil rights workers were murdered.

However, Hood also elicited testimony that the funeral home closed at 9:00 P.M. that Sunday night, leaving Killen plenty of time to meet other Ku Klux Klansmen on Rock Cut Road in rural Neshoba County, where Chaney, Goodman, and Schwerner were murdered.

Moving into his closing, State Attorney General Jim Hood called Killen "the main man" who recruited a group to kill the civil rights workers and dispose of their bodies. Hood told the jury that Killen was no better than a drug dealer, "one step removed but just as guilty as anyone else."

Taking apart Killen's alibi point by point, Hood said that Killen's family function was over by late afternoon. He had more than enough time to drive to Meridian and create the plan to first kidnap and then kill the three civil rights workers.

"Those three boys and their families were robbed of all the things that Edgar Ray Killen has been able to enjoy for these last forty years," District Attorney Mark Duncan said in his closing.

Defense attorney James McIntyre stood and pleaded with jurors to tap into the reasonable doubt in their minds about Killen's participation in the murders.

"Every witness that testified lied," the attorney from Jackson said. "They were paid [FBI] informants. This was paid testimony."

McIntyre, who worked with the defense in the 1967 federal trial, admitted Killen likely was a member of the Klan. But that didn't make him guilty as charged.

"You can't find him guilty if you're going to find the Klan guilty," he said. "This man is not guilty. The only thing he's guilty of is he had a big mouth and he was talking all the time."

It was time for the judge to charge the jury. Judge Gordon instructed the jury of their two options for conviction: murder or manslaughter. A conviction on the former was a life sentence for each count. A conviction on the latter was twenty years for each count. The judge had the option of having the sentences running consecutively or concurrently. Or the jury could find Killen not guilty on all counts.

For that matter, they could convict him of killing Schwerner, for example, but not Goodman or Chaney, or any permutation thereof. There isn't an honest lawyer alive who wouldn't acknowledge that you never know what a jury will do. At 2:53 P.M. Monday the judge sent the jury out to deliberate.

At 5:30 P.M., the jury told the judge that they were deadlocked six to six. Rather than give them the "Allen charge," Judge Gordon sequestered them in a local hotel for the night.

The next day, June 21, was the forty-first anniversary of the murders Killen was being judged for, and everyone in the courtroom felt the heavy weight of history. The jury began their deliberations at 8:30 A.M. In an article dated June 22, 2005, the *Chicago Sun Times* tells what happened next.

Justice after 41 years

June 22, 2005

By Emily Wagster Pettus

Edgar Ray Killen, an 80-year-old wheelchair-bound former Klansman, was convicted of manslaughter for masterminding the killings, a verdict of bittersweet justice for the families in a trial that marked Mississippi's latest attempt to atone for its bloodstained, racist past.

Upon hearing the verdict, Killen's wife, Betty Jo, ran to her husband with tears streaming down her face. She hugged him close. Still in a wheelchair from his logging accident, still sucking on his oxygen, Killen was surrounded by armed officers. As he was taken into custody for sentencing, then wheeled out of the courthouse to be taken to jail, Killen punched out a TV camera and two microphones. While publicly disappointed, Jim Hood was aware that manslaughter convictions went a long way for the state's atonement.

Warren Paprocki, a fifty-four-year-old engineer and thirteen-year resident of Neshoba County who served on the jury, told reporters after the verdict that prosecutors had failed to produce any evidence that showed Killen directly ordered his men to murder the three.

"If I had seen evidence that he had ordered murder, I would have found him guilty of murder and I would have hung the jury if I had to," said Paprocki. "But I didn't see it. What he [Killen] did say is, 'We got those civil rights workers up there and we need their butts tore up.'" Paprocki continued, quoting from witness testimony at the 1967 trial that was repeated during the present-day trial.

"Whatever they were going to do was going to rise to the level of a felony. In the commission of that, or the attempt to commit that, someone killed those people. There were a number of times in there where someone would make a statement like, 'I think this is what happened,' and 'I've always felt this is what happened,'" Paprocki said. "Then other jury members would stop them and say, 'Our instructions here are to go on the evidence.'

"For us to have been swayed by that emotional presentation [the prosecution's] and found him guilty of something in the absence of evidence would have been committing the very same crime that that man was on trial for. It would have been vigilantism under the color of law and it would have been just as wrong."

The next day, June 23, 2005, Killen was wheeled into court to hear sentence pronounced. Gazing down at the man who had once been his parents' preacher, Neshoba County Judge Marcus Gordon, seventy-three years old, said, "It is my responsibility to make that decision, and I have done it. Each life has value and each life is equal to other lives. There are three lives involved in this case, and three lives should be respected."

Then he sentenced Killen to three consecutive twenty-year prison terms for killing Andrew Goodman, James Chaney, and Michael Schwerner. Acknowledging Killen's age and condition, the judge nevertheless said that giving him time behind bars was justice under the law.

Killen's lawyers said they would appeal the verdict.

After the sentencing, Killen's wife ran again to her husband's side and kissed him three times before he was taken to the Central Mississippi Correctional Facility. Oscar Kenneth Killen, his brother, was quoted as saying, "Money will do anything."

Schwerner's widow, Rita Schwerner Bender, said afterward that the judge's comments struck a chord. The judge had "recognized that no one is valued more than others. Not only these men, but all the other people who were murdered and brutalized, they were all mothers' sons."

Attorney General Jim Hood claimed that the Klan no longer exists as an organized force in Mississippi. But thinking of the men like Killen who still believed fervently in the cause, Hood said: "At some point, there's got to be some remorse. You don't go to heaven unless you admit what you've done and ask for forgiveness."

Schwerner was twenty-four, Chaney twenty-one, and Goodman twenty when they died.

The system does work; it really does. It's just that sometimes it doesn't work the way we want it to. It works best when it takes into consideration the rights of the accused, regardless of the crime or conviction.

Under Mississippi state law, a person convicted of any felony other than sexual battery of a minor, child abuse, or a crime in which a death sentence or life imprisonment has been imposed, is allowed release on bail pending appeal if the convicted can show he is not a flight risk or a danger. Knowing this, Killen's attorneys petitioned for bail.

Judge Gordon held the bail hearing on August 12, 2005. How could the prosecution show the eighty-year-old guy hiccupping oxygen from a tube under his nose, confined to a wheelchair was a flight risk, let alone a danger? During the hearing, the eighty-year-old Killen was his own star witness. He took the stand to complain of his medical treatment behind bars since he entered the Central Mississippi prison in Pearl.

"They checked me through the line like a cattle auction," he testified. "I'm very unhappy with the treatment I've received."

Killen claimed to have bribed another convict to get him a pillow.

"I can barely sleep," he continued in his testimony. "I still don't understand how I could lie in severe pain for 24 hours and no one even brings me an aspirin. I'm not a drug addict."

To Judge Gordon, none of that really made a difference.

"It's not a matter of what I feel, it's a matter of the law," Judge Gordon reminded those in his crowded courtroom. He then released Edgar Ray Killen on a $600,000 bond. Thirty-eight thousand came from the pocket of Killan and his brother Bobby. The rest was posted by five of the old Klanner's friends. While Gordon took criticism from the victims' families for letting Killen out on bond, it was the right thing to do.

The State of Mississippi was showing that in 2005, even a white convict like Killen deserved everything the law allowed.

Epilogue

The Mudd case in particular, shows how a criminal case from another century can affect law in the current one. In Lizzie Borden's case, no one even thought that she might have been molested, which, if confirmed, might have made the killing of her father a form of justifiable homicide, which is argued in courtrooms today under similar circumstances.

Leo Frank was convicted because he was a Jew, pure and simple. Bruno Hauptmann was an idiot who got what he deserved. Pretty Boy Floyd was not guilty of the Kansas City Massacre. Julius Rosenberg was a sleazeball of an atomic spy. His wife Ethel was the Judy Holliday of spies.

Speaking of sleazeballs, Edgar Ray Killen is guilty of manslaughter in the case of the three murdered civil rights workers. Albert DeSalvo was the Boston Strangler, at least one of them. Hint to the Boston Police Department: one might still be out there. And Zacharias Moussaoui is not the twentieth hijacker. It's an urban fable destined for the dustheap of history.

How many other cases are out there, with unanswered questions? You know the ones . . . You're riding in your car late one night and you hear a news report that a famous murderer from decades past has died in his cell. That makes you think of other cases where you've had your doubts. And you know what you wonder as you pull into your driveway?

Did they really do it?

Appendix I

Thomas Ewing, Jr., Argument on the Law and Evidence in the Case of Dr. Samuel A. Mudd

May it please the Court: If it be determined to take jurisdiction here, it then becomes a question vitally important to some of these parties—a question of life and death—whether you will punish only offenses created and declared by law, or whether you will make and declare the past acts of the accused to be crimes, which acts the law never heretofore declared criminal: attach to them the penalty of death, or such penalty as may seem meet to you; adapt the evidence to the crime and the crime to the evidence, and thus convict and punish. This, I greatly fear may be the purpose, especially since the Judge Advocate said, in reply to my inquiries, that he would expect to convict "under the common law of war." This is a term unknown to our language—a quiddity—wholly undefined and incapable of definition. It is, in short, just what the Judge Advocate chooses to make of it. It may create a fictitious crime, and attach to it arbitrary and extreme punishment—and who shall gainsay it? The laws of war—namely, our Articles of War—and the habitual practice and mode of proceeding under them, are familiar to us all; but I know nothing, and never heard or read of a common law of war, as a code or system under which military courts or commissions in this country can take and exercise jurisdiction not given them by express legal enactment or constitutional grant. But I still hope the law is to govern, and if it do, I feel that my clients are still safe.

I will now proceed to show you, that on the part of one of my clients—Dr. Mudd—no crime known to the law, and for which it is pretended to prosecute, can possibly have been committed. Though not distinctly informed as to the offense for which the Judge Advocate claims conviction, I am safe in saying, that the testimony does not point to treason, and if he is being tried for treason, the proceedings for that crime are widely departed from. The prosecution appears to have been instituted and conducted under the proclamation of the Secretary of War, of April 20, 1865. This makes it a crime, punishable with death, to harbor or screen Booth, Atzerodt, or Herold, or to aid or assist them to escape. It makes it a crime to do a particular act, and punishes that crime with death. I suppose we must take this proclamation as law. Perhaps it is part of what the Judge Advocate means when he speaks of the "common law of war." If this be so, my clients are still safe, if we be allowed to construe it as laws are construed by cohorts of justice. But I will show, first, that Dr. Mudd is not, and cannot possibly be, guilty of any offense known to the law.

1. Not of treason. The overt act attempted to be alleged is the murder of the President. The proof is conclusive, that at the time the tragedy was enacted Dr. Mudd was at his residence in the country, thirty miles from the, place of the crime. Those who committed it are shown to have acted for themselves, not as the instruments of Dr. Mudd. He, therefore, cannot be charged, according to law and upon the evidence, with the commission of this overt act. There are not two witnesses to prove that he did commit it, but abundant evidence to show negatively that he did not.

Chief Justice Marshall, in delivering an opinion of the Court in Burr's case, says: "Those only who perform a part, and who are leagued in the conspiracy, are declared to be traitors. To complete the definition both circumstances must concur. They must 'perform a part' which will furnish the overt act, and they must be leagued with the conspiracy."

Now, as to Dr. Mudd, there is no particle of evidence tending to show that he was ever leagued with traitors in their treason; that he had ever, by himself, or by adhering to, and in connection with, others, levied war against the United States. It is contended that he joined in compassing the death of the President ("the King's death"). Foster, speaking of the treason of compassing the king's death, says: "From what has been said it followeth, that in every indictment for this species of treason, and indeed for levying war and adhering to the king's enemies, an overt act must be alleged and proved."

The only overt act laid in these charges against Mudd is the act of assassination, at which it is claimed he was constructively present and participating. His presence, and participation, or procurement, must be proved by two witnesses, if the charge be treason; and such presence, participation, or procurement, be the overt act.

Chief Justice Marshall., in Burr's case (Dall.,500), says: "Collateral points, say the books, may be proved according to the course of the common law; but is this a collateral point? Is the fact without which the accused does not participate in the guilt of the assemblage, if they were guilty (or in any way in the guilty act of others), a collateral point? This cannot be. The presence of the party, when presence is necessary, being part of the overt act, must be positively proved by two witnesses. No presumptive evidence, no facts from which presence may be conjectured or inferred, will satisfy the Constitution and the law. If procurement take the place of presence, and become part of the overt act, then no presumptive evidence, no facts from which the procurement may be conjectured or inferred, can satisfy the Constitution and the law. The mind is not to be led to the conclusion that the individual was present by a train of conjectures or inferences, or of reasoning. *The fact itself* must be proved by two witnesses, and must have been committed within the district."

2. Not of murder. For the law is clear, that, in cases of treason, presence at the commission of the overt act is governed by the same principle as constructive presence in ordinary felonies, and has no other latitude, greater or less, except that in proof of treason two witnesses are necessary to the overt act, and one only in murder and other felonies. "A person is not constructively present at an overt act of treason, unless he be aiding and abetting at the fact, or ready to do so, if necessary." Persons not sufficiently near to give assistance are not principals. And although an act be committed in pursuance of a previous concerted plan, those who were not present, or so near as to be able to afford aid and assistance, at the time when the offense is committed, are not principals, but accessories before the fact.

It is, therefore, perfectly clear, upon the law as enacted by the Legislature and expounded by jurists, that Dr. Mudd is not guilty of participating in the murder of the President; that be was not actually or constructively present when the horrid deed was done, either as a traitor, chargeable with it as an overt act, or a conspirator, connected as principal felon therewith.

3. The only other crimes defined by law for the alleged commission, of which the Judge Advocate may, by possibility, claim the conviction of the accused, are: 1st. The crime of treasonable conspiracy, which is defined by the law of 21st July, 1861, and made punishable by fine not exceeding $6,000, and imprisonment not exceeding six years, 2nd. The crime of being an accessory before, or after the fact to the crimes of murder, and of assault with intent to kill. That the accused is

not guilty of either of these crimes, will be clearly shown in the discussion of the evidence which follows.

4. Admitting the Secretary's proclamation to be law, it, of course, either supersedes or defines the unknown something or nothing which the Judge Advocate calls "the common law of war." If so, it is a definite, existing thing, and I can defend my clients against it; and it is easy to show that Dr. Mudd is not guilty of violating that proclamation. He did not, after the date of the proclamation, see either of the parties named therein— dress the wound, of Booth or point out the way to Herold— and the proclamation relates to future acts, not to past.

5. But of the common law of war, as distinct from the usages of Military Courts, in carrying out and executing the Articles of War: I know nothing, and on examining the books, I find nothing. All that is written down in books of law or authority I am, or ought to be, prepared to meet; but it were idle and vain to search for and combat a mere phantom of the imagination, without form and void.

I now pass to a consideration of the evidence, which I think will fully satisfy the Court that Dr. Mudd is not guilty of treasonable conspiracy, or of being an accomplice, before or after the fact in the felonies committed.

The accused has been a practicing physician, residing five miles north of Bryantown, in Charles county, Maryland, on a farm of about five hundred acres, given to him by his father. His house is between twenty-seven and thirty miles from Washington, and four or five miles east of the road from Washington to Bryantown. It is shown by Dr. George Mudd, John L. Turner, John Waters, Joseph Waters, Thomas Davis, John McPherson, Lewellen Gardiner, and other gentlemen of unimpeached and unquestionable loyalty, who are in full sympathy with the Government, that he is a man of most exemplary character—peaceable, kind, upright, and obedient to the laws. His family being slaveholders, he did not like the anti-slavery measures of the Government, but was always respectful and temperate in discussing them, freely took the oath of allegiance prescribed for voters (Dr. George Mudd), supported an Union candidate against Harris, the secession candidate, for Congress (T. L. Gardiner), and for more than a year past regarded the rebellion a failure. (Dr. George Mudd.) He was never known or reported to have done an act or said a word in aid of the rebellion, or in countenance or support of the enemies of the Government.

An effort was made, over all objections and in violation, I respectfully submit, of the plainest rules of evidence, to blacken his character as a citizen, by showing that he was wont, after the war broke out, to threaten his slaves to send them to Richmond "to build batteries." But it will be seen hereafter, that all that part of the testimony of the same witnesses, which related to the presence of Surratt and of rebel officers at the house of the accused, was utterly false. And Dyer, in presence of whom Eglent says the threat was made to him, swears he was not in the country then, and no such threat was ever made in his presence. The other colored servants of the accused, Charles and Julia Bloyce, and Betty and Frank Washington, say they never heard of such threats having been made; and J. T. Mudd and Dr. George Mudd, and his colored servants Charles and Julia Bloyce, and Betty and Frank Washington, describe him as being remarkably easy, unexacting and kind to all about him—slaves and freemen.

From this brief reference to the evidence of the character of the accused, I pass to a consideration of the testimony adduced to prove his connection with the conspiracy.

And, first, as to his acquaintance with Booth. J.C. Thompson says, that early in November last Booth went to the house of witness' father-in-law, Dr. William Queen, four or five miles south of Bryantown, and eight or ten from Dr. Mudd's, and presented a letter of introduction from a Mr. Martin, of Montreal, who said he wanted to see the county. It does not appear who Martin was. Booth said his business was to invest in land and to buy horses. He went with Dr. Queen's family to a church next day, in the neighborhood of Bryantown, and was there casually introduced, before service, by Thompson, to the accused. After service Booth returned to Queen's house, and stayed until the next morning, when he left. While at Queen's, he made inquiries of Thompson as to horses for sale, the price of lands, their qualities, the roads to Washington, and to the landings on the Potomac; and Thompson told him that the father of Dr. Samuel Mudd was a large landholder, and might sell part of his land. On Monday morning, after leaving Dr. Queen's, Booth came by the house of the accused, who went with him to the house of George Gardiner, to look at some horses for sale. The accused lives about one-quarter of a mile from Gardiner's (Mary Mudd, Thomas L. Gardiner), and on the most direct road to that place from Dr. Queen's, through Bryantown. (Mary Mudd, Hardy.) There Booth bought the one-eyed saddle-horse which he kept here, and which Payne rode after the attempted assassination of Mr. Seward. Mudd manifested no interest in the purchase, but after it was made Booth directed the horse to be sent to Montgomery's Hotel, in Bryantown, and Booth and the accused rode off together in the direction of the house of the accused, which was also the direction of Bryantown. Witness took the horse to Bryantown next morning, and delivered him in person to Booth there. Witness says the horse was bought on Monday; but he thinks in the latter part of

November; though he says he is "one of the worst hands in the world to keep dates."

Thompson further says, that after Booth's first introduction and visit to Dr. Queen's, "he came there again, and stayed all night, and left very early next morning. I think it was about the middle of December following his first visit there."

There is nothing whatever to show that Mudd saw Booth on this second visit, or at any other time, in the country, prior to the assassination; but a great deal of evidence that he never was at Mudd's house, or in his immediate neighborhood, prior to the assassination, except once, and on his first visit. I will refer to the several items of testimony on this point.

1st. Thomas L. Gardiner says he was back and forth at Mudd's house, sometimes every day and always two or three times a week, and never heard of Booth being there, or in the neighborhood, after the purchase of the horse and before the assassination.

2nd. Mary Mudd says she saw Booth on Sunday in November at church, in Dr. Queen's pew, and with his family, and that she heard of his being at the house of her brother the accused, on that visit, but did not hear that he stayed all night; and that on the same visit he bought the horse of Gardiner. She lives at her father's, on the farm adjoining that of accused, and was at his house two or three times a week, and saw him nearly every day on his visits to his mother, who was an invalid, and whose attending physician he was; and never saw or heard of Booth, except on that one occasion, before the assassination.

3rd. Fanny Mudd, sister of the accused, living with her father, testifies to the same effect.

4th. Charles Bloyce was at the house of the accused Saturday and Sunday of each week of last year until Christmas Eve (except six weeks in April and May), and never said or heard of Booth's being there.

5th. Betty Washington (colored) lived there from Monday after Christmas until now, and never saw or heard of Booth there before assassination.

6th. Thomas Davis lived there from 9th of January last. Same as above.

Nor is there any evidence whatever of Booth's having stayed with the accused on the visit when the horse was bought of Gardiner, or at any other time, except that of Col. Wells, who says, that after Mudd's arrest, "he said, in answer to another question, that he met Booth sometime in November. I think he said he was introduced by Mr. Thompson, a son-in-law of Dr. Queen, to Booth. I think he said the introduction took place at the chapel or church or Sunday morning; that, after the introduction had passed between them, Thompson said, Booth wants to buy farming lands; and they had some little conversation on the subject of lands, and then Booth asked the question, whether there were any desirable horses that could be bought in that neighborhood cheaply; that he mentioned the name of a neighbor of his who had some horses that were good travelers; and that he remained with him that night, I think, and the next morning purchased one of those horses. Now, it will be recollected that Thompson says Booth stayed at Dr. Queen's on that visit Saturday night and Sunday night, and Thomas L. Gardiner says the horse was bought Monday morning. So that, if Col. Wells is correct in recollecting what Mudd said, then Thompson must be wrong.

It is more probable that Thompson is right, as to Booth's having spent Sunday night at Queen's. Thompson's testimony is strengthened, too, by that of Mary Mudd, Fanny Mudd, and Charles Bloyce, who would, in all probability, have heard the fact of Booth spending Sunday night at the house of the accused, had he done so; but they did not hear it.

It is here to be observed, that though the accused was not permitted to show, by Booth's declarations here, that he was contemplating and negotiating purchases of lands in Charles county, yet evidence was admitted as to his declarations made there to that effect. Dr. Bowman, of Bryantown, says that Booth negotiated with him, on one of these visits, for the purchase of his farm, and also talked of buying horses. And a few days after witness had negotiated with Booth for the sale of his farm, he met Dr. Mudd, and spoke of the negotiation with Booth, and Mudd said, "Why that fellow promised to buy my land." It is also shown by Dr. Blanford, Dr. Bowman, M. P. Gardiner, and Dyer, that Mudd, for a year past, wanted to sell his land, and quit farming.

This, then, is all that is shown of any meeting between Mudd and Booth in the country before the assassination—a casual introduction at church on Sunday in November—Booth going next morning to Mudd's, talking of buying his farm, and riding with him a quarter of a mile to a neighbor's to buy a horse. They went off sliding together toward Mudd's and Bryantown, where the horse was delivered to Booth next morning.

We will now turn to consider the evidence as to the accuser's acquaintance with John H. Surratt. If he knew Surratt at all, the fact is not shown by, nor inferable from, the evidence. Miss Surratt was educated at Bryantown, before the war, and her family lived at Surrattsville, and kept the hotel there (which is on the road from Dr. Mudd's house to Washington), until they removed, in October last, to a house on H Street, in this city, where they have since resided. (Miss Surratt, Holahan, Weiehmann). Dr. Mudd probably had met Surratt at the hotel at Surrattsville, or, before the war, at Bryantown, while his sister was at school; but it is not shown by credible testimony that he knew him at all. Let us examine the evidence on this point.

1st. Mary Simms, formerly Dr. Mudd's slave, says that a man whom Dr. and Mrs. Mudd called Surratt was at Mudd's house from almost every Saturday night until Monday night through the latter part of the winter, and through the spring and summer of last year until apples and peaches were ripe, when she saw him no more; and that on the last of November she left Dr. Mudd's house. That he never slept in the house, but took dinner there six or seven times. That Andrew Gwynn, Benett Gwynn, Capt. Perry, Lieut. Perry, and Capt White, of Tennessee, slept with Surratt near the spring, on bed-clothes furnished from Dr. Mudd's house, and that they were supplied by witness and by Dr. Mudd with victuals from the house. That William Mudd, a neighbor, and Rachel Spencer, and Albin Brooke, members of Mudd's household, used to see Surratt there then. She says that the lieutenants and officers had epaulettes on their shoulders, gray breeches with yellow stripes, coat of same color and trimming. Their horses were kept in Dr. Mudd's stable, by Milo Simms.

2nd. Milo Simms, brother of Mary, fourteen years old, formerly slave of Dr. Mudd, left there Friday before last Christmas. Saw two or three men there last summer, who slept at the spring near Dr. Mudd's house. Bedding taken from the house; meals carried by Mary Simms, generally, though they sometimes ate in the house, and they all slept at the spring, except one called John Surratt, who slept once in the house. Don't say how long they stayed. It was in "planting tobacco time." He attended their horses in Dr. Mudd's stable.

3rd. Rachel Spencer, slave of Dr. Mudd and cook at his house, left him early in January 1865; saw five or six men around Dr. Mudd's house last summer; slept in the pines near the house, and were furnished with meals from it. Were dressed in black and blue. Were there only a week, and never saw them there before or since. She heard no names of the men except Andrew Gwynn and Watt Bowie. That Albin Brooke lived at Dr. Mudd's then, and was with these men occasionally.

4th. Elzee Eglent, formerly Dr. Mudd's slave, left him 20th August 1863; saw a party sleeping in the pines, by the spring, near the house, summer before last. Knew Andrew Gwynn, and he was one of them; did not recollect any other names. Mary Simms carried them meals, and Milo Simms attended the horses in Dr. Mudd's stable. Some wore gray clothes with brass buttons, but without other marks—some black clothes. Did not say how many there were, nor how long they stayed.

5th. Melvina Washington, formerly Dr. Mudd's slave, left him October 1863; saw party sleeping in the pines near the house summer before last; victuals furnished from the house. Party stayed there about a week and then left. Some were dressed in gray, and some in short jackets with little peaks behind, with black buttons. She saw them seven or eight times during one week, and then they all left, and she never saw any of them at any other time except during that week. That Andrew Gwynn's name was the only one she heard; that Mary Simms used to tell her, when the men were there, the names of others, but she had forgotten them.

• • •

That these five witnesses all refer to the same party of men and the same year is certain, from the fact that Elzee Eglen says that Mary Simms carried the party he describes as being there in the summer of their victuals, and that Milo Simms kept their horses in the stable, and Melvina, Washington says Mary Simms used to tell her the names of the party which she describes as being there in 1863; and also from the fact that all of them, except Milo Simms, named Andrew Gwynn as being one of the party. I will not waste the time of the Court in pointing out to it in detail the discrepancies in their evidence apparent from the foregoing synopsis of their testimony; and therefore, only calling its attention to the fact that all of these witnesses were living with Dr. Mudd during and after the year 1861 (Dyer), down to the several dates given above, when they respectively left, I will proceed to show from the evidence what and when the occurrences really were about which they have testified.

1st. Ben. Gwynn (named by Mary Simms as one of the party) says:

Q. Will you state whether during last summer, in company with Captain White, from Tennessee, Captain Perry, Lieut. Perry, Andrew Gwynn, and George Gwynn, or either of them, having seen Surratt, especially, says he knows you were about Dr. Samuel

A. Mudd's house for several days? I was not. I do not know any of the parties named, and I never heard of them, except Andrew Gwynn and George Gwynn.

Q. Were you with your brothers, Andrew Gwynn, and George Gwynn, about Dr. Mudd's house last year?

A. No, sir. I have not been in Dr. Mudd's house since about

the 1st of November 1861. I have not been on his place, or nearer his place than church, since about the 6th of November 1861.

Q. Where did you and the party who were with you near Dr. Mudd's sleep?
A. We slept in the pines near the spring.

Q. How long were you there?
A. Four or five days. I left my neighborhood, and went down there and stayed around in the neighborhood part of the time at his place, and part of the time elsewhere. He fed us there and gave us something to eat, and had some bed-clothing brought but of the house. That was all.

He further said that the party was composed of his brother, Andrew Gwynn, and Jerry Dyer, who, on the breaking out of the war, were, like all the people of that section panic-stricken, and apprehending arrest; that, he came up to Washington on the 10th of November, gave himself up, found there were no charges against him, took the oath, and went back home. That John H. Surratt, when this party were there, was at college, and witness never saw him in Charles county then or since. That his brother, Andrew Gwynn, went South in the fall of 1861, and was never, to his knowledge, back in that county but once since, and that was last winter sometime. He corrected his statement as to when the party were there, and fixed it in August 1861.

2nd. Jerry Dyer, brother-in-law of the accused, testifies to the same as Ben. Gwynn. Says he and the two Gwynns were members of companies organized by authority of Governor Hicks for home protection in 1860; were present on parade in

Washington at the inauguration of a statue, on the 22nd of February 1860. When the war broke out the companies were disbanded; many of the members going South, and many of those who remained in Charles county scattering about from rumors of arrests; that there was a general panic in the county then, and almost everybody was leaving home and "dodging about;" that while he and the two Gwynns slept in the pines these three or four days, Mary Simms carried them victuals from the house, and Milo Simms attended to the horses in Mudd's stables; that they were dressed in citizens' clothing; that Andrew Gwynn went South in the fall of 1861; witness never heard of his being back since; that Surratt was not there then, nor, so far as he knows, since.

3rd. William Mudd, a near neighbor of the accused, named by Mary Simms as having seen the party she describes, says he saw Benjamin Gwynn there in 1861, but saw none of the others, then or since.

4th. Albin Brooke, referred to by Mary Simms and Rachel Spencer as having seen the party they describe (and by Mary Simms as having seen Surratt especially), says he knows Surratt, having met him in another county once, and knew Benjamin Gwynn and Andrew Gwynn, but that he never saw Surratt with any of the men named by Mary Simms at Dr. Mudd's, nor heard of his having ever been there; never heard of Andrew Gwynn being back from Virginia since 1861. That he lived at Dr. Mudd's from the 1st of January to between the 1st and the 15th of September of last year, and was at the stable morning, noon, and night, each day, and was about the spring daily; while there, never saw any strangers' horses in the stable, nor any signs about the spring of persons sleeping there; but that, while living near Dr. Mudd's, in the summer of 1861, he knew of Ben, and Andrew Gwynn and Dyer sleeping in the pines there.

5th. Mrs. Mary Jane Simms boarded, or was a guest, at Dr. Mudd's all last year, except through March; knew Andrew, Ben. and George Gwynn, and George Surratt. Never saw or heard of any of them there, nor of any of them sleeping in the pines.

6th. Frank Washington (colored) lived at Dr. Mudd's all last year; knew Andrew Gwynn by sight; never saw or heard of him or Surratt (of whom a, photograph was shown him) or of any of the men named by Mary Simms, being there, or of any men being there in uniform; at the stable three times daily, and ten at the spring, and saw no strange horses in the stable; saw no signs of men sleeping about the spring,

7th. Baptist Washington, carpenter, at work there putting up kitchen, etc., from February till Christmas last year, except the month of August; same as above, except as to knowledge of Andrew Gwynn. (Photograph of Surratt shown him).

8th. Charles Boyce (colored), at Dr. Mudd's through every Saturday and Sunday all last year, except from 10th April to 20th May; same as Frank Washington, except as to knowing Andrew Gwynn.

9th. Julia Ann Bloyce (colored cook), there from early in July to 23rd December, 1864; same, substantially, as Frank Washington; knew Ben. and Andrew Gwynn. (Photograph of Surratt shown witness.)

10th. Emily Mudd and Fanny Mudd live on adjoining farm to Dr. Mudd, at his father's; at his house almost daily for years;

knew of the party in the pines in 1861, composed of Dyer and the two Gwynns; knew Andrew Gwynn well; never heard of his being back from Virginia since 1861, nor of Surratt ever being at Dr. Mudd's, nor of any of the others named by Mary Simms, except the Gwynns, in 1861.

11th. Henry L. Mudd, Jr., brother of the accused, living at his father's; same as above as to Surratt.

None of the live witnesses, whose testimony has been shown false in all essential parts by the evidence of the twelve witnesses for defense, referred to above said that Surratt was one of the party sleeping in the pines, except Mary and Milo Simms. These two witnesses are shown to have established reputations as liars, by the evidence of Charles Bloyce, Julia Ann Bloyce, and Frank, Baptist and Betty Washington. So all that testimony for the prosecution, of the "intelligent contrabands," who darkened the counsels of the court in this case, is cleared away. The only part of it at all admissible under the rules of evidence, or entitled to the consideration of the Court, was that showing Surratt was intimate with Mudd, and either being there, or the name of either mentioned in the family.

Another witness, who testifies to implicate Mudd as an associate of Surratt, is William A. Evans, who said he saw Mudd some time last winter enter a house on H Street, just as Judson Jarboe, of Prince George's county, was going out of it; and that Jarboe was then shaking hands with a young lady, whom witness took to be a daughter of Mrs. Surratt, from her striking likeness to her mother, having known or seen all the family; and that he stopped a policeman on the street, and asked whose house it was, and he said, "Mrs. Surratt's;" and that drove up to the pavement, and asked also a lady who lived near by and she said the same. He said this house was between

Eighth and Ninth, or Ninth and Tenth—he was not perfectly certain as to the streets, but was certain it was between the Patent Office and the President's. Through an hour's cross-examination, he fought by equivocation, or pleading defect of memory, against fixing any circumstance by which I could learn, directly or indirectly, the day or the month when it occurred, and, finally, he could only say it was "sometime last winter." Although his attention had been so strongly attracted to the house, he first said it was on one side of the street and then on the other; and could not tell whether it had any porch or any portico, nor describe its color, nor whether it had a yard in front, nor whether it was near the center of the square, nor describe a single house on either side of the same square. He said he knew Dr. Samuel Mudd, having met him first at Bryantown church, in December 1850.

Every material thing he did say, which was susceptible of being shown false, has been shown.

1st. Mrs. Surratt's house is not between the Patent Office and the President's, but next the corner of Sixth. (Weichmann, Holahan, Miss Surratt.)

2nd. Miss Surratt, an only daughter, says she never saw or heard of Samuel Mudd being at her mother's house, nor heard his name mentioned in the family, and never met Judson Jarboe there or elsewhere before the assassination,

3rd. Miss Fitzpatrick, who boarded at Mrs. Surratt's from the 6th of October last to the assassination, and Holahan, who was there from the first week of February last, never saw either Mudd or Jarboe there, or heard of either being there, or the name of either mentioned in the family.

4th. Weichmann who boarded there through last winter, never heard of Mudd being at the house.

5th. Judson Jarboe says he never was at Mrs. Surratt's house, or met Dr. Mudd or Miss Surratt in Washington before the assassination.

6th. Mary Mudd says Samuel Mudd was at Frederick College, at Fredericktown, Maryland, in December 1850, and was not at home during the collegiate year, beginning in September of that year; and Rev Dr. Stonestreet, who was president of that college until December of that year, testifies the accused was then entered as a student there, and could not by the rules of the college have gone home.

This witness, Evans, boasted often to the Court that he was a minister of the Gospel, and reluctantly admitted, on cross-examination, that he was also one of the secret police. In his reckless zeal as a detective, he forgot the ninth commandment, and bore false witness against his neighbor. It is to be hoped his testimony that he is a minister of the Gospel is as false as his material evidence. I feel bound in candor to admit, however, that his conduct on the stand gave an air of plausibility to one of his material statements—that for a month past he has "been on the verge of insanity."

I have now presented and considered all the testimony going to show that Mudd ever met Surratt at all, and all that he ever met Booth, before the assassination, and after the first visit Booth made to Charles county—except the testimony of Weichmann, which I will now consider.

That witness says that about the middle of January last, he and Surratt were walking down Seventh street one night, and passed Booth and Mudd walking up the street, and just after they had passed, Mudd called, "Surratt, Surratt." Surratt turned and recognized Mudd as an old acquaintance, and introduced Mudd to witness, and then Mudd introduced Booth to witness and Surratt. That soon after the introduction, Booth invited them all to his room at the National Hotel where wine and cigars were ordered. That Dr. Mudd, after the wines and cigars came, called Booth into the passage, and they stayed there five to eight minutes, and then both came and called Surratt out, and all three stayed thereabout as long as Mudd and Surratt had stayed, both interviews together making about ten to twenty minutes. On returning to the room, Dr. Mudd seated himself by witness, and apologized for their private conversation, saying, "that Booth and he had some private business—that Booth wished to purchase his farm." And that, subsequently, Booth also apologized to him, giving the same reason for the private conversation. Booth at one time took out the back of an envelope, and made marks on it with a pencil. "I should not consider it writing, but more in the direction of roads or lines." The three were at the time seated round a center table in the middle of the room. "The room was very large—half the size of this "courtroom." He was standing, when this was done, within eight feet of them, and Booth was talking in a low tone, and Surratt and Mudd looking on the paper, but witness heard no word of the conversation. About twenty minutes after the second return from the passage, and after a good deal of general conversation, they all walked round to the Pennsylvania House, where the accused sat with witness on a lounge, and talked about the war, "expressed the opinion that the war would soon be over, and talked like a Union man." Soon after getting there, Booth bid the accused good night, and after Booth left, witness and Surratt followed, at about half-past ten o'clock.

It will be observed that the only men spoken of by this witness as having seen the accused on this occasion are Booth, who is dead, and Surratt, who is a fugitive from the country. So there is no one who can be called to confirm or confute his statements, as to the fact of these men being together, or as to the character of the interview. But there was one fact about which he said he could not be mistaken, and by means of which his evidence against Mudd is utterly overthrown. That is, he alleges the meeting was about the middle of January, and fixes the time with certainty by three distinct circumstances:

1st. He made a visit to Baltimore about the middle of January, and near the date of this meeting.

2nd. He had, before the meeting, got a letter, which he received on the 16th of January.

3rd. It was after the Congressional holidays, and Congress had resumed its session. He recollects this fact of itself, and is confirmed in his recollection by the fact that Booth's room was one a member of Congress had occupied before the holidays, and which was given Booth, as he learned, until the member, who had been delayed beyond the time of the reassembling of Congress, should return. Booth told him this.

In refutation of this evidence, we have proved, beyond all controversy, that Dr. Mudd was not in Washington from the 23rd of December to the 23rd of March.

On the 23rd of December he came to Washington with J. T. Mudd, who says they left their horses at the Navy Yard, and went into the city at dark, on the streetcars, and registered at the Pennsylvania House. They then went out and got supper at a restaurant, and then went to the Metropolitan Hotel and stayed there together a quarter of an hour, and then to the National, where witness met a friend, and became separated in the crowd from the accused. Witness strolled out and went back to the Pennsylvania House, to which accused returned in a few minutes after he got there. He saw and heard no one with the accused, though there might have been persons with him in the front part of the room (which was separated from where witness sat by open folding doors), without witness seeing them. Witness and accused then went to bed; were together all next day; were about the market together, and at the store making purchases; were not at the National Hotel, and left the city about o'clock in the afternoon of the 24th, and returned home together. Witness never saw Booth, except on his visit to Bryantown in November. We have shown by the evidence of Lucas, Montgomery, Julia Bloyce, and Jerry Mudd, that accused came here on that visit on a sufficient and legitimate business errand—to purchase a cooking stove and other articles which he bought here then.

On the 23rd of March, Lewellyn Gardiner said accused again came to Washington with him to attend a sale of condemned horses but that the sale did not occur at that time. They got to Washington at four or five P.M., left their horses at Martin's, beyond the Navy Yard, and went about looking at some wagons for sale, and went then to the Island to the house of Henry Clark, where they took tea. They spent the evening at Dr. Allen's playing whist; slept together that night at Clark and after breakfast next morning went through the Capitol, looking at the paintings in the Rotunda, and returned to Martin's at dinner and after dinner left and returned home. Accused was not separated from or out of sight of witness five minutes during the whole visit and did not go to any of the hotels or to the post-office, or see or inquire for Booth. W Allen, Clark, Martin, Thomas Davis, Matt Mudd, Henry Mudd and Betty Washington confirm witness as to the objects or incidents of the visit.

On the 11th of April, three days before the assassination, while Booth, as appears by the hotel register, was at the National in this city, accused came to Giesboro to attend the sale of Government horses, which he and Lewellyn Gardiner had come on the 23rd of March to attend. Though in sight of Washington, he did not come into the city, but took dinner at Martin's, and after dinner left and returned home, on this visit he stayed all night at Blanford's, twelve miles from the city, coming up, but not returning. (Lewellyn Gardiner, Henry L. Mudd, Dr. Blanford, Martin, Davis, Betty Washington, Mary Mudd.)

On the 26th of January, he went with his wife to the house of his neighbor, George H. Gardiner, to a party, and stayed till daylight. (Betty Washington, Thomas Davis, Mary Mudd.) Except for one night on the occasion of each of those four visits—two to Washington, one to Giesboro, and one to an admirer's—the accused was not absent from home a night from the 23rd of December until his arrest. (Betty Washington, Thomas Davis, Henry L. Mudd, Mary Mudd, Frank Washington.)

After the evidence for the defense above referred to had been introduced, refuting and completely overwhelming Weichmann's testimony and all inferences as to Dr. Mudd's complicity with Booth, which might be drawn from it, a new accuser was introduced against him on the same point, in the person of Marcus P. Norton who said that at half-past 10 o'clock on the morning of the 3rd of March, as he was preparing his papers to go to the Supreme Court to argue a motion in a patent case there pending, (which motion the record of the Court shows he did argue on that day), a stranger abruptly entered his room and as abruptly retired, saying he was looking for Mr. Booth's room; and though witness never saw Dr. Mudd before or since, until the day of his testifying, he says that stranger is the prisoner at the bar. He could not tell any article of the stranger's clothing except a black hat. Wm. A. Evans, a part of whose evidence we have hereinbefore considered, comes to the support of Norton by saying that early on the morning of either the 1st, or 2nd, or 3rd of March (witness is certain it was one of those three days), Dr. Mudd passed witness on the road from Bryantown to Washington, a few miles from the city, driving a two-horse rockaway, and there was a man in with him, but whether a black or a white man witness could not recollect. Fortunately for the accused, the 1st day of March was Ash Wednesday—the first day of Lent—a religious holiday of note and observance in the community of Catholics among whom he lived. Fortunately for him, too, his sister Mary was taken ill on that day, and required his medical attendance (at her father's house, on the farm adjoining his own, thirty miles from Washington) each day, from the 2nd to the 7th of March, inclusive. By the aid of these two circumstances we have been able to show, by Thomas Davis, that accused was at home at work on the 28th of February the day before Ash Wednesday; by Dr. Blanford, Frank Washington and Betty Washington, that he was there at work at home on the 1st of March; by Mary, Fanny, Emily and Henry I, Mudd, Betty and Frank Washington and Thomas Davis, that he was there on the 2nd, 3rd, 4th, and 5th of March, at various hours of each day. Within two hours of the time when Norton says he saw the accused enter the room at the National (half past 10 A.M., 3rd of March), Mary, Emily; Fanny and Henry L. Mudd, Frank and Betty Washington, Thomas and John Davis, all testify most emphatically to having seen him at his house, on his farm, or at his father's house adjacent to his own—six hours' ride from Washington! We have shown, too, by Mary Mudd, that the accused has always worn a lead-colored hat whenever she has seen him this year, and that she has seen him almost daily; and by Henry Mudd, Dr. Blanford and Mary Mudd, that neither he nor his father owns a rockaway. Now, Norton either saw the accused enter his room on the morning of the 3rd of March, or not at all, for his evidence, clinched as to the date by of record of the Supreme Court, excludes the supposition that he could have been mistaken as to the day. Nor can these eight witnesses for the defense be mistaken as to the day, for the incidents by which they recollect Mudd's presence at the house, fix the time in their memories exactly. With all this evidence before the Court, it cannot hesitate to hold the alibi established beyond all cavil.

The only other item of evidence as to anything done or said by Dr. Mudd, or by anybody, before the assassination, tending in the least to show him implicated in the conspiracy, is the evidence of Daniel J. Thomas, who says that several weeks before the assassination he met Mudd at the house of his neighbor, Downing, and there, in the course of conversation, Mudd said (laughingly) that "Lincoln and his whole Cabinet, and every Union man in the State of Maryland, would be killed within six weeks." Witness said he wrote to Col. John C. Holland, provost marshal of that district, at Ellicott's Mills, before the assassination, advising him of Mudd's statement, But Col. Holland says he got a letter from witness about that time, and there was not a word of the statement in it, nor a reference to the accused, nor to any statement by anybody about killing anybody. Thomas says he told his brother, Dr. Thomas, of the declaration before the President was killed, but his brother says emphatically he did not tell him until after Mudd's arrest—the boot found at Mudd's house having been named in the same conversation. Thomas says he told Mr. Downing about it before the assassination, but Downing says emphatically he did not tell him a word about it at any time. Downing also says that he himself was present every moment of the time Mudd and Thomas were together at his house, and heard every word said by either of them, and Mudd did not make that statement, nor refer to the President, or the Cabinet, or the Union men of Maryland, at all, nor say a word about anybody being killed. He says, however, Mudd, when Thomas was bragging and lying about being a provost marshal, did tell him, "he was a jack," which insult was doubtless an incentive to the invention of the calumny. But it was not the only incentive. Thomas knew that if that lie could be palmed off on the Judge Advocate and the Court for truth, it might lead to Mudd's arrest and conviction as one of the conspirators. He had, on Tuesday, before Mudd's arrest, and before this lie was coined and circulated, been posting handbills, containing the order of the War Department offering liberal rewards for any information leading to the arrest of Booth's accomplices, and he then doubtless conceived the idea of at once getting reward in money from the Government for his information, and revenge on Mudd for his insult in Downing's house.

That he gave that evidence corruptly is shown by Wm. Watson, John R. Richardson and Benjamin Naylor, who say that Thomas, after testifying against Mudd, went to see them, and said that "*if Dr. Mudd was convicted upon his testimony, he would then have given conclusive evidence that he gave the information that led to the defection of the conspirator.*" He then asked Mr. *Benjamin J. Naylor if he did not mention to him and Gibbons, before the killing of the President, the language that Dr. Mudd had used. Mr. Naylor said that he had never done it before or after!*" "*He said his portion of the reward ought to be $10,000—and asked me (Watson) if I would not, as the best loyal man in Prince George's county, give him a certificate of how much he ought to be entitled to.*"

The testimony of Richards, and of Eli J. Watson, coupled with Thomas' testimony in denial of these statements, fill the record of infamy of this false witness.

To accumulate evidence that Thomas' statement is utterly unreliable, the defense brought over twenty of his neighbors, who testified that he could not be believed on oath—among whom were Naylor, Roby, Richards, Orme, Joseph Waters, John Waters, J. F. Watson, Eli Watson, Smith, Baden, Dickens, Hawkins, Monroe, and others, of undisputed loyalty, nearly all of whom had known him from boyhood. His brother, Dr. Thomas, testifies that he is at times deranged; and Dr. George Mudd says that he is mentally and morally insane. And, although Thomas' evidence was the most important in the case against Dr. Mudd, the Judge Advocate has not seriously attempted to sustain him—has not tried to show that he ever told or hinted at this story to anybody before the assassination—and has not asked one of the scores of witnesses for the prosecution in attendance from Thomas' neighborhood question as to his reputation for veracity except Wm. Watson, who said it was decidedly bad. A feeble attempt was made to sustain him, by endeavoring to show that he was a zealous supporter of the Administration, and that, therefore, the general voice of his community was against him. But we showed that he was a rebel at the beginning of the war, and an opponent of the Administration at the last election—and then the Judge Advocate dropped him.

This is all the evidence of every act or word done or said by anybody, prior to the assassination, tending in the remotest degree to connect Mudd with the conspiracy. It consists, in large part, of the testimony of the five negroes, as to the Confederate officers frequenting Mudd's house last year and the year before—two of them, Mudd and Mary Simms, as to Surrat's visiting his house last year—of Evans, as to Mudd's going to Surratt's house last winter—of Evans and Norton, as to Mudd's being here on the 3rd of March—of Weichmann, as to the interview between Mudd, Booth and Surratt, about the middle of January, and of Thomas, as to Mudd's prediction of the assassination in March. I venture to say that rarely in the annals of criminal trials has the life of an accused been assailed by such an array of false testimony as is exhibited in the evidence of these nine witnesses—and rarely has it been the good fortune of an innocent man, arraigned and on trial for his life, to so confute and overwhelm his accusers. I feel it would be a waste of time, and an imputation on the intelligence of the Court to delay it with fuller discussion of the evidence of these witnesses, and feel sure it will cast their testimony from its deliberations, or recollect it only to reflect how foully and mistakenly the accused has been assailed.

Having now discussed all the evidence adduced that calls for discussion, or may by possibility be relied on as showing Mudd's acquaintance with Booth, or connection with the conspiracy, and having, I think, shown that there is no reliable evidence that he ever met Booth before the assassination but once on Sunday, and once the day following, in November last, I will proceed to a consideration of the testimony relied on to show that he knowingly aided the escape of the assassin.

First. Why did Booth go to Dr. Mudd's and stop there from daybreak till near sundown on his flight? I answer, because he had a broken leg, and needed a physician to set it. And as to the length of the stay, the wonder is he was able to ride off on horseback with his broken and swollen limb at all, not that he took twelve hours rest. The Court will observe from the map in evidence, that Booth, taking Surrattsville in his route to Pope's creek, opposite Matthias Point, where he crossed the Potomac (Capt. Doherty traveled at least eight or ten miles out of his way to go, after leaving Surrattsville, by Dr. Mudd's.

(See Dyer's testimony.) Would he have gone that far out of his route to the Potomac crossing if he had not broken his leg? Or was it part of his plan to break it? Obviously, be could not in advance have planned to escape by crossing the Patuxent, nor to evade his pursuers by lying concealed in Charles county, within six hours ride of Washington. He must, as a sane man, have contemplated and planned escape across the Potomac into Virginia, and thence South or abroad; and it could never have been part either of the plan of abduction, or of that of assassination, to go the circuitous route to a crossing of the Potomac by Bryantown or Dr. Mudd's. So that the fact of Booth going to the house of the accused and stopping to get his leg set and to rest, does not necessarily lead to any conclusion unfavorable to the accused.

Booth got there, with Herold, about daybreak (Frank Washington). He usually wore a mustache (see photograph), but he then wore heavy whiskers, and had his face muffled in a shawl, so as to disguise him. The disguise was kept up all day. (Col. Wells.) He was taken to a lounge in the hall, and then to a front room upstairs. where the broken bone was set, where a fee of $25 was paid for the service, and where, it is probable, he slept most of the day. They represented that the bone had been broken by a fall of the horse; that they had come from Bryantown, and were going to Parson Wilmer's. After breakfast accused went to his field to work. Herold, whom Mudd had never met (Colonel Wells), came down to breakfast and dinner with the family, and after dinner he and Mudd went off together to the house of Mudd's father to get a family carriage to take the wounded man to the house of Parson Wilmer, five miles off, at Piney Chapel. (Lovett Wells.) Now, can any man suppose for a moment that Mudd, at this time, had the slightest suspicion or intimation of the awful tragedy of the night before? Could he, knowing or suspecting the crime or the criminal, have thus recklessly given himself up to arrest and trial, by publicly aiding the escape of the assassin? Could he have been ready to expose his old father to suspicion by thus borrowing his carriage, which would have been noticed by every man, woman and child on the road, to carry off the assassin? Impossible! I need nothing more of the Court than its consideration of this fact, to clear the accused of all suspicion of having, up to that time, known or suspected that a crime had been committed by the crippled stranger, whom he was thus openly and kindly seeking to aid.

But the carriage could not be got, and Mudd and Herold rode off toward Bryantown to get one there. Col. Wells thinks the accused told him that Herold turned back when getting one and a half miles from the elder Mudd's house, saying he could take his friend off on horseback. Betty Briscoe and Eleanor Bloyce, however, say they saw a man riding toward Bryantown with the accused, who turned back at the bridge at the edge of the town.

Mudd made some purchases of calico and other articles, and heard of the assassination. (Bean.) It was not generally known then among the citizens who was the assassin. (Bean, Roby, Trotter, B. W. Gardiner, M. L. McPherson, John McPherson.) In fact it was not generally known with certainty at the theater, or in Washington, Friday night, whether Booth was the murderer. (Gobright.) In Bryantown it was commonly understood that Boyle, a noted desperado of that region, who assassinated Capt. Watkins last fall, was one of the assassins. (M. L. McPherson, Bean, Trotter, Roby.) It was not known that the murderer had been tracked into that neighborhood. (Bean, Dr. Geo. Mudd.) Lieutenant Dana told Dr. Geo. Mudd, Saturday afternoon, that Boyle assassinated Mr. Seward, and Booth the President, but that he thought Booth had not then got out of Washington. Even next day (Sunday) it was reported there that it was Edwin Booth who killed the President.

The accused left Bryantown about four o'clock to return home. Betty Briscoe says the same man who had turned back at the bridge stopped in the edge of a branch, which the road crosses a couple of hundred yards from the bridge, until Mudd returned from the town, and then they rode off together across the branch, "up the road." But Booz says he saw Mudd a couple of hundred yards beyond that crossing leisurely going through the farm Booz lives on, by a near-cut which he usually traveled, alone; and that he would himself have probably noticed the man at the crossing, which was in full view of where he was, had he been waiting there; and would have certainly noticed him had he been with Mudd traveling the main road, when Mudd turned into the cut-off through the farm— but he saw no one but the accused. Susan Alzewart also saw Mudd in the by-road returning home alone, and did not see any man going the main road, which was in full view. I call the attention of the Court to the plate by which the branch and these roads are shown, and to the fact that there is no road turning off from the main road between Booz's place and Bryantown, except the side road by Booz's house. If further refutation of the testimony of Betty Briscoe on this point be required, it is found in the evidence of Primus Johnson, who saw Herold pass the elder Mudd's in the main road, going toward the house of the accused and some time after that, himself caught a horse in the pasture, and rode toward Bryantown, and met and passed Dr. Mudd coming leisurely from Bryantown, alone, at Booz's farm; and that from the time he saw Herold until he met and passed Mudd was full an hour and a half. And in the evidence of John Acton, who was on the roadside, three miles from, Bryantown, when Herold passed, at between three and four o'clock, and who remained there an hour, and Dr. Mudd did toward Bryantown and the time Herold returned alone, was but three-quarters of an hour. From the fact that Herold could not have ridden to the bridge and back in that time (six miles), it seems highly probable that he did not go to the bridge, but turned back about where Colonel Wells thinks Mudd said he did. But however that may be is not important, as it is certain from the evidence of these four witnesses that Herold did not wait at the branch for Mudd's return from Bryantown.

As Mudd rode home, he turned out of his way to see his neighbor, Hardy (who lives half-way between the house of the accused and Bryantown), about some rail timber he had engaged there. The house is not in view of the road, a clump of pines intervening. He told Hardy and Farrell of the news. Hardy says: "He said to me that there was terrible news now, that the President and Mr. Seward and his son had been assassinated the evening before. Something was said in that connection about Boyle (the man who is said to have killed Captain Watkins) assassinating Mr. Seward. I remember that Booth's name was mentioned in the same connection, and I asked him if Booth was the man who had been down there. His reply was that he did not know whether it was that man or one of his brothers; he understood that he had some brothers. That ended the conversation, except that he said it was one of the most terrible calamities that could have befallen the country at this time.

Q. Did you say that it was understood or said that Booth was the assassin of the President?

A. There was some such remark made, but I do not exactly remember the remark.

They both say he seemed heartily sorry for the calamity,

and that he said he had just come from Bryantown, and heard the news there. Hardy says he stayed there only about ten minutes, and left just about sundown. Farrell corroborates Hardy as to the conversation, except that he reports nothing as to Boyle's name being mentioned; but he says the conversation was going on when he joined Hardy and Mudd. He says the house is less than a quarter of a mile off the road, and that accused stayed there about fifteen minutes.

Now, I ask the Court, what is there up to this point to indicate that Mudd knew or had any suspicion that the broken-legged man was implicated in the crime? If there is anything in proof showing that fact, I fail to find it. True, he had met Booth twice in November five months before. Had seen him that dark, cloudy morning, at day-break, faint with fatigue and suffering, muffled in his shawl and disguised in a heavy beard; had ministered to him in the dim light of a candle, whose rays struggled with the dull beams of the opening day; had seen him, perhaps, sleeping in the darkened chamber, his mustache then shaved off, his beard still on, his effort at concealment still maintained. (Wells.) And here let me remind the Court, that, between the time Herold and Mudd went that there is nothing in the evidence showing that Booth spoke a word, but where either of the men are referred to as saying anything, "the smaller man" was the spokesman. Let it be remembered, too, that Booth was an actor, accustomed by years of professional practice to disguise his person, his features, and his tones, so that if Mudd had been an intimate associate, instead of a mere casual acquaintance, it would have been easy for Booth to maintain a disguise even when subjected to close scrutiny under circumstances favorable to recognition. If the Court will also consider with what delicacy a physician and a gentleman would naturally refrain from obtrusive scrutiny of a patient coming to his house under the circumstances, they will appreciate how easy it was for Booth to avoid recognition, and how probable that Mudd had no suspicion who his patient was. Had he recognized Booth before he went to Bryantown, and heard there that name connected with the "terrible calamity," would he have jogged quietly home, stopping to chat with Booz, to look after his rail-timber, to talk of the names of the assassins with his neighbors? Unless the Court start out with the hypothesis of guilt, and substitute unsupported suspicion for proof—which I respect them too highly to fear for a moment they will do—they can not charge him with a recognition of Booth before he returned home from Bryantown.

Hardy says it was about sundown when Mudd left; Farrell says about 6 o'clock. He had two miles to ride home. It must have been sundown when he got home, and the men had just gone. Betty Washington says that three or four minutes after Herold (the last of the two) disappeared toward the swamp, Mudd came through the hall to the kitchen, and was then first seen by her after his return from Bryantown. The other servants had not come from the field when the men started, and we are, therefore, left to that one witness to show that the statement of Simon Gavacan, one of the detectives, who says "he thinks" Mudd said he went with them part of the way, is incorrect. It is inconsistent too with Mudd's statement to Col. Wells on the subject, which is as follows: "The Doctor said that as he came back to the house he saw the person, that he afterward supposed to be Herold, passing to the left of the house, and toward the barn or the stable; that he did not see the other person at all after he left him at the house, which was about one o'clock, I think." This statement, and that of Betty Washington, last above quoted, coincide with, and strengthen each other.

It is true, Dr. Mudd did say to all, who asked him, that he

had shown Herold the way to Parson Wilmer's by the short route, but this was in the morning, soon after the parties reached the house, and before the idea of the carriage appears to have been suggested. This is shown by the statement of Col. Wells, who says that the accused, in the same conversation in which he said that Booth and Herold had just gone from the house as he came up, told him that "Herold, the younger of them, asked him the direct route to Pincy Chapel, Dr. Wilmer's, saying that he was acquainted with Dr. Wilmer." He described the main traveled road, which leads to the right of his house, and was then asked if there was not a shorter or nearer road. He said, "Yes; there is a road across the swamp that is about a mile nearer, I think;" he said it was five miles from his house to Piney Chapel by the direct road and four miles by the marsh, and undertook to give him (as he said) a description by which they could go by the nearer route. He said that the directions were these: "They were to pass down by his barn, inclining to the left and then pass straight forward in a new direction across the marsh, and that, on passing across the marsh, they would come to a hill; keeping over the hill, they would come in sight of the roof of a barn, and, letting down one or two fences, they would reach the direct road."

The accused meant, of course, that this inquiry and explanation occurred before his return to the house from Bryantown, and so Col. Wells understood him, for he so in effect says. The statement of the accused to Dr. George Mudd, the next day after Booth left, is to the same effect. He said: "That these parties stated that they came from Bryantown, and were inquiring the way to the Rev. Dr. Wilmer's," thus putting their inquiry for the route to Parson Wilmer's in direct connection with their early explanation as to whence they came.

I have no doubt that Gavacan, the detective, recollects an inference which he and, perhaps, also his associate detective,

Williams, drew from Dr. Mudd saying that he had shown
Herold the route to Person Wilmer's; that he showed it as Booth
and Herold were leaving. But the inferences of detectives,
under the strong stimulus of prospective rewards, are inferences
generally of guilt; and that these gentlemen were not free from
the weaknesses of their profession, and that they grossly mis-
represented Dr. Mudd in other important statements, will
presently be shown to the satisfaction of the Court.

Now, if Mudd did not know, when he talked with Hardy
about the assassination, and spoke of Booth in connection with
it, that the assassin was at his house—as I think the evidence
shows he did not—then when did he first suspect it? Col. Wells
says his inference was, from something the accused said, that he
suspected the crippled man to be Booth before he left the
premises. The evidence not only shows that when Mudd
returned Booth had gone out of sight, but it also shows what
fact it was that, added to the undue excitement of the strangers,
and to the fact that the crippled man shaved off his moustache,
thoroughly aroused his suspicion. It was the fact, that his wife
said to him, after they left, that, as the crippled man came down
to go, his false whiskers became detached from his face. (Lieut.
Lovett.) When she told him this, and what he said or proposed
to do, was not shown by the prosecution, and, by the rules of
evidence, could not be by the defense. But that was a fact which
could not probably have been communicated to Mudd by his
wife until Booth had gone.

In the evidence adduced as to Mudd's subsequent conduct
and statements, I need only call the attention of the Court to
two points, for in it there is nothing else against. He did not
tell, on Tuesday, that the boot was there, far down in the leg of
which was found, by the officers, "J. Wilkes," written in pale
ink. I answer, the boot was not found by his wife until several
days after the assassin left, and was then found in sweeping

under the bed. (Hardy.) We have every reason to suppose it was not found until after Tuesday, for the accused, on Friday, before a question was asked, or a word communicated to him, told of the boot himself, and had it produced, and said, in presence of his wife, it was found by her after the officers were there before. (Hardy.)

2nd. Of the three detectives who went to the house of accused Tuesday, Williams says: Accused denied throughout that two men had been there; yet he says, on cross-examination, that accused, in the same conversation, pointed out the route the men had taken toward Wilmer's. Gavacan said he at first denied two men had passed there, and then admitted it. Lloyd says he denied it from beginning to end, on Tuesday. But Lieut. Lovett, who went with and in command of these detectives, speaking of this interview on Tuesday, says: "We first asked whether there had been any strangers at his house, and he said there were." The three detectives are manifestly mistaken; either from infirmity of memory, or from some less pardonable cause, they have failed to recollect and truthfully render what Dr. Mudd did say on that subject.

The commentators upon the law of evidence give a caution which it may be well for the Court to observe. They admonish us how easy it is for a corrupt witness to falsify a conversation of a person accused, and as the accused can not be heard, how difficult, if not impossible, contradiction is. How easy for an honest witness to misunderstand, or in repeating what was said, to substitute his own language or inference for the language which was really used, and thus change its whole meaning and import. In no case can the caution be more pertinent than in this. The very frenzy of madness ruled the hour. Reason was swallowed up in patriotic passion, and a feverish and intense excitement prevailed most unfavorable to a calm, correct hearing and faithful repetition of what was said, especially by the suspected. Again, and again, and again accused was catechised by detectives, each of whom was vying with the other as to which should make the most important discoveries, and each making the examination with a preconceived opinion of guilt, and with an eager desire, if not determination, to find in what might be said the proofs of guilt. Again, the witnesses against the accused have testified under the strong stimulus of a promised reward for information leading to arrest and followed by convictions. (See order of Secretary of War.) At any time and in any community, an advertisement of rewards to informers would be likely to be responded to—at a time, and on an occasion like this, it would be a miracle if it failed of effect. In view of these considerations, the Court can not be too vigilant in its scrutiny of the evidence of these detectives, or too circumspect in adjusting the influence to be given to it.

No more effective refutation of this statement, that Mudd denied on Tuesday that two strangers had been at his house, can be given than to ask how came Lieut. Lovett and the detectives at Dr. Mudd's? They did not scent out the track for themselves. They were at Bryantown on Saturday, and were at fault, and had they been let alone, would probably have remained at fault, and not have gone to Dr. Mudd's. By whom and when was the information given which brought them there? The next morning after the startling news of the assassination reached him, the accused went to Dr. George Mudd, a man of spotless integrity and veracity, and of loyalty unswerving through all the perilous and distressing scenes of the border war, and fully informed him of all that had occurred—the arrival of the two strangers, the time and circumstances under which they came, what he had done for them, the suspicions he entertained, when they departed, and what route they had taken; and requested him, on his behalf and in his name, to communicate this information to the military authorities on his return that day to Bryantown. Dr. George Mudd did make the communication as requested, on Monday morning, to Lieut. Dana, and further informed him of Dr. Samuel Mudd's desire to be sent for any further information which it might be in his power to give. In consequence of this, and of this alone, Lieut. Lovett and the detectives did, on Tuesday, go to the house of the accused, accompanied by Dr. George Mudd, who prefaced his introduction by informing the accused that, in accordance with his request, he had brought Lieut. Lovett and the detectives to confer with him in reference to the strangers who had been at his house Saturday. Of these facts there is no doubt or dispute. They stand too prominently upon the record to be ignored or evaded. But for this information the detectives would not have been at the house of the accused at all. They came at his request, and when they came it is absurd and idle to say that he denied, almost in the presence of Dr. George Mudd, who had been his messenger and was then in the house, that the two strangers had been there. On the contrary, the evidence shows he imparted all he knew, and pointed out the route which the strangers took when they left—but which Lieut. Lovett and the detectives did not at once pursue, because they chose to consider his statement un-candid and intended to put them upon a false scent. Indeed, so accurate was the description given by the accused to Lieut. Lovett, Tuesday, of the persons who had been at his house, that the lieutenant says he was satisfied, from Mudd's description, they were Booth and Herold.

It was in great part by reason of Dr. Mudd's having delayed from Saturday night until Sunday noon to send to the authorities at Bryantown information as to the suspected persons who had been at his house, that he was arrested and charged as a conspirator; and yet I assert this record shows he moved more promptly in communicating his information than they did in acting on it. His message was communicated to Lieut. Dana Monday morning. Tuesday, Lieut. Lovett and the detectives came, and that officer got such information from Dr. Mudd as convinced him the suspected persons were Booth and Herold, and yet it was not until Col. Wells came, on Saturday, that an energetic effort was made to find the route of the assassin. On that day, Dr. Mudd himself went with that officer, and followed the tracks on the route indicated beyond the marsh into a piece of plowed ground, where the tracks were lost. But Col. Wells had got the general direction, and it was in consequence of the information sent by the accused to the authorities the day after Booth left his house, that he was tracked to the Potomac.

But the evidence does not show that Dr. Mudd delayed at all in communicating his information, for it does not show when his wife told him of the false whisker of the crippled man. But admit she told him on Saturday evening, as soon as the men left. It was four miles to Bryantown, and his wife may have feared to be left alone that night. Boyle, who haunted that neighborhood, was understood by Dr. Mudd to have been one of the assassins (Hardy), and may not his or his wife's fear of the vengeance of that desperado have prevented him communicating his suspicions direct and in person to the officer at Bryantown? He told Dr. George Mudd next day, when asking him to go to the authorities with the information, to caution them not to let it be publicly known that he had volunteered the statement, lest he might be assassinated in revenge for having done it.

Having thus presented and discussed somewhat in detail the testimony in this case I now ask the indulgence of the Court while I briefly review some of its leading features.

Booth and Mudd met first in November last at church, near Bryantown, casually, and but for a few minutes. Their conversation was in the presence of many others, including men of unquestioned loyalty. Next morning, Booth left Dr. Queen's, rode by Mudd's, talked of buying his farm, got him to show him over to Gardiner's, a quarter of a mile off, where he bought a horse, Mudd manifesting no interest in the purchase. They rode away together toward Mudd's house, and toward Bryantown where Gardiner found Booth next morning at the village hotel. Booth was again at Dr. Queen's in the middle of December. But the evidence shows that he did not go into Mudd's neighborhood, or seek or see him. So far as we dare speak from the evidence—and we should dare speak from nothing else—that is all the intercourse between Mudd and Booth in that neighborhood before the assassination.

What was there in that to attract attention or excite remark toward Mudd more than to Dr. Queen or Mr. Gardiner, or any other gentleman in Charles county, to whom Booth had been introduced, and with whom he had conversed? All that is shown to have passed between them was perfectly natural and harmless, and nothing is to be presumed which was not shown. True, they might have talked of and plotted assassination; but did they? Is there, in the intercourse which had thus far occurred, any incident from which such a deduction could be drawn, or which would justify a suspicion that any such thing was thought of or hinted at? Nor did they ever meet again anywhere before the assassination unless the testimony of Weichmann is to be accepted as true, which, upon this point, at least, is quite unworthy of credence. He swears to having met Dr. Mudd and Booth in the city of Washington, about the middle of January—certainly after the holidays. But it is in proof by many witnesses, who can not be mistaken, have not been impeached, and who unquestionably stated the truth, that Dr. Mudd was from home but one night from the 23rd of December to the 23rd of March, and that night at a party in his own neighborhood. If this be so, and there is no reason to doubt it, then Weichmann's statement can not be true. The mildest thing that can be said of him, as of Norton, is, that he was mistaken in the man. That which was attempted to be shown by this contradicted witness (Weichmann) was, that Dr. Mudd and Booth, who were almost strangers to each other, met Surratt, to whom Booth was unknown, at the National Hotel, and within half an hour after the meeting, plotted the assassination of the President, his Cabinet, the Vice-President, and General Grant—all this in Washington, and in the presence of a man whom one of the supposed conspirators knew to be an employee of the War Department, and had reason to believe was a Government detective! It is monstrous to believe any such thing occurred. It outrages all that we have learned of the philosophy of human nature, all that we know of the motives and principles of human actions. And yet, if Mudd was not then and there inducted into the plot, he never was. He never saw Booth again until after the assassination, and never saw any of the other conspirators at all. Twice, then, and twice only unless the Court shall accept the testimony of Weichmann against the clear proofs of an alibi, and then only three times—he and Booth had met. None of these meetings occurred later than the 15th of January. They are shown to have been accidental and brief. The parties had but little conversation, and portions of that little have been repeated to the Court. So far as it has been disclosed, it was as innocent as the prattle of children and not a word was breathed that can be tortured into criminality—not a word or an act that betokens malign purposes. Against how many scores of loyal persons, even in this community, may stronger evidence be adduced than against Mudd, if the mere fact of meeting and conversing with Booth is to be accepted as evidence of guilt? Booth was a guest at the National Hotel intelligent, agreeable, of attractive manner, with no known blemish on his character as a man or a citizen. He had the entree of the drawing-rooms, and mingled freely with the throngs that assembled there. His society, so far from being shunned, was courted; and the fairest ladies of the land, the daughters of distinguished statesmen and patriots deemed it no disparagement to them to accept his escort and attentions. It is not extravagant to say, that hundreds of true, Union-loving, loyal people in this and in other cities, were on terms of cordial and intimate association with him. And why should they not have been? He was under no suspicion. They did not shun him. Why should Mudd? And why shall what was innocent in them be held as proof of guilt in him? Let it be remembered, in this connection, that Dr. Mudd's house was searched and his papers seized; that Surratt's house was seized and searched; that all the effects of Booth, Atzerodt, Arnold, Herold, Spangler, and Mrs. Surratt, that could be found, were seized and examined; and among them all not a letter, a note, a memorandum, not the scrape of a pen by any person or in any form, has been found implicating Dr. Mudd. Let it further be remembered, that all these persons have been subjected to repeated examinations, under appalling circumstances, by various officials of the Government, eager to catch the faintest intimation of Mudd's complicity, and that not one of them has mentioned or hinted at his name. Let it also be remembered, that anonymous letters have been picked up in railroad cars, found in pigeon-holes at hotels, rescued from the waves, and that the continent has been traversed and the ocean vexed in search of proofs of the conspiracy, its instigators, leaders, and abettors, and that in all this written and oral testimony there is not a word making the remotest allusion to Dr. Mudd. The probabilities are as a thousand to one that he never knew, or heard, or imagined, of a purpose, much less plotted in a conspiracy, either to capture or to assassinate the President. There is not only a failure to show his connection affirmatively, but., if the rules of law be reversed, and guilt be presumed until innocence be shown, then, I say, he has carried his proofs in negation of complicity to a point as near demonstration as it is possible for circumstantial evidence to reach. I once more concede, that (if the Court accept Weichmann's statement) it is possible he may have talked treason and plotted assassination with Booth and Surratt, but it is indefinitely removed from the probable; and neither liberty nor life is to be forfeited upon either probabilities or possibilities. I can not bring myself to fear that this Commission will sanction what, in my judgment, would be so shocking and indefensible a conclusion.

If he and Booth had, at the alleged meeting in January, confederated for the perpetration of one of the most stupendous and startling crimes in the annals of human depravity, who can doubt that frequent meetings and consultations would thereafter have occurred, and that they would have increased in frequency as the time for the consummation of the atrocious plot approached? Yet, though within six hours' ride of each other, they had no Meetings, no consultations, no intercourse, no communication, no concert. He was not here for the purpose of seeing Booth, nor did he see him. He made no inquiry for him,—did not call at his hotel; saw none of his associates; did not speak of him; did not, so far as appears, even think of him. On the 11th of April, only three days before the frightful tragedy was enacted, Mudd was at Geisboro, in sight of Washington. Booth was then at the National Hotel; and if Mudd was leagued with him, that was the time of all others, from the conception to the consummation of the deed, when he would have seen and conferred with him. If Mudd was a conspirator, he knew of Booth's presence here then; yet he did not come to the city—did not inquire for Booth, see him, hold communication with him, learn whether he was in Washington or Boston, Nassau or London. Three days only before the frightful tragedy—three days before the world was astounded by its enactment! Imagine, if you can—if he was a conspirator—what a tumult of thought and emotion must have agitated him then—what doubts and misgivings—what faltering and rallying of resolution—what invocations to "stop up the access and passage to remorse" and then ask your own hearts and judgments if it is natural, or possible, that, at such a moment and under such circumstances, he could quietly have transacted the business that brought him to Geisboro, then turn his back upon Washington, indifferent to the failure or success of the events with which his own life, the happiness of his family, and all that was dear to him on earth, were bound up? If a conspirator, he knew what had been, and what was to be, done. He knew that the hour for the bloody business was at hand, and that everything depended upon the secrecy and success of its execution. Yet he was indifferent. He sought no interview with his supposed confederate—gave them no counsel or assistance—took no precautions for Security gave no signs of agitation or concern—but, in sight of the place and the agents selected for the enactment of the horrible deeds, turned his back upon them all, with an indifference that bordered upon idiocy, quietly trafficked at Geisboro, and returned to the seclusion of his family and farm. You know, gentlemen, that this is impossible. You know that it could not have happened without outraging every law of human nature and human action. You know that at such an hour his soul would have been shaken with the maddest storm and tempest of passion, and that no mere business affair on earth could have seduced his thoughts for a moment from the stage slaughter he had in hand. It would have engrossed all his thoughts; and shaped all his actions. No one can, in the strong light of the evidence, believe he was a conspirator.

I then confidently conclude that Dr. Mudd can not be convicted as a principal in the felony. He did not participate in its commission, and was more than thirty miles distant from the scene when it was committed. He can not be convicted as an accessory before the fact, for the evidence fails to show that he had any knowledge or suspicion of an intention to commit it. If, then, he is to be held responsible at all, it is an accessory after the fact. Does the evidence implicate him in that character? What is an accessory after the fact?

An accessory after the fact is when a person, knowing a felony to have been committed, receives, relieves, comforts, or assists him whom he knows to be the felon. He must know that the felon is guilty to make him an accessory.

Any assistance given to him to hinder his being apprehended, tried, or punished, is sufficient to convict the offender—as lending him a horse to escape his pursuers; but the assistance or support must be given in order to favor an illegal escape. If a man receives, harbors, or otherwise assists to elude justice, one whom he knows to be guilty of a felony, he becomes thereby an accessory after the fact in the felony. Obviously, a man to be an accessory after the fact must be aware of the guilt of his principal; and, therefore, one can not become an accessory by helping to escape a prisoner convicted of felony, unless he has notice of the conviction, or at least of the felony committed. The charge against an accessory consists of two parts: First, of the felonious situation of the principal: and, secondly, of the guilty knowledge and conduct of the accessory. It will thus be seen that knowledge of the crime committed, and of the guilt of the principal who is aided and aid and assistance after acquiring that knowledge, are all necessary to charge one as accessory after the fact.

Now let us apply the facts to the law, and see whether Dr. Mudd falls within the rule. On the morning after the assassination, about daybreak, Booth arrived at his house. He did not find the doctor on watch for him, as a guilty accomplice, expecting his arrival, would have been, but he and all his household were in profound sleep. Booth came with a broken leg, and his companion, Herold, reported that it had happened by the fall of his horse, and that they had come from Bryantown, and were going to Parson Wilmer's. The doctor rose from his bed, assisted Booth into the house, laid him upon a sofa, took him up stairs to a bed, set the fractured bone, sent him a razor to shave himself, permitted him to remain there to sleep and rest, and had a pair of rude crutches improvised for his use. For all this he received the ordinary compensation for services rendered to strangers. He then went to his field to work. After dinner, while the day was still dark, and Booth still resting disguised in his chamber, Mudd left the house with Herold. Even though he had known of the assassination, and that his patient was the assassin, none of these acts of assistance would have made him an accessory after the fact. "If a person supply a felon with food, or other necessaries for his sustenance, or professionally attend him sick or wounded, though he know him to be a felon, these acts will not be sufficient to make a party an accessory after the fact." But he did not know, and had no reason to suspect, that his patient was a fugitive murderer. The most zealous advocate would not venture to assert that the evidence warrants such conclusion; much less will it be assumed by one acting under the solemn responsibilities of judge. Down, then, to the time Mudd left home with Herold, after dinner, the evidence affords no pretext for asserting he was accessory after the fact.

But if he was not then an accessory, he never was. It is shown that Herold turned back on the way to Bryantown, and when Mudd returned, he and Booth had gone. And the evidence does not show that he suspected them of having been guilty of any wrong, until his wife told him, after they had gone, that the whiskers of the crippled man fell off as he came down stairs to go. True, Booth was guilty, and Mudd had shown his companion the route to Wilmer's; which was the only thing done by Mudd, from first to last, that could have implicated him, even had he from the first known the crime and the criminal. But when he did that, he did not know either; for he did not know the crime until he went to Bryantown, not have even the least suspicion of the criminal, until after Booth had gone. I have read you the law—the scienter must be shown. Things not appearing and not existing stand before the law in the same category; and the guilty knowledge not appearing in evidence, in the eye of the law it does not exist. In this case it is not only not shown, but is negated by the evidence. The conclusion most unfavorable to Mudd which the evidence can possibly justify is, that, having had his suspicions thoroughly aroused Saturday night, he delayed until Sunday noon to communicate them to the authorities. "If A knows B hath committed a felony, but doth not discover it, this doth not make A an accessory after the fact." "Merely suffering a felon to escape will not charge the party so doing—such amounting to a mere omission."

Can, then, Dr. Mudd be convicted as a conspirator, or an accessory before or after the fact, in the assassination? If this tribunal is to be governed in its findings by the just and time-honored rules of law, he can not; if by some edict higher than constitutions and laws, I know not what to anticipate or how to defend him. With confidence in the integrity of purpose of the Court and its legal advisers, I now leave to them.

APPENDIX II

JAMES SPEED, OPINION ON THE CONSTITUTIONAL
POWER OF THE MILITARY TO TRY AND EXECUTE THE
ASSASSINS OF THE PRESIDENT,

Washington, July—, 1865.

SIR: You ask me whether the persons charged with the offense of having assassinated the President can be tried before a military tribunal, or must they be tried before a civil court. The President was assassinated at a theater in the city of Washington. At the time of the assassination a civil war was flagrant, the city of Washington was defended by fortifications regularly and constantly manned, the principal police of the city was by Federal soldiers, the public offices and property in the city were all guarded by soldiers, and the President's House and person were, or should have been, under the guard of soldiers. Martial law had been declared in the District of Columbia, but the civil courts were open and held their regular sessions, and transacted business as in times of peace.

Such being the facts, the question is one of great importance—important, because it involves the constitutional guarantees thrown about, the rights of the citizen, and because the security of the army and the government in time of war is involved; important, as it involves a seeming conflict between the laws of peace and of war.

Having given the question propounded the patient and earnest consideration its magnitude and importance require, I will proceed to give the reasons why I am of the opinion that the conspirators not only may but ought to be tried by a military tribunal.

A civil court of the United States is created by a law of Congress, under and according to the Constitution. To the Constitution and the law we must look to ascertain how the court is constituted, the limits of its jurisdiction, and what its mode of procedure. A military tribunal exists under and according to the Constitution in time of war. Congress may prescribe how all such tribunals are to be constituted, what shall be their jurisdiction, and mode of procedure. Should Congress fail to create such tribunals, then, under the Constitution, they must be constituted according to the laws and usages of civilized warfare. They may take cognizance of such offenses as the laws of war permit; they must proceed according to the customary usages of such tribunals in time of war, and inflict such punishments as are sanctioned by the practice of civilized nations in time of war. In time of peace, neither Congress nor the military can create any military tribunals, except such as are made in pursuance of that clause of the Constitution which gives to Congress the power "to make rules for the government of the land and naval forces." I do not think that Congress can, in time of war or peace, under this clause of the Constitution, create military tribunals for the adjudication of offenses committed by persons not engaged in, or belonging to, such forces. This is a proposition too plain for argument. But it does not follow that because such military tribunals can not be created by Congress under this clause, that they can not be created at all. Is there no other power conferred by the Constitution upon Congress or the military, under which such tribunals may be created in time of war?

That the law of nations constitutes a part of the laws of the land, must be admitted. The laws of nations are expressly made laws of the land by the Constitution, when it says that "Congress shall have power to define and punish piracies and felonies committed on the high seas and offenses against the laws of nations." To define is to give the limits or precise meaning of a word or thing in being; to make, it is to call into being. Congress has the power to define, not to make, the laws of nations; but Congress has the power to make rules for the government of the army and navy. From the very face of the Constitution, then, it is evident that the laws of nations do constitute a part of the laws of the land. But very soon after the organization of the Federal Government, Mr. Randolph, then Attorney General, said: "The law of nations, although not specifically adopted by the Constitution, is essentially a part of the law of the land. Its obligation commences and runs with the existence of a nation, subject to modification on some points of indifference." The framers of the Constitution knew that a nation could not maintain an honorable place among the nations of the world that does not regard the great and essential principles of the law of nations as a part of the law of the land. Hence Congress may define those laws, but can not abrogate them, or as Mr. Randolph says, may "modify on some points of indifference."

That the laws of nations constitute a part of the laws of the land is established from the face of the Constitution, upon principle and by authority. But the laws of war constitute much the greater part of the law of nations. Like the other laws of nations, they exist and are of binding force upon the departments and citizens of the Government, though not defined by any law of Congress. No one that has ever glanced at the many treatises that have been published in different ages of the world by great, good and learned men, can fail to know that the laws of war constitute a part of the law of nations, and that those laws have been prescribed with tolerable accuracy.

Congress can declare war. When war is declared, it must be, under the Constitution, carried on according to the known laws and usages of war among civilized nations. Under the power to define those laws, Congress can not abrogate them or authorize their infraction. The Constitution does not permit this Government to prosecute a war as an uncivilized and barbarous people.

As war is required by the frame-work of our government to be prosecuted according to the known usages of war among the civilized nations of the earth, it is important to understand what are the obligations, duties, and responsibilities imposed by war upon the military. Congress, not having defined, as under the Constitution it might have done, the laws of war, we must look to the usage of nations to ascertain the powers conferred in war, on whom the exercise of such powers devolve, over whom, and to what extent to those powers reach, and in how far the citizen and the soldier are bound by the legitimate use thereof.

The power conferred by war is, of course, adequate to the end to be accomplished, and not greater than what is necessary to be accomplished. The law of war, like every other code of laws, declares what shall not be done, and does not say what may be done. The legitimate use of the great power of war, or rather the prohibitions against the use of that power, increase or diminish as the necessity of the case demands. When a city is besieged and hard pressed, the commander may exert an authority over the non-combatants which he may not when no enemy is near.

All wars against a domestic enemy or to repel invasions, are prosecuted to preserve the Government. If the invading force can be overcome by the ordinary civil police of a country, it should be done without bringing upon the country the terrible scourge of war; if a commotion or insurrection can be put down by the ordinary process of law, the military should not be called out. A defensive foreign war is declared and carried on because the civil police is inadequate to repel it; a civil war is waged because the laws cannot be peacefully enforced by the ordinary tribunals of the country through civil process and by civil officers. Because of the utter inability to keep the peace and maintain order by the customary officers and agencies in time of peace, armies are organized and put into the field. They are called out and invested with the powers of war to prevent total anarchy and to preserve the Government. Peace is the normal condition of a country, and war abnormal, neither being without law, but each having laws appropriate to the condition of society. The maxim *arma silent leges is* never wholly true. The object of war is to bring society out of its abnormal condition; and the laws of war aim to have that done with the least possible injury to persons or property.

Anciently, when two nations were at war, the conqueror had, or asserted, the right to take from enemy his life, liberty and property: if either was spared, it was as a favor or act of mercy. By the laws of nations, and of war as a part, thereof, the conqueror was deprived of this right.

When two governments, foreign to each other, are at war, or when a civil war becomes territorial, all of the people of the respective belligerents become by the law of nations the enemies of each other. As enemies they can not hold intercourse, but neither can kill or injure the other except under a commission from their respective governments. So humanizing have been, and are the laws of war, that it is a high offense against them to kill an enemy without such commission. The laws of war demand that a man shall not take human life except under a license from his government; and under the Constitution of the United States no license can be given by any department of the Government to take human life in war, except according to the law and usages of war. Soldiers regularly in the service have the license of the government to deprive men, the active enemies of their government, of their liberty and lives; their commission so to act is as perfect and legal as that of a judge to adjudicate, but the soldier must act in obedience to the laws of war, as the judge must in obedience to the civil law. A civil judge must try criminals in the mode prescribed in the Constitution and the law; so, soldiers must kill or capture according to the laws of war. Non-combatants are not to be disturbed or interfered with by the armies of either party except in extreme cases. Armies are called out and organized to meet and overcome the active, acting public enemies.

But enemies with which an army has to deal are of two classes:

1. Open, active participants in hostilities, as soldiers who wear the uniform, move under the flag, and hold the appropriate commission from their government. Openly assuming to discharge the duties and meet the responsibilities and dangers of soldiers, they are entitled to all belligerent rights, and should receive all the courtesies due to soldiers. The true soldier is proud to acknowledge and respect those rights, and very cheerfully extends those courtesies.

2. Secret, but active participants, as spies, brigands, bushwackers, jayhawkers, war rebels and assassins. In all wars, and especially in civil wars, such secret, active enemies rise up to annoy attack an army, and must be met and put down by the army. When lawless wretches become so impudent and powerful as to not be controlled and governed by the ordinary tribunals of a country, armies are called out, and the laws of war invoked. Wars never have been and never can be

conducted upon the principle that an army is but a posse comitatus of a civil magistrate.

An army, like all other organized bodies, has a right, and it is its first duty, to protect its own existence and the existence of all its parts, by the means and in the mode usual among civilized nations when at war. Then the question arises, do the laws of war authorize a different mode of proceeding, and the use of different means against secret active enemies from those used against open, active enemies? As has been said, the open enemy or solider in time of war may be met in battle and killed, wounded or taken prisoner, or so placed by the lawful strategy of war as that he is powerless. Unless the law of self-preservation absolutely demands it, the life of a wounded enemy or a prisoner must be spared. Unless pressed thereto by the extremest necessity, the laws of war condemn and punish with great severity harsh or cruel treatment to a wounded enemy or prisoner.

Certain stipulations and agreements, tacit or express, betwixt the open belligerent parties, are permitted by the laws of war, and are held to be of very high and sacred character. Such is the tacit understanding, or it may be usage, of war, in regard to flags of truce. Flags of truce are resorted to as a means of saving human life, or alleviating human suffering. When not used with perfidy, the laws of war require that they should be respected. The Romans regarded ambassadors betwixt belligerents as persons to be treated with consideration, and respect. Plutarch, in his Life of Caesar, tells us that the barbarians in Gaul having sent some ambassadors to Caesar, he detained them, charging fraudulent practices, and led his army to battle, obtaining a great victory.

When the Senate decreed festivals and sacrifices for the victory, Cato declared it to be his opinion that Caesar ought to be given into the hands of the barbarians, that so the guilt which this breach of faith might otherwise bring upon the State might be expiated by transferring the curse on him who was the occasion of it.

Under the Constitution and laws of the United States, should a commander be guilty of such a flagrant breach of law as Cato charged upon Caesar, he would not be delivered to the enemy, but would be punished after a military trial. The many honorable gentlemen who hold commissions in the army of the United States, and have been deputed to conduct war according to the laws of war, would keenly feel it as an insult to their profession of arms for any one to say that they could not or would not punish a fellow-soldier who was guilty of wanton cruelty to a prisoner, or perfidy toward the bearers of a flag of truce.

The laws of war permit capitulations of surrender and paroles. They are agreements betwixt belligerents, and should be scrupulously observed and performed. They are contracts wholly unknown to civil tribunals. Parties to such contracts must answer any breaches thereof to the customary military tribunals in time of war. If an officer of rank, possessing the pride that becomes a soldier and a gentleman, who should capitulate to surrender the forces and property under his command and control, be charged with a fraudulent breach of the terms of surrender, the laws of war do not permit that he should be punished without a trial, or, if innocent, that he shall have no means of wiping out the foul imputation. If a paroled prisoner is charged with a breach of his parole, he may be punished if guilty, but not without a trial. He should be tried by a military tribunal, constituted and proceeding as the laws and usages of war prescribe.

The laws and usages of war contemplate that soldiers have a high sense of personal honor. The true soldier is proud to feel and know that his enemy possesses personal honor, and will conform and be obedient to the laws of war. In a spirit of justice, and with a wise appreciation of such feelings, the laws of war protect the character and honor of an open enemy. When by the fortunes of war one enemy is thrown into the hands and power of another, and is charged with dishonorable conduct and a breach of the laws of war, he must be tried according to the usages of war. Justice and fairness say that an open enemy to whom dishonorable conduct is imputed, has a right to demand a trial. If such a demand can be rightfully made, surely it can not be rightfully refused. It is to be hoped that the military authorities of this country will never refuse such a demand, because there is no act of Congress that authorizes it. In time of war the law and usage of war authorize it, and they are a part of the law of the land.

One belligerent may request the other to punish for breaches of the laws of war, and, regularly, such a request should be made before retaliatory measures are taken. Whether the laws of war have been infringed or not, is of necessity a question to be decided by the laws and usages of war, and is cognizable before a military tribunal. When prisoners of war conspire to escape, or are guilty of a breach of appropriate and necessary rules of prison discipline, they may be punished, but not without trial. The commander who should order every prisoner charged with improper conduct to be shot or hung, would be guilty of a high offense against the laws of war, and should be punished therefor, after a regular military trial. If the culprit should be condemned and executed, the commander would be as free from guilt as if the man had been killed in battle.

It is manifest, from what has been said, that military tribunals exist under and according to the laws and usages of war, in the interest of justice and mercy. They are established to save human life, and to prevent cruelty as far as possible. The commander of an army in time of war has the same power to organize military tribunals and execute their judgments that he has to set his squadrons in the field and fight battles. His authority in each case is from the laws and usages of war.

Having seen that there must be military tribunals to decide questions arising in time of war betwixt belligerents who are open and active enemies, let us next see whether the laws of war do not authorize such tribunals to determine the fate of those who are active, but secret, participants in the hostilities. In Henry Wheaton's *Elements of International Law*, he says: "The effect of a state of war, lawfully declared to exist, is to place all the subjects of each belligerent power in a state of mutual hostility. The usage of nations has modified this maxim by legalizing such acts of hostility only as are committed by those who are authorized by the express or implied command of the State; such are the regularly commissioned naval and military forces of the national and all others called out in its defense, or spontaneously defending themselves, in case of necessity, without any express authority for that purpose. Cicero tells us in his offices, that by the Roman feudal law no person could lawfully engage in battle with the public enemy without being regularly enrolled, and taking the military oath. This was a regulation sanctioned both by policy and religion. The horrors of war would indeed be greatly aggravated, if every individual of the belligerent States were allowed to plunder and slay indiscriminately the enemy's subjects, without being in any manner accountable for his conduct. Hence it is that, in land wars, irregular bands of marauders are liable to be treated as lawless banditti, not entitled to the protection of the mitigated usages of war as practiced by civilized nations. In speaking on the subject of banditti, Patrick Henry said in the Virginia Convention, "The honorable gentleman has given you an

elaborate account of what he judges tyrannical legislation, and
an ex post facto law (in the case of Josiah Phillips); he has mis-
represented the facts. That man was not executed by a tyrannical stroke of power; nor was he a Socrates; he was a fugitive
murderer and an outlaw; a man who commanded an infamous
banditti, and at a time when the war was at the most perilous
stage, he committed the most cruel and shocking barbarities;
he was an enemy to the human name. Those who declare war
against the human race may be struck out of existence as soon
as apprehended. He was not executed according to those
beautiful legal ceremonies which are pointed out by the laws
in criminal cases. The enormity of his crime did not entitle
him to it. I am truly a friend to legal forms and methods, but,
sir, the occasion warranted the measure. A pirate, an outlaw, or
a common enemy to all mankind, may be put to death at any
time. It is justified by the law of nature and nations." (3rd
volume, *Elliott's Debates on Federal Constitution,* page 140.)

No reader, not to say student, of the law of nations, can
doubt but that Mr. Wheaton and Mr. Henry have fairly stated
the laws of war. Let it be constantly borne in mind that they
are talking of the law in a state of war. These banditti that
spring up in time of war are respecters of no law, human or
divine, of peace or of war, are hostes humani generis, and may
be hunted down like wolves. Thoroughly desperate, and perfectly lawless, no man can be required to peril his life in ven-
turing to take them prisoners—as prisoners, no trust can be
reposed in them. But they are occasionally made prisoners.
Being prisoners, what is to be done with them? If they are
public enemies, assuming and exercising the right to kill, and
are not regularly authorized to do so, they must be apprehended and dealt with by the military. No man can doubt the
right and duty of the military to make prisoners of them, and
being public enemies, it is the duty of the military to punish

them for any infraction of the laws of war. But the military can not ascertain whether they are guilty or not without the aid of a military tribunal.

In all wars, and especially in civil wars, secret but active enemies are almost as numerous as open ones. That fact has contributed to make civil wars such scourges to the countries in which they rage. In nearly all foreign wars the contending parties speak different languages and have different habits and manners; but in most civil wars that is not the case; hence there is a security in participating secretly in hostilities that induces many to thus engage. War prosecuted according to the most civilized usage is horrible, but its horrors are greatly aggravated by the immemorial habits of plunder, rape and murder practiced by secret, but active participants. Certain laws and usages have been adopted by the civilized world in wars between nations that are not kin to one another, for the purpose and to the effect of arresting or softening many of the necessary cruel consequences of war. How strongly bound we are, then, in the midst of a great war, where brother and personal friend are fighting against brother and friend, to adopt and be governed by those laws and usages.

A public enemy must or should be dealt with in all wars by the same laws. The fact that they are public enemies, being the same, they should deal with each other according to those laws of war that are contemplated by the Constitution. Whatever rules have been adopted and practiced by the civilized nations of the world in war, to soften its harshness and severity, should be adopted and practiced by us in this war. That the laws of war authorized commanders to create and establish military commissions, courts or tribunals, for the trial of offenders against the laws of war, whether they be active or secret participants in the hostilities, can not be denied. That the judgments of such tribunals may have been sometimes harsh, and sometimes even tyrannical, does not prove that they ought not to exist, nor does it prove that they are not constituted in the interest of justice and mercy. Considering the power that the laws of war give over secret participants in hostilities, such as banditti, guerrillas, spies, etc., the position of a commander would be miserable indeed if he could not call to his aid the judgments of such tribunals; he would become a mere butcher of men, without the power to ascertain justice, and there can be no mercy where there is no justice. War in its mildest form is horrible; but take away from the contending armies the ability and right to organize what is now known as a Bureau of Military Justice, they would soon become monster savages, unrestrained by any and all ideas of law and justice. Surely no lover of mankind, no one that respects law and order, no one that the instinct of justice, or that can be softened by mercy, would, in time of war, take away from the commanders the right to organize military tribunals of justice, and especially such tribunals for the protection of persons charged or suspected with being secret foes and participants in the hostilities. It would be a miracle if the records and history of this war do not show occasional cases in which those tribunals have erred; but they will show many, very many cases in which human life would have been taken but for the interposition and judgments of those tribunals. Every student of the laws of war must acknowledge that such tribunals exert a kindly and benign influence in time of war. Impartial history will record the fact the Bureau of Military Justice, regularly organized during this war, has saved human life and prevented human suffering. The greatest suffering, patiently endured by soldiers, and the hardest battles gallantly fought during this protracted struggle, are not more creditable to the American character than the establishment of this bureau. This people have such an educated and profound respect for law and justice—such a love of mercy—that they have, in the midst of this greatest of civil wars, systematized and brought into regular order, tribunals that before this war existed under the law of war, but without general rule. To condemn the tribunals that have been established under this bureau, is to condemn and denounce the war itself, or justifying the war, to insist that it shall be prosecuted according to the harshest rules, and without the aid of the laws, usages, and customary agencies for mitigating those rules. If such tribunals had not existed before, under the laws and usages of war, the American citizen might as proudly point to their establishments as to our inimitable and inestimable constitutions. It must be constantly borne in mind that such tribunals and such a bureau can not exist except in time of war, and can not then take cognizance of offenders and offenses against the laws of war.

But it is insisted by some, and doubtless with honesty, and with a zeal commensurate with their honesty, that such military tribunals can have no constitutional existence. The argument against their constitutionality may be shortly, and I think fairly, stated thus: Congress alone can establish military or civil judicial tribunals. As Congress has not established military tribunals, except such as have been created under the articles of war, and which articles are made in pursuance of that clause in the Constitution which gives to Congress the power to make rules for the government of the army and navy, and any other tribunal is and must be plainly unconstitutional, and all its acts void.

This objection thus stated, or stated in any other way, begs the question. It assumes that Congress alone can establish military judicial tribunals. Is that assumption true? We have seen that when war comes, the laws and usages of war come also, and that during the war they are a part of the laws of the land. Under the Constitution, Congress may define and punish offenses against those laws, but in default of Congress defining those laws and prescribing a punishment for their infraction, and the mode of proceeding to ascertain whether an offense has been committed, and what punishment is to be inflicted, the army must be governed by the laws and usages of war as understood and practiced by the civilized nations of the world. It has been abundantly shown that these tribunals are constituted by the army in the interest of justice and mercy, and for the purpose and to the effect of mitigating the horrors of war.

But it may be insisted that though the laws of war, being a part of the law of nations, constitute a part of the laws of the land, that those laws must be regarded as modified so far, and whenever they come in direct conflict with plain constitutional provisions. The following clauses of the Constitution are principally relied upon to show the conflict betwixt the laws of war and the Constitution:

> The trial of all crimes, except in cases of impeachment, shall be by the jury; and such trial shall be held in the State where the said crime shall have been committed; but when not committed within any State, the trial shall be at such or places as the Congress may by law have directed."(Art. III of the original Constitution, sec. 2.)
>
> No person shall be held to answer for a capital or otherwise infamous crime unless on a presentment or indictment of a grand jury, except in cases arising in the land or naval forces, or in the militia when in actual service, in time of war or public danger; nor shall any person be subject for the same offense to be twice put in jeopardy of life or limb, nor shall be compelled, in any criminal case,

to be witness against himself, nor be deprived of
life, liberty or property, without due process of law;
nor shall private property be taken for public use
without just compensation. (Amendments to the
Constitution, Art. V.)

In all criminal prosecutions, the accused shall
enjoy the right of a speedy and public trial by an
impartial jury of the State and district wherein the
crime shall have been committed, which district
shall have been previously ascertained by law, and
be informed of the nature and cause of the accusation; to be confronted with the witnesses against
him, to have compulsory process for obtaining witnesses in his favor; and to have the assistance of
counsel for his defense." (Art. VI of the amendments to the Constitution.)

These provisions of the Constitution are intended to fling
around the life, liberty and property of a citizen all the guarantees of a jury trial. These constitutional guarantees can not
be estimated too highly, or protected too sacredly. The reader
of history knows that for many weary ages the people suffered
for the want of them; it would not only be stupidity, but madness in us not to preserve them. No man has a deeper conviction of their value, or a more sincere desire to preserve and
perpetuate them than I have.

Nevertheless, these exalted and sacred provisions of the
Constitution must not be read alone and by themselves, but
must be read and taken in connexion with other provisions.
The Constitution was framed by great men—men of learning
and large experience, and it is a wonderful monument of their
wisdom. Well versed in the history of the world, they knew
that the nation for which they were forming a government

would, unless all history is false, have wars, foreign and domestic. Hence the government framed by them is clothed with the power to make and carry on war. As has been shown, when war comes, the laws of war come with it. Infractions of the laws of nations are not denominated crimes, but offenses. Hence the expression in the Constitution that "Congress shall have power to define and punish offenses against the law of nations." Many of the offenses against the law of nations for which a man may lose his life, his liberty or his property are not crimes. It is an offense against the law of nations to break a lawful blockade, and for which a forfeiture of the property is the penalty, and yet the running of a blockade has never been regarded a crime; to hold communication or intercourse with the enemy is a high offense against the laws of war, and for which those laws prescribe punishment, and yet it is not a crime; to act as a spy is an offense against the laws of war, and the punishment for which in all ages has been death, and yet it is not a crime; to violate a flag of truce is an offense against the laws of war, and yet not a crime of which a civil court can take cognizance; to unite with banditti, jayhawkers, guerrillas or any other unauthorized marauders is a high offense against the laws of war; the offense is complete when the band is organized or joined. The atrocities committed by such a band do not constitute the offense, but make the reasons, and sufficient reasons they are, why such banditti are denounced by the laws of war. Some of the offenses against the laws of war are crimes, and some not. Because they are crimes they do not cease to be offenses against those laws; nor because they are not crimes or misdemeanors do they fail to be offenses against the laws of war. Murder is a crime, and the murderer, as such, must be proceeded against in the form and manner prescribed in the Constitution; in committing the murder an offense may also have been committed against the laws of war; for that offense he must answer to the laws of war, and the tribunals legalized by that law.

There is, then, an apparent but no real conflict in the constitutional provisions. Offenses against the law must be dealt with and punished under the Constitution, as the laws of war, they being part of the law of nations; crimes must be dealt with and punished as the Constitution and laws made in pursuance thereof, may direct.

Congress has not undertaken to define the code of war nor to punish offenses against it. In the case of a spy, Congress has undertaken to say who shall be deemed a spy, and how he shall be punished. But every lawyer knows that a spy was a well-known offender under the laws of war, and that under and according to those laws he could have been tried and punished without an act of Congress. This is admitted by the act of Congress, when it says that he shall suffer death "according to the law and usages of war." The act is simply declaratory of the law.

That portion of the Constitution which declares that "no person shall be deprived of his life, liberty or property without due process of law," has such direct reference to, and connection with, trials for crime or criminal prosecutions, that comment upon it would seem to be unnecessary. Trials for offenses against the laws of war are not embraced or intended to be embraced in those provisions. If this is not so, then every man that kills another in battle is a murderer, for he deprived a "person of life without that due process of law" contemplated by this provision; every man that holds another as a prisoner of war is liable for false imprisonment, as he does so without that same due process. The argument that flings around offenders against the laws of war these guarantees of the Constitution would convict all the soldiers of our army of murder; no prisoners could be taken and held; the army could not move. The absurd consequences that would of necessity flow from such an argument show that it can not be the true construction—it can not be what was intended by the framers of the instrument. One of the prime motives for the Union and a Federal Government was to confer the powers of war. If any provisions of the Constitution are so in conflict with the power to carry on war as to destroy and make it valueless, then the instrument, instead of being a great and wise one, is a miserable failure, a *felo de se*.

If a man should sue out his writ of habeas corpus, and the return shows that he belonged to the army or navy, and was held to be tried for some offense against the rules and articles of war, the writ should be dismissed, and the party remanded to answer to the charges. So, in time of war, if a man should sue out a writ of habeas corpus, and it is made to appear that he is in the hands of the military as a prisoner of war, the writ should be dismissed and the prisoner remanded to be disposed of as the laws and usages of war require. If the prisoner be a regular unoffending soldier of the opposing party to the war, he should be treated with all the courtesy and kindness consistent with his safe custody; if he has offended against the laws of war, he should have such trial and be punished as the laws of war require. A spy, though a prisoner of war, may be tried, condemned and executed by a military tribunal without a breach of the Constitution. A bushwacker, a jayhawker, a bandit, a war rebel, an assassin, being public enemies, may be tried, condemned and executed as offenders against the laws of war. The soldier that would fail to try a spy or bandit after his capture, would be as derelict in duty as if he were to fail to capture; he is as much bound to try and to execute, if guilty, as he is to arrest; the same law that makes it his duty to pursue and kill or capture, makes it his duty to try according to the usages of war. The judge of a civil court is not more strongly bound under the Constitution and the law to try a criminal than is the military to try an offender against the laws of war.

The fact that the civil courts are open does not affect the right of the military tribunal to hold as a prisoner and to try. The civil courts have no more right to prevent the military, in time of war, from trying an offender against the laws of war than they have a right to interfere with and prevent a battle. A battle may be lawfully fought in the very view and presence of a court; so a spy, or bandit or other offender against the law of war, may be tried, and tried lawfully, when and where the civil courts are open and transacting the usual business.

The laws of war authorized human life to be taken without legal process, or that legal process contemplated by those provisions in the Constitution that are relied upon to show that military judicial tribunals are unconstitutional. Wars should be prosecuted justly as well as bravely. One enemy in the power of another, whether he be an open or a secret one, should not be punished or executed without trial. If the question be once concerning the laws of war, he should be tried by those engaged in the war; they and they only are his peers. The military must decide whether he is or not an active participant in the hostilities. If he is an active participant in the hostilities, it is the duty of the military to take him a prisoner without warrant or other judicial process, and dispose of him as the laws of war direct.

It is curious to see one and the same mind justify the killing of thousands in battle because it is done according to the laws of war, and yet condemning that same law when, out of regard for justice and with the hope of saving life, it orders a military trial before the enemy are killed. The love of law, of justice and the wish to save life and suffering, should impel all good men in time of war to uphold and sustain the existence and action of such tribunals. The object of such tribunals is obviously intended to save life, and when their jurisdiction is confined to offenses against the laws of war, that is their effect. They prevent indiscriminate slaughter; they prevent men from being punished or killed upon mere suspicion.

The law of nations, which is the result of the experience and wisdom of ages, has decided that jayhawkers, banditti, etc., are offenders against the laws of nature and of war, and as such amenable to the military. Our Constitution has made those laws a part of the law of the land.

Obedience to the Constitution and the law, then, requires that the military should do their whole duty; they must not only meet and fight the enemies of the country in open battle, but they must kill or take the secret enemies of the country, and try and execute them according to the laws of war. The civil tribunals of the country can not rightfully interfere with the military in the performance of their high, arduous and perilous, but lawful duties. That Booth and his associates were secret active public enemies, no mind that contemplates the facts can doubt. The exclamation used by him when he escaped from the box on to the stage, after he had fired the fatal shot, sic semper tyrannis, and his dying message, "Say to my mother that I died for my country," show that he was not an assassin from private malice, but that he acted as a public foe. Such a deed is expressly laid down by Vattel, in his work on the law of nations, as an offense against the laws of war, and a great crime. "I give, then, the name of assassination to treacherous murder, whether the perpetrators of the deed be the subjects of the party whom we cause to be assassinated or of our sovereign, or that it be executed by any other emissary introducing himself as a suppliant, a refugee, or a deserter, or, in fine, as a stranger." (Vattel, 339.)

Neither the civil nor the military department of the Government should regard itself as wiser and better than the

Constitution and the laws that exist under or are made in pursuance thereof. Each department should, in peace and in war, confining itself to its own proper sphere of action, diligently and fearlessly perform its legitimate functions, and in the mode prescribed by the Constitution and the law. Such obedience to and observance of law will maintain peace when it exists, and will soonest relieve the country from the abnormal state of war.

My conclusion, therefore, is, that if the persons who are charged with the assassination of the President committed the deed as public enemies, as I believe they did, and whether they did or not is a question to be decided by the tribunal before which they are tried, they not only can, but ought to be tried before a military tribunal. If the persons charged have offended against the laws of war, it would be as palpably wrong of the military to hand them over to the civil courts, as it would be wrong in a civil court to convict a man of murder who had, in time of war, killed another in battle.

I am, sir, most respectfully, your obedient servant,

JAMES SPEED.
Attorney General to the President

BIBLIOGRAPHY

Aiuto, Russell. 2004. *The Case of Leo Frank.* New York, NY. Crime Library Website. Available from World Wide Web: http://www.crimelibrary.com/classics/Frank.

Apodaca, Patrick. May 24, 1978. *Memorandum for Bob Lipschutz from Apodoca. Subject: Conviction of Dr. Samuel Mudd [online].* Washington, DC: The White House. Pages 1–6. Available from World Wide Web: file:///c:/Documents%20and%20Settings/Owner/My%20Documents/May%2024,%201978.htm.

Associated Press. April 28, 2005. *Moussaoui Requests Burial in a Muslim Country-Admitted Terrorist Says he Hopes to Avoid Death Sentence.* Washington, D.C. Available from World Wide Web: http://www.msnbc.msn.com/id/7664966/.

Ibid. June 18, 2005. *Defense Opens in 1964 Civil Rights Workers . . .* Available from World Wide Web: www.sunherald.com/mld/sunherald/news/politics/11923718.htm.

Ball, Julian. 2005. *Moussaoui On Trial For His Life Using Terrorism to Justify The Death Penalty.* Chicago, IL: The New Abolitionist. Available from World Wide Web: http://www.nodeathpenalty.org/newab024/terrorism.html.

Barry, Ellen. June 24, 2005. *Judge Gives Killen Twenty Years Per Murder. LA Times.* Available from World Wide Web: http://www.ricross.com/reference/kkk/kkk85.html.

Bardsley, Marilyn. 2005. *The Boston Strangler.* New York, NY: Court TV's Crime Library website. Available from World Wide Web: http://www.crimelibrary.com/serial_killers/notorious/boston/2.html.

Century Foundation. Dec. 8, 2003. *Schulhofer. Stephen J.—Testimony before the 9/11 Commission on Domestic Intelligence-Gathering.* Washington, DC: Homelandsecurity.org. Available from World Wide Web: http://www.homelandsec.org/commentary.asp?opedid=394

CNN. June 22, 2005. *Former Klansman Found Guilty of Murder.* Philadelphia, Mississippi. Available online: http://www.cnn.com/2005/LAW/06/21/mississippi.killings/.

Dinnerstein, Leonard. 2003. *Leo Frank Case.* Georgia: University of Georgia Press. *The New Georgia Encyclopedia.* Available from World Wide Web: http://www.georgiaencyclopedia.org/nge/Article.jsp?id=h-906.

FBI. 2005. *Pretty Boy Floyd and Kansas City Massacre.* Washington, D.C.: FBI Electronic Reading Room. Available from World Wide Web: http://foia.fbi.gov/foiaindex/floydsum.htm.

FBI. 2005. *FBI Case Summary: Rosenberg, Julius and Ethel.* Washington, DC. Available from World Wide Web: http://foia.fbi.gov/rosen/rosen1.pdf, http://foia.fbi.gov/rosen/rosen2.pdf.

FBI. 2005. *Charles Lindbergh.* Washington, D.C.: FBI Electronic Reading Room. Available from World Wide Web: http://foia.fbi.gov/foiaindex/lindberg.htm.

Helmer, William and Mattix, Rick. 1998. *Public Enemies: America's Criminal Past, 1919–1940 (Hardcover).* New York: Facts on File.

Feklisov, Alexander. 1999. *Interview with Alexander Feklisov, Russian KGB Agent.* Moscow, Russia: Public Broadcasting Service (PBS). Secret Victories of the KGB. Available from World Wide Web: chttp://www.pbs.org/redfiles/kgb/deep/interv/k_int_alexander_feklisov.htm.

Frank, Gerald. 1966. *The Boston Strangler.* NY: New American Library.

Gehringer, Joseph. 1999. *Charles Arthur Floyd: "Pretty Boy" from Cookson Hills.* New York, NY: Court TV's Crime Library website. Available online: http://www.crimelibrary.com/gangsters_outlaws/outlaws/floyd/1.html.

Hopkins, A.L., Investigator. Sept. 29, 1966. *Investigation in Philadelphia and Neshoba County Mississippi for the Purpose of Ascertaining if Known Subversives are Still Operating in the Area.* Mississippi Dept. of Archives and History. Available from World Wide Web: http://www.mdah.state.ms.us/arlib/contents/er/result.php?image=/data/sov_commission/images/png/cd05/038521.png&otherstuff=2|112|2|43|1|1|1|37927.

Johnson, Andrew. May 1, 1865. *Order Establishing a Military Commission to Try the Lincoln Assassination Conspirators: Order of the President.* Washington, DC: The White House. Available from World

Wide Web: http://www.law.umkc.edu/faculty/projects/ftrials/lincolnconspiracy/commissionorder.html.

Lindner, Douglas. *The Trial of the Lincoln Assassination Conspirators, 1865.* Kansas City: University of Missouri, Kansas City School of Law. Available from World Wide Web: http://www.law.umkc.edu/faculty/projects/ftrials/lincolnconspiracy/lincolnconspiracy.html.

Ibid. *1893. The Trial of Lizzie Borden,* Kansas City: University of Missouri, Kansas City School of Law. Available from World Wide Web: http://www.law.umkc.edu/faculty/projects/ftrials/Lizzie Borden/bordenhome.html.

Ibid. *1935. Bruno Hauptmann: (Lindberg Kidnapping) Trial,* Kansas City: University of Missouri, Kansas City School of Law. Available from World Wide Web: http://www.law.umkc.edu/faculty/projects/ftrials/Hauptmann/Hauptmann.htm.

Ibid. *1967. U. S. vs Cecil Price et al. ("Mississippi Burning" Trial) 1967. A Trial Account by Douglas Lindner.* Kansas City: University of Missouri, Kansas City School of Law. Available from World Wide Web: http://www.law.umkc.edu/faculty/projects/ftrials/price&bowers/price&bowers.htm.

Locy, Toni. Nov. 5, 2003. *FBI has new 9/11 Hijacking Suspect.* Washington, DC: *USA Today.* Available from World Wide Web: http://www.usatoday.com/news/washington/2003-11-04-hijacker-usat_x.htm.

Meyers, Debbie Burt; Foreman, Josh; and Prince, Jim. June 16, 2005. *Killen Taken by Ambulance from Courthouse; Proceedings Delayed. Neshoba Blade Democrat.* Available from World Wide Web: http://www.neshobademocrat.com/main.asp?FromHome=1&TypeID=1&ArticleID=10521&SectionID=36&SubSectionID=371.

Ibid. June 22, 2005. *Former Mayor Lauds Klan.* Available from World Wide Web: http://www.neshobademocrat.com/main.asp?FromHome=1&TypeID=1&ArticleID=10596&SectionID=2&SubSectionID=297.

Ministère des Affaires Etrangères. *April 25, 2005. Statement made by the French Ministry of Foreign Affairs Spokesperson (excerpt)* Paris, France: Ministry of Foreign Affairs. Available from World Wide Web: http://www.diplomatie.gouv.fr/actu/articletxt.gb.asp?ART=48990Mudd.

Mitchell, Jerry. June 4, 2000. *Experts: Autopsy reveals beating. Clarion Ledger*. Available from World Wide Web: http://orig.clarion ledger.com/news/0006/04/04miburn.html.

Ibid. June 18, 2000. *Killen Tied to Slayings*. Available from World Wide Web: http://www.clarionledger.com/apps/pbcs.dll/article?AID=/20050618/NEWS010702/506180358/1240.

Ibid. August 13, 2005. *Killen Free on $600,000 Bond*. Available from World Wide Web: http://www.clarionledger.com/apps/pbcs.dll/article?AID=/20050813/NEWS010702/508130352/1240.

Mudd, Samuel. 1865. Two *Statements Made By Dr. Mudd to Authorities, 1865*. Washington, D.C.: National Archives Records Administration (NARA), M-599, reel 5, frames 0212-0239.

Pettis, Emily Wagner. *Justice After 41 Years*. Philadelphia: Mississippi. *Chicago Sun-Times*. Available from World Wide Web: file:///c:/Documents%20and%20Settings/Owner/My%20Documents/Did/Justice%20after%2041%20years.htm.

Rosen, Fred. July 22, 2005. *President Carter's Reply to Letter of July 12*.

Rowley, Coleen. May 21, 2002. *Memo to FBI Dr. Robert Mueller*. Available from World Wide Web: http://www.time.com/time/nation/article/0,8599,249997,00.html.

Speed, James. May 1865. *Opinion on the Constitutional Power of the Military to Try and Execute the Assassins of the President*. Washington, D.C.: Office of the Attorney General. Available from World Wide Web: http://www.law.umkc.edu/faculty/projects/ftrials/lincolnconspiracy/commissionorder.html.

Surratt House Museum. April 12, 2003. *Regarding the Case for Dr. Mudd: A Chronology [online]*. Maryland: Surratt House. Available from World Wide Web: http://www.surratt.org/mudd/mudd chron.html.

USA. 2001. USA v Zacarias Moussaoui, a/k/a "Shaqil," a/k/a "Abu Khalid al Sahrawi." Defendant. Alexandria, VA. Available from World Wide Web: http://www.usdoj.gov/ag/moussaouiindict ment.htm.

White House. March 2002. *Press Briefing Index by Ari Fleischer—Zacharias Moussaoui*. Washington, D.C. Available from World Wide Web: http://www.whitehouse.gov/news/releases/2002/03/20020319-7.html#19.

BBC News. Dec. 6, 2001. *DNA Doubts Over Boston Strangler*. London, England. Available from World Wide Web: http://news.bbc.co.uk/1/hi/world/americas/1696552.st.

Index

Acton, John, 235
Adams, John, 50
Alcock, John, Captain, 77–78
Allen, Dr., 226
Allen, W., 226
Allen, Willliam, 86
Apodaca, Patrice, 183
Arnold, Benedict, 126
Arnold, Reuben, 69, 70
Arnold, Samuel, 6, 7, 10, 14, 27, 247
Asgiersson, Jon, 156–57
Ashcroft, John, 169, 170, 174
Atzerodt, George A., 6, 8, 10, 14, 23, 27, 206, 247

Baden, 231
Bailey, F. Lee, 43, 157–58, 159
Beck, Irmgard, 154
Bence, Eli, 34, 35, 49
Bender, Rita Schwerner, 194, 200
Benny, Jack, 90, 94
Bentley, Elizabeth, 125–26
bin Laden, Osama, 173–74
Birdwell, George, 108–9, 112
Bissette, Patricia, 152
Blake, Helen, 152
Blanford, Dr., 214, 228, 229
Bloch, Emmanuel, 122, 124, 126, 128
Bloyce, Charles, 210, 213, 214, 221
Bloyce, Julia Ann, 210, 220, 221, 226
Bodman, Henry A., 43
Bonnie and Clyde, 108, 113
Booth, John Wilkes, 4, 5–6, 7–8, 9, 10, 21, 22, 23–24, 25, 26, 180, 184, 189, 190, 206, 211, 212, 213, 214, 223–24, 225, 226, 227, 228, 232–33, 235, 236–38, 239, 243, 244, 245, 246–47, 248–49, 251, 252, 273
Booth, Junius, 5
Booz, 235, 238
Borden, Abby Durfree, 31, 33, 35, 37, 38, 41, 42, 44, 52
Borden, Alice, 32
Borden, Andrew Jackson, 29, 30, 33, 35, 37, 38, 41, 42–43, 44, 45, 54, 56
Borden, Emma, 31, 40, 52, 54
Borden, Elizabeth Andrew ("Lizzie"), xiv, 29, 31, 32, 33, 34, 35, 36, 39–45, 47–50, 52, 53–56, 203
Bottomley, District Attorney, 158
Bowen, Seabury W., Dr., 29–34, 39
Bowers, Sam, 135–36, 144, 147
Bowie, Walter, 15, 216
Bowman, Dr., 214
Boyce, Charles, 220
Boyle, 234, 244
Boynton, Thomas Jefferson, Judge, 181, 188
Brinkema, Leonie, 172, 173, 174, 175, 176
Briscoe, Betty, 235
Brooke, Albin, 215, 216, 219
Brooke, Edward, 158
Brown, Arthur Whitten, Lieutenant, 78
Brown, John, 6, 58
Brown, Mary, 152
Brown, Sue, 137
Buckley, Travis, 146

Burrage, Olen, 147
Bush, George W., 170, 175, 190

Caesar, 259–60
Caffrey, Raymond J., 110, 111
Carter, Jimmy, 177, 183–86
Caruso, Assistant Director, 167
Cato, 259–60
Chaney, James, xiii, 133, 134, 135, 136, 138, 139–40, 142, 143, 144, 147, 192, 195, 197, 199
Cherry, Bobby Frank, 192
Clark, Henry, 226
Clark, Sophie, 152
Clark, William D., 187
Clay, Cassius, 145
Clendenin, David, 14
Condon, John, 83–86, 88, 92, 94
Conkle, Widow, 115
Conley, Jim, 65–66, 67, 68, 69, 70, 71, 74
Corbin, Evelyn, 152
Coughlin, John, 39
Cox, William Harold, Judge, 143, 144, 145–46, 148
Cronkite, Walter, 134

Davis, John, 228
Davis, Thomas, 209, 213, 226, 228
Dawning, John S., 22
de la Beckwith, Byron, 192
Dennis, Delmar, 144–45
DeSalvo, Albert, 153–57, 158–60, 203
DeSalvo, Charlotte, 153
DeSalvo, Frank, 153
DeSalvo, Michael, 154
Diana, Princess, 97
Dickens, 231
Dickey, James, 146
Dillinger, John, 105, 108, 113, 117
Doar, John, 140, 144, 146–47
Dolan, Max, Dr., 37–38
Dorsey, Hugh, 65, 66, 67, 68
Doster, William, 14
Downing, 229–30
Doyle, Conan, 55
Driscoll, John, 151

Duncan, Mark, 193, 197
Dutton, George W., 181
Dyer, Sarah Frances (Mrs. Mudd), 5, 9, 210, 214, 215
Dyer, Jerry, 218, 220, 221

Edwards, Governor, 81
Eglent, Elzee, 16, 17, 18, 216, 217
Eglent, Frank, 18
Eglent, Sylvester, 18, 210
Ekin, James, 14
El Ramein, Omar, 173
Evans, William A., 221, 223, 228, 231, 232
Evers, Medgar, 192
Ewing, Thomas, Jr., 12–13, 17, 19, 20, 23, 25–26, 205
Ewing, Thomas, Sr., 13

Farrell, 236, 237, 238
Featherston, William, Dr., 142, 143, 146
Ferlisov, Alexander, 130–32
Fitsch, Isidor, 89, 94, 95
Fitzpatrick, Miss, 222
Fleischer, Ari, 169–70
Flitcher, Max, 123, 124
Floyd, Charles Arthur (aka Pretty Boy, Choc), 101–18, 203
Floyd, Charles Dempsey, 103
Floyd, Glendon, 113
Floyd, Walter, 101, 102
Forrest, Nathan Bedford, 58, 59, 60
Foster, Robert, 14
Frank, Leo, 57, 62, 63–64, 66, 67, 68, 69, 70–74, 75
Franks, Harold, 103
Freud, Sigmund, 56
Friedman, Paul L., Judge, 188, 189
Fuchs, Karl, 119–20

Galliher, Chief, 107
Gardiner, 245
Gardiner, Ben, 20, 21
Gardiner, George, 227
Gardiner, Llewellen, 209, 226, 227
Gardiner, M. P., 214

Gardiner, Thomas L., 211, 212
Gardner, Dick, 18
Gardner, Erle Stanley, xiii
Gardner, Lou, 18
Garza, Juan Raul, 170
Gavacan, 239, 241
Gifford, Charles, 52
Goering, Hermann, Marshal, 907
Gold, Harry, 120, 125, 126
Golos, Jacob, 126
Gonzalez, Albert, 175–76
Goodman, Andrew, xiii, 133, 134, 135, 136, 137, 138, 144, 147, 192, 195, 197, 199
Goodman, Carolyn, 195
Gordon, Marcus, Judge, 193, 197, 199, 200, 201
Gow, Betty, 79, 92
Graff, Joann, 152
Grant, Ulysses S., 7, 246
Greenglass, David, 120, 122, 124–25
Greenglass, Ruth, 121, 122, 125
Grooms, W. J., 110–11
Guthrie, Woody, 117–18
Gwynn, Andrew, 17, 216, 217, 218, 219, 220, 221
Gwynn, Benjamin, 217, 218, 219, 220
Gwynn, George, 217, 218, 220

Handy, Benjamin, Dr., 52
Hansom, Pike, 40–41
Hardy, 236, 237, 238, 240
Hargraves, Ruby, 103
Harkrider, J. H., 102
Harris, T. M., 14
Harrison, Andrew, 13
Hartranft, Brevet Major-General, 12
Hatcher, Joseph, 195
Hauptmann, Bruno Richard, xiv, 77, 89–90, 92, 93–94, 95–96, 97, 203
Hawkins, 231
Hawkins, Ben, 58
Helmer, William, 112, 116
Henry, Mr., 263
Hermanson, Frank, 110–11
Herndon, Frank, 147

Herold, David E., 6, 8, 10, 14, 27, 180, 206, 233, 234, 235, 236, 237, 238, 239, 240, 243, 244, 247, 251, 252
Hilderbrand, John, 103–4
Hilliard, Sam, 34, 36, 37, 39
Hlavatry, Joe, 104
Hochmuth, Amandus, 92
Holahan, 222
Holland, John C., Col., 229
Holmes, H. H. (aka Herman Mudgett), 150
Holmes, Oliver Wendell, 71
Holmes, Sherlock, 55
Holt, J., 10
Hood, Jim, 192, 193, 195–97, 198, 200
Hoover, J. Edgar, 112–13, 114, 117, 122, 132, 141
Hopkins, Anthony, 143
Howe, Albion, 14
Hughes, Charles Evans, 71
Hunter, David, General, 14, 18, 20

Irga, Ida, 152

Jackson, Andrew, President, 5
James, Frank, 37
James, Jesse, 37
Jameston, Willie, 20
Jarboe, Judson, 221, 222, 223
Jennings, Andrew, 43, 52
Johnson, Andrew, 8, 12, 182, 184
Johnson, Charles, Reverend, 145
Johnson, Lyndon, President, 141
Johnson, President, 5, 27, 179, 185
Johnson, Primus, 235
Jordan, James, 144, 145, 194

Kaczynski, Theodore (aka "The Unabomber"), 174, 176
Kaufman, Irving, Judge, 128
Kautz, August, 14
Killen, Betty Jo, 198
Killen, Edgar Ray, xiii, 138, 139, 144, 146, 147–48, 192, 193, 194–95, 196–201, 203
Killen, Oscar Kenneth, 200

Killen, Bobby, 201
Kirby, Uriah, 52
Klarsfeld, Beate, 191
Knowlton, Hosea M., 43, 44, 53
Koehler, Arthur, 93
Koski, Walter, 124

LaSabine, Lafayette, 8
Lebranchu, Marylise, 169
Lee, Newt, 62, 63, 66, 67
Lee, Robert E., 7, 58
Lewis, Clayton, 145
Lincoln, Abraham, President, 1, 3, 5, 6, 7,
    8, 10, 11, 13, 15, 16, 18, 20, 21, 26,
    28, 181–82, 184, 185, 187, 189, 190,
    229
Lindbergh, Anne, 78, 82, 96
Lindbergh, Charles, 77, 78, 79, 80, 82,
    83, 84, 85–86, 90, 91, 93, 95, 96,
    97–98, 99
Lindbergh, Charles, Jr., 77, 85–86, 87,
    89, 94, 96
Lipshutz, Bob, 183
Lister, Sara, 188
Lloyd, 241
Lovett, Lieut., 241, 242, 243, 244

Majors, Lee, 161
Majure, Harlan, 196
Mann, Alonzo, 74
Marshall, William, Chief Justice, 20–21,
    206, 207
Mattix, Richard, 112, 116
Maynor, Harry, 141
McCarthy, Eugene, Senator, 121
McIntyre, James, 193, 197
McPherson, John, 209
McVeigh, Timothy, 170
Mellon, James, 151
Miller, Vernon, 110
Miller, Wallace, 144
Miller, William, 106–7, 112
Monroe, 231
Montgomery, Lucas, 226
Moody, Thomas, 43, 44, 50
Morse, John, 31–32

Moussaoui, Zacharias, xiii, 161, 162,
    163–76, 203
Mudd, Emily, 220, 228
Mudd, Fanny, 212, 214, 220, 228
Mudd, George, Dr., 209, 231, 242, 243,
    244
Mudd, Henry, 229
Mudd, Henry I., 228
Mudd, Henry Lowe, 9, 226
Mudd, Jerry, 226
Mudd, J. T., 225
Mudd, Lillian Augusta, 9
Mudd, Mary, 212, 214, 223, 228, 229
Mudd, Matt, 226
Mudd, Richard D., Dr., 182–84, 187,
    188, 189
Mudd, Richard, II, Dr., 189, 190
Mudd, Samuel A., Dr., xiii, 1–5, 9–10,
    11, 12, 14, 15, 16, 17, 18–21, 22–28,
    177, 179–85, 187–90, 205–52
Mudd, William, 215, 219
Mueller, Robert, 162, 167, 174
Mullen, Mary, 152
Murray, "Alfalfa Bill," Governor, 109

Nash, Frank, 110–11, 112
Nasser, George, 157
Naylor, Benjamin, 230, 231
Nichols, Nina, 152
Nichols, Terry, 174
Norton, Marcus P., 24–25, 227, 228,
    229, 232

O'Laughlen, Michael, 6, 10, 14, 27, 177,
    179
O'Neill, William, 99
Orme, 231

Paine, Lewis. See Powell, Lewis
Paprocki, Warren, 198–99
Parker, Bonnie, 113. See also Bonnie and
    Clyde
Payne, Lewis, 10
Perry, Captain, 217
Perry, Lieut., 217
Pettus, Emily Wagster, 198

Phagan, Mary, 57, 58, 62, 63, 65, 67, 70, 72–73, 74, 75
Plutarch, 259
Porter, Edwin H., 37
Powell, Lewis 6, 8, 14, 27
Price, Cecil, 137, 138–40, 141, 147, 192
Proctor, John, 141, 142
Purvis, Melvin, 114, 115–16, 117

Queen, William, Dr., 211, 213, 214, 245

Rainey, Lawrence, 137, 141, 147
Raymond, George, 138
Reagan, Ronald, 129–30
Reed, Otto, 110, 111
Reeves, Sarah Ann, 9
Reid, Richard (aka "The Shoe Bomber"), 174, 176
Reilly, Edward J., 91, 92, 93, 94
Richards, 231
Richardson, John R., 230
Richetti, Adam, 110, 112, 113–14
Roberts, Wayne, 140, 147
Roan, Judge, 69–70, 71
Robinson, George, 43, 48, 49, 50, 52
Roby, 231
Roosevelt, Franklin Delano, 98, 99
Rosenberg, Ethel, xiv, 120, 122, 123, 126, 127, 128, 129, 131, 132, 203
Rosenberg, Julius, xiv, 120, 121–23, 124, 126–27, 128–29, 130, 131, 132, 203
Rowley, Colleen, 162–68, 172, 174
Runyon, Damon, 90
Russell, Alice, 40, 47–48, 54

Samans, Beverly, 152
Saypol, Irving, 123, 124
Schneider, Ben, 127
Schulhofer, Stephen J., 171–72
Schwartzkopf, H. Norman, 80–81, 82, 83, 86, 87, 92
Schwerner, Michael, xiii, 133, 134, 135, 136, 137, 138, 144, 145, 147, 192, 194, 197, 199
Selig, Lucille, 64, 74
Sellers, Charles, 93

Seward, William H., 8, 11, 14, 234, 236
Simms, Billy, 19
Simms, Mary, 15–16, 18, 19, 215, 216, 217, 219, 220, 221, 231
Simms, Mary Jane, 220
Simms, Milo, 19–20, 215, 216, 217, 219
Slaton, John, 71, 72, 75
Slesers, Anna, 150–51
Slesers, Juris, 151
Smith, D. R., 34
Smith, Chester, 115 116, 117
Smith, Howard K., 134
Smith, William M., 71
Sobell, Morton, 123, 124, 126, 128
Spain, David, Dr., 142–43
Spangler, Edman, 14, 27, 177, 179, 247
Speed, James, 13, 274
Speed, Joshua, 13
Spencer, Rachel, 19, 215, 216
Stanton, Secretary of War, 11
Starrs, James, Dr., 159, 160
Stonesstreet, Rev Dr., 223
Sullivan, Bridget, 34, 35, 40, 44, 45
Sullivan, Jane, 152
Sullivan, Joe, 133, 134, 141–42
Sullivan, Margaret, 159–60
Sullivan, Mary, 152
Surratt, John H., 6, 7, 10, 15, 19, 20, 21, 24, 25, 180, 214–15, 216, 217, 218, 220, 221, 223–24, 225, 232, 246
Surratt, Mary, 7, 14, 27, 180, 214–15, 221, 222, 223, 247
Surratt, George, 220

Tartakow, Jerome, 127
Taylor, Zachary, 13
Thaw, Harry K., 90
Thomas, Daniel J., 22–23, 229, 230
Thomas, Dr., 229, 231
Thomas, G. C., 181
Thompson, J. C., 211–12, 213–14
Tomkins, C. H., Colonel, 14
Trenchard, Thomas, Judge, 95
Turner, John L., 209
twentieth Hijacker. See Moussaoui, Zacharias

Tyrell, John, 93

Wallace, Lewis, 14
Washington, Baptist, 220, 221
Washington, Betty, 210, 213, 221, 227, 228, 238
Washington, Frank, 210, 220, 221, 228
Washington, George, 81
Washington, Melvina, 18, 216, 217
Waters, John, 209, 231
Waters, Joseph, 209, 231
Watkins, Capt., 234
Watson, Eli J., 231
Watson, J. F., 231
Watson, Tom, 72
Watson, Wm., 230, 231
Weichmann, Louis, 7, 24, 223, 232, 245, 246
Weir, Laurel, 145
Welles, Gideon, 11
Wells, H. H., Colonel, 1, 2, 5, 213, 234, 236, 239, 240, 244
Westlake, Donald E., 86
Wheaton, Mr., 262, 263
White, Captain, 217
White, Stanford, 90
Wiesenthal, Simon, 191
Wilder, Billy, 80
Wilentz, David, 90–91, 93, 94
Wilkes, J., 240
Williams, 240, 241
Wilmer, John, Dr., 3–4, 239
Wilmer, Parson, 233, 240, 241, 251, 252
Wilson, President, 70
Winchell, Walter, 90
Winstead, Mike, 195
Wolf, Joseph, Corporal, 92
Wood, Edward S., Professor, 38, 45–47, 55
Woods, James, 192

Yakovlev, Anatoli, 125